SA D0405552

A tale of hard work, musical discovery, and faith, Charlie Daniels's journey has been one of a kind. Equal parts rebel-rouser and apostle, it's no small coincidence he launched his career by beating the Devil with a fiddle in hand. I love this man, the things he stands for, and his music. What a story.
—BRAD PAISLEY, Grammy Award-Winning
Singer and Songwriter

Charlie Daniels has entertained people around the world for decades, including America's troops in war-torn countries. But what impressed me most over the years is that he brought his legendary band to perform at evangelistic crusades, attracting audiences that would never have heard me or my father, Dr. Billy Graham, proclaim the saving Gospel of the Lord Jesus Christ. When we looked out from the platform we didn't concentrate on the sea of people; we looked into the faces of individuals who longed to know God. I was reminded of this when I heard that Charlie had written this memoir, *Never Look at the Empty Seats*. Thank you Charlie Daniels for caring about those who fill the seats! You are a giant of a man.
—FRANKLIN GRAHAM, President and CEO, Billy Graham
Evangelistic Association, Samaritan's Purse

Charlie Daniels's personal stories are lessons in self-reliance, accountability, and responsibility, and they are as relevant today as they were when Charlie was learning them. These are inspiring words from a great patriot and a great friend.
—GENERAL TOMMY FRANKS, Former Commander,
United States Central Command,
Author of *New York Times* Bestseller *American Soldier*

Charlie takes you inside stories of his amazing family, his discovery of music, and his fight to make it in a profession that most just don't! He shares the why, who, and how of really hard times that taught him life lessons, and those wonderful events and people that he is proud of and celebrates in his book. Read it for yourself . . . this amazing man has a story for us all.

—PHILLIP FULMER, 2012 College Football Hall of Fame

Finally, Charlie Daniels, the Tar Heel, singer-songwriter, tells all! If you love our Lord, our country, and great American music, you will love every word in this book—and learn why US Marines at Camp Lejeune, North Carolina, really matter to my friend Charlie!

—LtCol OLIVER NORTH, USMC (RET.),
Host of *War Stories* on Fox News Channel

Charlie Daniels is a true American icon. He's a patriot who loves God and country and a Country Music Hall of Famer. I am blessed to call him my friend. Trust me, there will never be another Charlie Daniels!

—DARRELL WALTRIP, NASCAR Hall of Famer

Country is the heart and soul of Charlie Daniels—the music, the land, the people, and the uniquely American freedoms that make our country the greatest in the world.

—WAYNE LAPIERRE, Executive Vice President,
National Rifle Association

Charlie is so up-front and friendly, we all assume we know everything there is to know about him. Not so. There is so much about Charlie's life in this book that it would and could make a great movie, or even better, a long-running series . . . very informative and interesting. We all love Charlie, me more than most. Enjoy the book. I did.

—DOLLY PARTON, Grammy Award-Winning Singer,
Songwriter, and Actress

My friend Charlie Daniels is not only a country music legend and icon, he's also a Great American, and a lover of all that matters—God, faith, family, country, and our military. If you want to live life to the fullest, read this book, as it is a road map to everything great.

—SEAN HANNITY, Host of *Hannity* and
Author of *New York Times* Bestseller *Deliver Us from Evil*

I particularly enjoyed Charlie's chapter on Louis L'Amour. Clearly, Louis and Charlie are kindred spirts.

—TOM SELLECK, Actor and Film Producer

NEVER LOOK AT THE EMPTY SEATS

NEVER LOOK AT THE EMPTY SEATS

A MEMOIR

CHARLIE DANIELS

W PUBLISHING GROUP

AN IMPRINT OF THOMAS NELSON

© 2017 Charlie Daniels

Published in Nashville, Tennessee, by W Publishing, an imprint of Thomas Nelson.

Published in association with the literary agency of WTA Services, LLC, Franklin, TN.

Thomas Nelson titles may be purchased in bulk for educational, business, fundraising, or sales promotional use. For information, please e-mail SpecialMarkets@ ThomasNelson.com.

Unless otherwise noted, Scripture quotations are taken from the Holy Bible, New International Version®, NIV®. Copyright © 1973, 1978, 1984, 2011 by Biblica, Inc.® Used by permission of Zondervan. All rights reserved worldwide. www.zondervan.com. The "NIV" and "New International Version" are trademarks registered in the United States Patent and Trademark Office by Biblica, Inc.®

Scripture quotations marked AMPC are from the Amplified® Bible, Classic Edition. Copyright © 1954, 1958, 1962, 1964, 1965, 1987 by The Lockman Foundation. Used by permission. (www.Lockman.org)

Any Internet addresses, phone numbers, or company or product information printed in this book are offered as a resource and are not intended in any way to be or to imply an endorsement by Thomas Nelson, nor does Thomas Nelson vouch for the existence, content, or services of these sites, phone numbers, companies, or products beyond the life of this book.

ISBN 978-0-7180-7476-0 (eBook)
ISBN 978-0-7180-7496-8 (HC)

Library of Congress Control Number: 2017909961

Printed in the United States of America
17 18 19 20 21 LSC 10 9 8 7 6 5 4 3 2 1

To my friend, mentor, and teacher, Bob Johnston, whose influence on my life and my career cannot be overestimated.

CONTENTS

CONTENTS

CONTENTS

Contents

The proposition of making a living as a professional musician can be confusing and challenging. To take it a step further and join the few who have ascended the slippery slope of the big time is a daunting task, to say the least.

After so many years in the business, I guess it's only natural for young men and women who want to chase the dream to ask an old-timer like me questions about the decades I've devoted and the miles I've traveled in my half-century-plus roller coaster ride as a professional musician.

The two most frequently asked questions are, "How do you make it in the music business?" and "How do you have a long career like yours?"

I am writing this book with two primary thoughts in mind. First of all, I'd like to answer these and other questions. Most of all, I have a story to tell. It is a story about trial and error, hard work, hard times, and the myriad of encouraging little things that give you hope and a reason to go on when it seems it's uphill all the way.

I want to tell you about the people who have been a part of my life and the miles I've traveled. But most of all, I want to tell you about the music, the creation and performance, and the undying love that I have for it and my God-given gift that makes it possible.

I'd also like to give you an inside view of what the life of a professional musician is like and a look at the business from my view and attitude.

The truth about the music business is that there is no yellow brick road to get you there. There is no academic degree that guarantees the success you seek. There is no safety net to catch you when you fall.

There's only you, your talent, your determination, your belief in yourself, and, most important of all, your attitude.

While, as I said, there is no yellow brick road, there are some time-proven absolutes, many that I've learned the hard way over the years. I'll pass them on to you, laced with a goodly portion of knowledge earned by beating my head against various walls over the years.

I have had many unique experiences in my eight-plus decades. I've ridden on everything from an Eskimo dog sled to the Concorde and *Air Force One*. I've performed in every state in our union and in some twenty-one foreign countries, in war zones, on an aircraft carrier at sea, and on remote forward operating bases where only a few lonely soldiers make up one of the most cherished audiences of all.

I've stood at the 38th parallel that separates South and North Korea, knocked a few chips out of the Berlin Wall, and worked cattle with the cowboys in Texas and the buckaroos in Nevada. I've seen the polar ice cap, seen the Negev in Israel, been baptized in the Jordan River, and marveled at the beauty of the ceiling of the Sistine Chapel.

I've seen whales in the Pacific and watched the mustang herds run wild and free across the endless expanses of the high desert country.

This account is not written in exact chronological order. I tend to jump around a bit in my narrative, relating memories and lessons learned as I recall them and not always in sequence, reliving times and events as they come to me, one memory prompting another, one instance remembered triggering a vivid recollection of something that could well have happened years on down or back up the road.

It's a little different route, I know, but we still end up at the same place.

One of life's most important lessons I've learned, as it relates to the path I've chosen, is like the old song says, "accentuate the positive; eliminate the negative."[1]

Walk onstage with a positive attitude. Your troubles are your own and are not included in the ticket price.

Some nights you have more to give than others, but put it all out there every show.

You're concerned with the people who showed up, not the ones who didn't. So always give them a show, and never look at the empty seats!

CHAPTER 1

FIRST THINGS FIRST

The first things I remember are frosty Carolina mornings with a cheery fire crackling in my momma's big, black woodstove.

There's no particular reason why you should remember October 28, 1936, unless you happen to be one of the handful of history buffs who know it was the fiftieth anniversary of the Statue of Liberty standing in the harbor in New York.

The mood of the time was laid back and lethargic, the waning era of the Great Depression, and the last year of FDR's New Deal. Polio was a dreaded childhood disease. The Dodgers were in Brooklyn, the Empire State Building was the tallest in the world, and streetcars still rumbled down the streets of small-town America.

Cokes cost a nickel, hot dogs were a dime, and hemlines were well below the knee. Radio was king, and Eddie Cantor and Al Jolson were big stars.

It was seventy-one years after the end of the Civil War, twenty-three years since the Wright brothers made their short but historic flight up the coast at Kitty Hawk, and one year before Amelia Earhart's ill-fated attempt to fly around the world. But 1936 itself was a bland and ordinary year, absent of earth-shaking happenings and grandiose events.

One thing for sure is that the most inauspicious occurrence on October 28, 1936, took place at approximately 2:00 a.m. at James Walker Memorial Hospital in Wilmington, North Carolina, when eighteen-year-old LaRue Daniel and nineteen-year-old William Carlton Daniel had their first and only child—me.

The bureaucratic foul-ups started on the first day of my life when somebody put an "s" on the family name of Daniel on my birth certificate. I became the first and only Daniels in my family.

They named me Charles Edward and took me home as hairless as a billiard ball and probably hungry, a state of affairs that has existed ever since, except that I did manage to grow a modicum of hair over time.

My very first memories are of snowflakes as big as goose feathers, a moon the color of new-made country butter, and a night sky like Van Gogh's "Starry Night." I remember cold mornings with a cheery fire crackling in Momma's big, black woodstove and waking up with the smell of breakfast cooking and how the early morning sunshine would make frost diamonds on the winter-brown broom grass in the field next to the house.

We had electricity but no plumbing. Our water source was a hand pump on the back porch. We cooked and heated with wood and took baths in the same galvanized washtub Momma used to do the laundry.

Did you ever take a bath in a galvanized washtub on a cold night? The side next to the fire is roasting, and the side away from the fire is close to hypothermia. You're red on one side and blue on the other.

Our sanitary facility was the kind you had to walk to. And yes, it's true, folks; the back issues of the Sears and Roebuck catalog really did spend their dotage in the little house behind the big house, growing thinner by the day, titillating the imaginations of little boys who sat there ogling the scantily clad models in the lingerie section.

It was a time when hardly anybody locked a door. We always had a handout for the occasional itinerant, or "tramp" as we called them, and most men's word was better than any contract a lawyer could draw up.

There were no atheists in my world. We believed that everything that existed was created by an all-seeing, all-knowing, all-powerful God. We believed in heaven and hell, the virgin birth, and Jesus Christ's atoning sacrifice on the cross. We believed He rose from the dead and would one day return to claim His rightful place as King of kings and Lord of lords.

That's just how it was and how it still is with me.

I was about the forty-leventh grandchild born on my daddy's side of the family. But I was the very first on my mother's side, a fact that carried a considerable bit of weight until the advent of several more grand-siblings, who siphoned off a goodly portion of my exclusive adult adoration.

My maternal grandparents lived just down the Carolina Beach Road from us. At the time I came along, my mother's two sisters, Ruby and Greta, and her brother Buster were still living at home. Of course, I was the epicenter of attention, and don't think I didn't take advantage of the situation.

My mother was an exceptionally pretty woman who had tremendous respect for education, which I think stemmed from never finishing high school. She had to quit school and stay home to help with the work and the younger children.

This was not an uncommon practice in those days. Times were hard, and keeping food on the table and the family taken care of was considered much more important than finishing high school.

My mother never stopped educating herself and worked hard learning the things she missed out on in school. She eventually became a book-keeper, dealing with intricate math. This was in the days before computers, when columns of numbers were added on hand-operated adding machines and the sums entered into a book with a fountain pen.

Although she had regretted not getting a high school diploma, more than anything else she had wanted her class ring. When I got mine, she was some kind of proud.

I never told her that years later, on a wild night in El Paso, I pawned it for three dollars and never got it back. Just one of the many things I've done in my life that I'm not proud of.

My daddy knew more about timber than any man I ever knew. He could look at a pine tree and tell you how many board feet of lumber it had in it or what kind of pole or piling it would make. He could cruise a tract of standing timber and tell you what it was worth. Millions of dollars changed hands on nothing more than Carl Daniel's word.

My maternal grandfather was the epitome of a man's man: physically strong and capable, a mighty hunter and fisherman. He was a natural leader with the instincts of a frontiersman and was definitely the undisputed patriarch of our family.

He could build a house or a boat, raise a crop, skin a deer, or run a trotline. Once, in his youth, he picked up a bale of cotton by himself. Graham Hammonds was gentle, charitable, and strongly devout in his later years, and I don't believe there was anything he feared other than his Creator.

He commanded a great deal of respect, and everybody knew him as Mr. Graham.

My maternal grandmother, Mattie, stood just over five feet tall, and if God ever made a sweeter woman, I never had the pleasure of making her acquaintance.

When it came to Southern cooking, she was the master, and in my book, she had no equal. She was loving and gentle, and I'm sure that the time I spent with her helped make up the positive side of me.

I never got to know my paternal grandfather, as Poppa Billy died when I was only four years old, but Grandma Daisy lived until I was in my late teens. She was the prototype of a grandma: good-natured and jolly, a righteous woman who loved the Lord and could quote Scripture to fit just about any situation.

Grandma Daisy and Poppa Billy raised nine children on a small Carolina tobacco farm in a house with no electricity and no running water and instilled in them a sense of right and wrong and a strong work ethic.

They're all gone now. But I know in my heart that this world is a better place for having them pass through it.

My early childhood consisted of tricycles, puppies, swimming in the creek, picking sand spurs out of my toes, and trying to avoid red ant hills, or at least that's how I remember it.

The first songs I learned to sing were the gospel song "Kneel at the Cross" and "You Are My Sunshine." I don't even remember learning them. It just seemed I had always known them.

The first song I remember getting emotional about was one my dad sang to me titled "Hobo Bill," the tale of a railroad bum dying alone in a cold boxcar. It could literally reduce me to tears.

I don't recall how old I was when we got our first radio. But I do remember bringing it home and turning it on and, right then, beginning a lifelong fascination with a little box that rocked my world.

There was *The Lone Ranger, Fibber McGee and Molly*, and *Jack Benny*. Then there was a scary show called *Inner Sanctum* that Momma and Daddy would listen to after they went to bed with the lights off. I'd hunker down under the covers in my little bed and see boogers all over the room.

But most of all, what radio brought into our home was music, all kinds of music. Big bands were popular in those days, and the Dorsey Brothers, Benny Goodman, Harry James, and scores of others were all the rage. Many of them had their own radio programs or were featured on comedy or variety shows.

Sunday featured gospel music, from the dignified choirs of the big churches to the energetic, guitar-powered Pentecostal praise and worship to the earthy harmonies of black spiritual songs. It all poured out of our radio.

There were even shows like *Afternoon with the Masters* that featured classical, or what we called "long-haired music." Everybody I knew avoided it like the plague.

But the premier night of the week was Saturday and the radio show that our whole neighborhood was glued to. The fifty-thousand-watt clear-channel voice of WSM boomed into coastal Carolina at night like a local station, bringing the *Grand Ole Opry* into the homes of adoring fans all over the Eastern Seaboard and Midwest.

There was Roy Acuff, Ernest Tubb, Minnie Pearl, and Bill Monroe. Uncle Dave Macon would pick his five-string banjo and sing about ten-cent cotton and forty-cent meat, how in the world can a poor man eat. The square dancers would prance around to the lively hoedown sounds of the Fruit Jar Drinkers, the taps on their shoes clapping out the rhythm as they sashayed across the stage. We all listened and tried to imagine what it would be like to actually be there.

It was an energetic, entertaining, and unparalleled hunk of Americana and made a profound impression on my young life. I listened in awe, having not a clue that one day I would stand on that same stage and go out over those same airwaves.

I was raised in an atmosphere of love by parents who believed that to spare the rod was to spoil the child. My mother could wield a switch with the aplomb of an Olympic fencer, a talent she shared with most of the mothers of that era.

The corporal punishment was meted out in accordance with the degree of the transgression. If it was a minor infraction, Momma would do the honors. However, if I stepped too far over that fragile line, Momma would bring out the big guns, "We'll just wait until your daddy gets home," which doubled the punishment because you had to dread it the rest of the day.

My parents always explained exactly why I was being punished, and looking back, as the old saying goes, "I never got a lick amiss."

My love and respect for cowboys and all things Western started with those black-and-white cowboy movies that played in almost every theater in the South every Saturday afternoon. There was Gene Autry, Roy Rogers, Sunset Carson, Tex Ritter, Bob Steele, and Lash LaRue. Of course I had my favorites, but I loved them all.

They all had basically the same theme. The man who ran the local saloon had a gang of outlaws who robbed stagecoaches, rustled cattle, and tried to run people off their land. Usually the same bunch of actors played the outlaws in all the movies, and as soon as they appeared on the screen, every kid in the place knew who the bad guys were.

They wore the same clothes and hats and rode the same horses whether they were robbing a stagecoach or hanging around the saloon. Except for the bandanna masks they donned for their dastardly deeds, they looked exactly the same. But for some reason, nobody could figure out who was making all the mischief.

The country would be in chaos, terrorized by a band of desperadoes nobody could identify.

Enter the hero. He'd walk into the saloon, beat up five or six guys, shoot the gun out of somebody's hand, foil the evil plans of the outlaws, say goodbye to the girl, hop onto his silver mounted saddle, and lope off into the setting sun.

They would never do anything as boring as kiss a girl. The mushier stuff was reserved for John Wayne and Randolph Scott and the guys who made what we called "high-class Westerns." They ran during the week, along with the dreaded "love movies," which were anything that didn't feature cowboys or Tarzan.

The boys who did the high-class Westerns kissed girls, got married, and occasionally even got shot, but Saturday's heroes had never been known to take a bullet. They were tall in the saddle, fast on the draw, and the undisputed darlings of the short-pants set.

Every boy's prized possession was his cap pistol. You usually got it for Christmas and ran out of caps in a couple of days. Then you had to make the sound of gunfire with your mouth, "Pow, pow. Got him."

Those old Saturday Westerns were so heavily scored that the music was about as important as the plot and had to be included when you mounted your broomstick horse and played cowboy. "Make out like me and you are coming down off this mountain and see this bunch of fellers rustling cattle. Let's go! Dun de dun. Pow Pow. Dun de dun. Pow Pow." We never missed.

Occasionally, the theaters would have live acts between the movies, sometimes variety shows. I guess they were the dregs of a dying vaudeville. But my favorite was when some country music artists would bring their road show to town. The music, the costumes, the lights, and the overall ambiance would totally enthrall me, and I think that's where the fantasy of being onstage first started. The idea of standing in front of a crowd of people playing an instrument and singing has always excited me. It still does.

When I was five years old, something happened that would change our world and help form many of my attitudes for the rest of my life.

It was a bleak, cold Sunday afternoon in December. The whole family was gathered at my grandmother's house when word came over the radio that the Imperial Japanese Air Force had bombed the US naval base in Pearl Harbor.

President Roosevelt declared war. The news fell like a ton of bricks on the shoulders of a nation already deeply concerned about losing sons on the battlefields of Europe. President Roosevelt said that December 7, 1941, would be a day that would live in infamy.

It was also the day America got her back up. The shock wore off and the mobilization was on. Provoked by aggression, fueled by patriotism, and empowered by almighty God, the American people had no doubt they would be victorious. Even in the darkest days of the war when the fighting went badly and the casualty lists were high, we listened to FDR and war commentator Gabriel Heatter and said our prayers knowing full well that no swastika or rising sun would ever fly above our beloved United States of America.

Brokenhearted mothers buried their sons, hung a gold star in the window, and got back to the business at hand. The war effort was in high gear, and seeing this nation operating at 100 percent was an awesome sight.

Recycling is not a new idea. It peaked during the war years as tin cans, old newspapers, scrap metal, and even used cooking grease were saved and collected to play some small part in winning. Hollywood did its part with movies like *The Fighting Seabees* and *The Sands of Iwo Jima*. When you saw John Wayne up there on the big screen, you got the feeling we just couldn't lose.

Besides making scores of patriotic films, movie stars volunteered for active duty. Others did USO tours or appeared at war bond rallies. The Hollywood of the war years and the Hollywood of today are a stark contrast.

Wilmington, North Carolina, is a seacoast town and was strategically important to the war efforts because of the port facilities and a shipyard. German U-boats lay in wait in the waters a few miles off our coastline to sink the oil tankers leaving the port of Wilmington to supply our troops fighting the war in Europe.

It was said that sometimes the ships were sunk close enough to the shoreline that the glow of the burning tankers could be seen from the beaches along our coast.

The war was very real to us. In the days before sophisticated communications and satellite technology to keep up with the enemy, we never knew if the Germans would try to bring the fight on shore.

Slogans like "loose lips sink ships" were prominently on display, and we had air raid drills and rationing. The enlistment offices did a brisk business, and everybody had a father, brother, or uncle who had gone to war.

Due to a badly set broken arm that wouldn't straighten out, my dad was classified as 4F, which meant unfit for service.

CHAPTER 2

SCHOOL DAYS AND THE REAL WORLD

W ell, life goes on, even in the middle of a war. The day came for young Charles to start school, which I did at William Hooper Elementary in Wilmington. I had gone there all of two weeks when Daddy changed jobs and we moved to Valdosta, Georgia, which might as well have been South Africa to a Tarheel first grader who had never been a hundred miles from home or out of reach of the sheltering arms of his doting grandparents.

With the war going on, there was a housing shortage even in a small town in South Georgia. So we spent the first few weeks in the Daniel Ashley Hotel. I thought I was ruined. You take a wet-behind-the-ears country boy used to climbing trees and running through open fields and coop him up in a small hotel room with nothing outside the window but city streets, and you've got yourself a mighty sad little feller.

I had no playmates, no creek to swim in, not even a front porch. About the only bright spot in my life was our trusty old Zenith radio that brought the world into my tiny domain and helped my vivid imagination run wild as I listened to the daily adventures of my radio heroes and pretended to take part in the action.

As people went into the military and took jobs in the defense industry, the manpower shortage was acute. It even affected the schools, which had to scramble to find enough teachers, resorting to calling back into service some who had been retired for many years.

My first-grade teacher in Valdosta was an elderly lady. I wish I could remember her name because I owe her a great deal. She came from a day before the modern teaching methods so adversely affected American education. A time when phonetics and basic math were taught in a hands-on, easy-to-understand way referred to as the "Three Rs"—reading, riting, and rythmetic.

In my opinion, when the school system stopped teaching phonetics and instituted the "new math," they left a lot of students behind. They never got caught up, unable to pronounce simple words or solve or even understand basic math problems. It's a shame.

In the meantime, the Daniels family finally got a house. Well, it was not really a house. It was an apartment, but it meant getting out of that hotel room, and it was in a neighborhood with trees to climb and kids to play with. I set out on a quest to make new friends, a task that was to become all too familiar over the next several years.

Valdosta, Georgia, was not really all that different from the surroundings I'd lived in in Wilmington. The kids in the neighborhood came from working-class families, the basic environment was the same, and soon I was part of the bunch.

During my Christmas vacation that year, I had a serious case of measles and stayed in bed for several days with an extremely high fever. I will always believe that is where my eyesight started going bad.

It was a rude awakening the next year in second grade when I found out I had gone from normal to impaired vision in very short order and would need glasses. I would wear some sort of corrective lenses for the next sixty years of my life until 2014, when I had cataract surgery and a permanent lens implant.

I'll always remember a hot morning in June 1944 when Momma got me up early. We made our way to the Methodist church to join our fellow Americans who were praying for the sixteen thousand Allied troops who at that moment were landing on the coast of France.

It was D-Day.

The church was packed to the rafters, as mothers, fathers, sisters, and brothers came together to beseech almighty God to protect the sons of America who were storming the beaches of Normandy.

It was a bloody day, and German machine gun emplacements and artillery cut the landing force to ribbons. But on they came, wave after wave, until at the end of the longest day the backs of Adolph Hitler's Nazis had been broken. The march to Berlin and the end of the war in Europe were in sight.

The D-Day operation was to cost more than nine thousand Allied lives, and the courage of those men should and will be honored as long as there's an America.

After I finished first grade in Valdosta, the family moved again. I started second grade in Elizabethtown, North Carolina, moved back to Valdosta for a couple of months, and finished the year back at William Hooper Elementary in Wilmington, where it all began.

This was to become a pattern in my early school years. Between my dad's company transferring him around and him changing jobs, it seemed like we moved constantly. I was always having to leave a set of friends in one place and make a new set somewhere else.

Always being the new kid and wearing glasses made me a prime target for the class bully, and I had to take the glasses off and defend myself many times. I learned early about bullies. Most of them are really cowards at heart. They use intimidation and sometimes superior numbers to torment someone who is afraid to fight back.

I knew I had to fight back and tried to give as good as I got. They soon learned that they could beat me in a fight but they were going to get bruised up in the process every time they tried it. They soon got the idea.

One of the reasons we moved so much was that my daddy was an alcoholic. This has always been a hard subject for me to talk about in public. When you say "alcoholic," the first thing that pops into someone's mind is some disheveled, dirty, pathetic bum stumbling down the street, trying to find another drink, and this was not the case with my dad.

Far from it. Carl Daniel was one of the best, if not the best, and most-respected timbermen in the business. Everybody knew it, and there was always a job available for him, even from a company he had been fired from before. He was just that good and that well thought of.

My father fought his alcohol problem all his life and would go for as long as four years without touching a drop. But alcoholism is a disease and is always lurking just under the surface, waiting for a weak moment. Its victim gets confident enough to think he can have "just one." Then it pounces like a tiger, and it takes almost superhuman strength to make it let go.

My dad used to say he was one drink away from a drunk all the time. Although he would give in to the temptation once in a while, he always took care of his family and always provided for us. He was an affectionate, responsible father, and his love for music was passed on to his only son.

My dad couldn't play an instrument, but he loved to sing. He was a welcome sight at any church in the country. While most churchgoers did little but pay a timid lip service to the worship music, my dad sang the old songs with an exuberance and a decibel level that was downright infectious.

I proved myself to be a chip off the old block when my daddy attended a Wednesday night prayer service at a holiness church across the street from my grandmother's house in Wilmington. The congregation was good people who loved the Lord and didn't mind letting the world know about it in song. I was sitting in my grandmother's front porch swing when they went into a rafter-shaking rendition of "Power in the Blood," and I joined in by singing at the top of my lungs.

"Oh, would you be free from the burden of sin? There's power in the blood, power in the blood."[2] I was swinging and singing along with all my might when I saw my daddy come out of the church and make a beeline across the street.

"Charles, you've got to stop. Everybody in the church is turning around to see who's singing so loud!" All this from all the way across the street. I was about eight years old.

It was while I was going to school in Valdosta, Georgia, that World War II finally ended. The little town went wild. The sidewalks were full of people. The streets were full of cars, drunk people, sober people, people laughing and crying, and horns blowing. I don't believe the people in Times Square in New York City celebrated any harder than the good people of that little South Georgia town.

Our long national nightmare was finally over, and America would get on with the business of becoming the greatest nation the world had ever known.

America would soon face the Cold War and the Korean War, but the technical and industrial advances we had learned during World War II would soon be put to use in a peacetime setting. The results would be the most advanced and productive nation on the planet.

There was also a dark side to the advances that were made during the war, as the nuclear genie was let out of the bottle and would forever cast its ominous shadow on civilization around the world. It had ended the war with Japan practically overnight, but the awful specter of nuclear destruction would forever haunt planet Earth.

I went to third and fourth grades in Baxley, Georgia. The summer between grades I got my first job, carrying water in a tobacco warehouse for the princely sum of around nine dollars a week, which I thought was pretty good money for a ten-year-old.

There was one movie theater right across the square from where we lived. Admission for kids my age was nine cents, and I was there just about every time the picture changed. I made friends and loved living in Baxley, Georgia, but about the time I finished fourth grade, we moved again.

I won't bore you with any more of the vagabond nature of my early school days. But I did spend all four of my high school years at Goldston High School in Goldston, North Carolina, located three miles up Highway 421 from where we lived in Gulf, or "The Gulf," as many of the locals called it.

Gulf had a post office, a brick mill, a general store, and a couple of small gas station–type places, as well as the General Creosoting Company, where my dad worked.

Now, Gulf might have been a one-horse town, but we rode that old horse for all he was worth. We had a swimming hole in the Deep River, a baseball field with the emphasis on field, and plenty of woods to squirrel hunt in.

Gulf was to play an intricate and lasting role in my life as the years there unfolded. While in Gulf I drank my first beer, had my first real girlfriend, took my first trip to the Grand Ole Opry, and made friendships that lasted more than sixty years.

Goldston High School was actually an elementary, middle, and high school combined. With all twelve grades under one roof, the student body constituted a little more than three hundred, and with the rare exception of a few people like me, they went to school together for all twelve years. It was small by any standard. We didn't have some of the advantages of larger schools, but in my book the advantages far outweighed the disadvantages.

Some of the kids would show up for registration on the first day of school and not return to class for two weeks or so, or however long it took to get the family's tobacco crop harvested and to market. I can't imagine a larger school tolerating it, but that was how life was in a farming community, where feeding a family took priority during the first couple of weeks of school.

I played center on the football team my senior year and formed a lifelong passion for the game. I learned a lot about life by going out for the football team. I have little or no natural athletic ability and only made the team because I wanted it so badly and put all I had into it.

The late summer workouts in the hot, humid Carolina afternoons, the daily practices, pounding away at tackling dummies and blocking sleds, and the soreness and discipline all paled in comparison to running onto a football field and facing off with another bunch of kids who had worked just as hard as you had and were ready to go head-to-head to prove which team wanted to win the most.

The prize was indeed worth the effort. I found out how gratifying it is to compete hard and, whether win, lose, or draw, know that you had given it your best. Competition is good, and the only way to win is to try a little harder than everybody else in the game. The sooner young people find that out, the better off they'll be.

I really loved my last couple of years in high school and playing on the Goldston football team. Pittsboro, the county seat of Chatham County, was the largest town and therefore the biggest school in our football district. Being a larger school gave it a larger pool of potential athletes and made it the dominant football power. Therefore, they were the big boys in our neighborhood.

On a fall Friday afternoon, our little rag-tag single wing went up against the mighty Pittsboro team, and against all odds, we won. There is no feeling in the world like being a giant slayer, and I think we all learned a lesson about never giving up no matter what. To win against such superior odds is a feeling like none other, bordering on euphoria. I took my football jersey home and wore it around all the next day.

No description of Gulf, North Carolina, would be complete without at least a cursory mention of Richard Moore's store. It was a combination grocery, hardware, drugstore, and farm supply; it stocked just about anything you might happen to need.

You could buy anything from a candy bar to a mule collar at J. R. Moore and Son. You could get five pounds of finishing nails or a hundred pounds of hog feed. There were blue jeans, plow line, pocketknives, boots, shotgun shells, nuts and bolts, shoestrings, kitchen matches, straw hats, bib overalls, and flashlight batteries.

There was a big hoop of cheese, and you could buy the whole hoop or Mr. Richard would carve you off a nickel's worth. There was hand-cut bologna and a sure-enough potbellied stove with a collection of old boys who sat around it and solved the world's problems on a daily basis.

There were some world-class characters around Gulf, also. I would like to just name a couple.

There was Frank Walden, who walked down the side of the road laughing and talking to himself and could quote the Bible, chapter and verse.

There was also Uncle Bud, who lived alone. He smoked Granger pipe tobacco rolled up in brown-sack paper and claimed to be a statue, or a "statue of the nation," as he put it.

Then there were Charley Brewer and Alford Davis. They built a cubby hole to sleep in on the back of their pulpwood truck and drove it to the Grand Ole Opry.

I was really happy in Gulf, and the memories from that part of my life are vivid and warm. We had a real home there. I liked the school and the slow pace of life, and I made friendships that have lasted more than six decades.

Suppertime was always a special time of day for me. The sun would be going down, and smoke would be rising from the chimneys of the cookstoves. The family would sit down at the table, and you'd get a warm, the-hunter-is-home-from-the-hill kind of feeling, a feeling of security and togetherness, of really being a family.

I had a lot of friends. There was Jimmy Phillips, Tommy Wilkie, and Ernest and Ralph Willett, but my very best friend was Russell Palmer. We did everything together and occasionally got into a bit of trouble.

We had a 1948 Ford coupe for a family car. One night well before I got a driver's license, Momma and Daddy went somewhere and drove

Dad's company pickup, leaving the keys to the Ford on the mantelpiece. I grabbed the keys and took off up to Russell's house. We proceeded to cruise the Chatham County back roads for an hour or so, after which I dropped Russell off, drove back home, put the keys back on the mantelpiece, and was sitting there the picture of underage innocence when my parents came home.

Well, unbeknownst to me, my parents had come back home in my absence and had been out looking for me. That's the night that the ship hit the sand.

In those days, I'd usually spend part of the summer on my Uncle Edgebert's farm in Bladen County, where I helped harvest the tobacco crop.

Growing bright leaf tobacco in those days was physical labor on a grand scale. From the time the young plants were pulled from the plant beds and set out in the field, it was pretty much a sunup until sundown proposition. It had to be hoed, suckered, fertilized, plowed, and, finally, harvested. Harvesting was done by picking one leaf at a time, stringing it on sticks, hanging it in a barn to be heat cured, taking it out of the barn and off the stick, grading and tying it in small bundles, and finally hauling it to market.

But it wasn't all work and no play. At precisely the stroke of noon on Saturdays, my cousin Murray and me would drop what we were doing, go to the house, clean up, and head for Elizabethtown to spend the rest of the day eating junk and seeing every movie available in the town's two movie houses. Murray's older brother Walton said that Murray and me would go to the movies if all they showed was a pile of horse manure on the screen. He was probably right.

In those days, almost everybody in Bladen County was in town on Saturdays buying the week's groceries, getting haircuts, visiting, or just goofing off like us. Rural small-town Saturdays were a social event, a country boy's delight, an institution, and a long-lost piece of Americana gone the way of modern times and fondly recalled.

I learned a lot about hard work those summers on my uncle's farm. I learned what it's like to get up at two o'clock in the morning to take the cured tobacco out of the barn and turn right around and spend the day filling it back up with green tobacco. I learned about holding up my part of the job and taking pride in doing it well.

I learned a lot about personal responsibility. For the farmers of that day, there was no safety net. They were at the mercy of the elements and market forces. There was nobody that was coming to bail them out if the crop failed. They just had to tighten their belts, go deeper in debt, and pray that next year would be better.

I don't even remember when I started smoking cigarettes, but it was at a very early age. Carrying a pack around in my shirt pocket became as natural as putting on my pants. It would take me many years to truly learn the dangers of smoking and finally kick the habit.

On one of those days I spent in Bladen County, Murray got hold of a plug of chewing tobacco, and we took off back in the woods to give it a try. I stuck a big chunk of it in my mouth and was chewing away, thinking that the warnings I'd heard about how chewing tobacco would make you deathly sick were way overrated. I was chewing and spitting and having a fine old time one minute. The next minute I was lying on my back, as sick as a dog, the world spinning around above me. I was throwing up and so dizzy I couldn't tell up from down.

Although I stayed with the cigarettes, I swore off chewing tobacco. It was to be many a day before I worked up the nerve to try chewing tobacco again.

The summer ended and I headed back to another school year, a little older, hopefully a little wiser. Little did I know that something exciting was about to happen to me, something that would affect my outlook, concepts, and horizons, and I would never look at the world the same way again.

CHAPTER 3

THAT'S A BIG OL' WORLD OUT THERE

The first time I ever saw a picture on a television set was at Russell Palmer's house when I was about fifteen years old. TV sets were expensive in those days, and Russell's family had one of the few in our neighborhood. Every night his buddies would crowd into the Palmer family room to watch television. I don't know why they put up with us, but they did.

There was never any question about what to watch since there was only one channel. It was from Greensboro, about sixty miles away, necessitating a tall antenna that the wind would blow around sometimes. Somebody would have to go to the attic and turn it in the right direction while somebody else watched the set and relayed instructions.

"Go a little farther. No, that's too far. You've gone past it; turn it back."

One of my favorite shows was *Your Hit Parade*, a weekly Saturday night show where the top ten tunes in the country were performed on live TV, starting at number ten and working down to number one.

There were the Friday night fights, wrestling matches, *Dragnet*, and of course Ed Sullivan and Jackie Gleason. For the first time, us folks in the boondocks got a live look at what was going on in the rest of the world.

Television has become a taken-for-granted, mundane appliance these days, where you can zip through two-hundred-plus channels and find something to your liking. But in the early days, especially in the rural areas, the choices were limited and the whole country was watching the same shows.

One appearance on a show like *Ed Sullivan* could mean overnight stardom, and performers who were little known were catapulted to instant national status and success.

Upstart rock and rollers like Jerry Lee Lewis and Little Richard started appearing on television alongside Frank Sinatra and Pearl Bailey. And as Bob Dylan would so succinctly put it a few years later, "The Times They Are A-Changin'."

The most amazing show-business phenomenon I've ever witnessed was the meteoric rise of Elvis Presley.

The first time I ever heard his name was on Ernest Tubb's *Midnight Jamboree*, a live radio show that took place directly after the *Grand Ole Opry* and broadcast on WSM. It originated at the Ernest Tubb Record Shop on Broadway around the corner from the Opry and featured guests from established stars to up-and-comers.

I was listening the night Elvis was on, and the first thing I thought was, what kind of name is *Elvis Presley*? Sounds silly. Then he sang one of my favorite Bill Monroe songs, "Blue Moon of Kentucky" and, from my point of view, murdered it. I never expected to hear from him again.

How wrong can you be?

Elvis joined a country package tour with *Grand Ole Opry* stars Hank Snow and the Louvin Brothers and had the lowest billing on the show, his name in tiny print at the bottom of the show placards. But after a couple of performances, for all practical purposes, the rest of the entertainers could have gone home. The crowds came to see Elvis and made it difficult for anybody else to perform. They screamed "Elvis, Elvis, Elvis" until the other stars just gave up and brought him on.

The rumor mill went wild about this young singer with the guitar and sideburns. Little was known about him other than that he was tearing up crowds wherever he went. But what really got his career in high gear was one appearance on the Dorsey Brothers' television show. After that night, Elvis Presley became a household name and the public could not get enough of him.

Nobody has ever impacted the entertainment business like the kid from Tupelo, Mississippi. He was the first true modern superstar. He lived the Cinderella story and took us all along for the ride. He played out our fantasies for us, buying a Cadillac for every day of the week, giving fabulous gifts to anybody he wanted to, buying his mom a big house in Memphis, and causing young girls to swoon and faint just by walking onstage.

The world was changing right before our eyes, as the East Coast, West Coast, and all points in between were tied together by this emerging monolith known as television. It seemed that one day we were just a sleepy backwater and the next day the whole world was coming into our living rooms. We knew what the people in Los Angeles were wearing, what weather was expected in Chicago, and what Times Square looked like on New Year's Eve. For the first time, we saw football games, presidential inaugurations, and the World Series in real time.

The sleepy giant known as the South was coming of age. People in the other part of the country were able to see Dixie for the vibrant, culturally rich place it was rather than the backward, slow-talking caricature many of them perceived it to be. Television expelled stereotypes and exploded myths as articulate Southerners came to the fore in entertainment and national politics and the rich legacy of the music of the South and the artists who created it were going mainstream.

The world was changing fast, and I was just about to do the same thing.

CHAPTER 4

Three Chords that Changed My Life

Meanwhile, back in The Gulf, I was about to go through a life-altering experience. It happened one afternoon when I went to Russell Palmer's house and found him messing with a guitar. When I say "messing," I mean that he knew about two and a half chords he could haltingly string together.

As long as I had known Russell, I had no idea he had a guitar he'd forgotten about stashed somewhere and that he could actually play it a little.

It was an old Stella with a neck about the size of half a fence post, and the strings were rough and rusty, but little did I know that that old beat-up Stella guitar was going to change the course of my life. I had always had a fantasy and a burning desire to play a guitar, and here was my best friend who knew two and a half chords and was willing to teach them to me.

I don't believe I ever worked as hard or had as difficult a time on anything in my life as I did learning those first chords on Russell's guitar. My fingers got sore and my patience wore thin, but I stuck with it until I could play G, C, and sometimes a D chord. If you knew three chords, you could play a whole song, and that was just about the most exciting thing that had ever happened to me.

I am not a natural musician. Even to this day, I have to work hard to achieve any degree of proficiency. And in those early days, I had a trying time, but I hung in there. I've never been short on tenacity when I really wanted something, and I wanted this more than anything I'd ever wanted in my life.

Life for Russell and me became music. We wore that old guitar out, and a few months later Russell's daddy bought him a genuine Gibson flat-top acoustic guitar. It was by far the best instrument we'd ever had our hands on and excited us even more.

I had just gotten to where I could play G, C, and D with some degree of regularity when Tommy Wilkie came by one day with a mandolin, and I just had to get my hands on it. I don't even remember how I learned those first few mandolin chords, but sometime later I bought one of my own and practically lived with it.

Joe Phillips started coming by once in a while with a five-string banjo; he could play a little bit. As soon as we got to the point where we could play a few simple songs together, we decided we'd form a band.

Lester Flatt and Earl Scruggs and the Foggy Mountain Boys were a daily feature on WPTF in Raleigh. Since they were our idols, we named our band the Misty Mountain Boys. Imagine that.

One night while we were picking and talking, we figured it was time for the Misty Mountain Boys to make a public appearance; it was time for the world to learn about this new phenomenon springing forth from The Gulf. After all, we could play three whole chords and actually play them together once in a while.

Joe Phillips came up with the idea of doing a benefit show for a needy local gentleman. That very night we went out and found some old movie posters, flipped them over on the blank side, and hand printed the fact that the Misty Mountain Boys would be making their maiden voyage at the Gulf Community Building on a Saturday night in the not-too-distant future.

We didn't ask anybody about using the building. We didn't even inform the gentleman we were doing the benefit for. We just block printed it all up on the back of those old movie posters and put them up around town.

Now don't go getting any delusions of grandeur about the Gulf Community Building. It was just an old brick structure about thirty by forty feet with electricity and a few benches.

Our first problem was that we didn't have a sound system, and the only person in our area having anything approaching one was a young black kid named Poochie Reeves. Well, it wasn't really a sound system—it was just a National guitar amplifier. But with a borrowed microphone, we were in business.

We made a stage by laying boards across a couple of saw horses and hung a blanket across a piece of wire for a curtain.

The stage was set for the worldwide debut of the Misty Mountain Boys. When the big night arrived, we had about twenty-five or thirty people in the audience, including our parents. The red light on Poochie Reeves's amplifier was shining like a beacon in the night, beckoning us on to fame and glory.

We took the stage: Russell Palmer on guitar, Joe Phillips on banjo, and Charlie Daniels on mandolin. My dad even came up and sang a song with me. We played our limited repertoire, which the crowd seemed to enjoy, or at least endure. But the biggest hit of the evening was when Ralph Willet took Russell's guitar, which he couldn't play at all, and accompanied himself on an out-of-tune, out-of-time rendering of a song called "I'm Gonna Kill Myself." Ralph had a speech impediment and absolutely no concept of rhythm or pitch whatsoever, but he was by far the hit of the night. The place broke up.

When it was over, we were ecstatic. We had raised a few dollars for a good cause, and our first public appearance had been a success. Sure that fame and fortune lay just over the next hill, we went back in practice mode with a vengeance.

In the early 1950s, it was fairly common for small radio stations around our part of the country to have local bands doing weekly and sometimes daily radio shows. The stations got some free programming, and the bands could advertise the square dances and other functions they were playing. Most of the time the bands averaged from mediocre to downright terrible.

After we had learned a few more songs and become a little more efficient on our instruments, we figured we had progressed to the point that we should get our own radio show.

Russell worked up the nerve to call WWGP in Sanford and ask for an audition, which was so promptly granted that we figured we were off and running. The big day arrived, and we took off for Sanford with phrases like "Y'all are as good as some of 'em I hear on the radio" ringing in our ears.

We knew we were in trouble when we first laid eyes on the station manager who handled our audition. He was a business-like, no-nonsense kind of a guy. He listened to us play, made some valid criticism, and promptly burst our bubble. We headed back to Gulf to inform the home folks that there would be no radio show forthcoming for the Misty Mountain Boys.

Joe Phillips just gave up and stopped coming to practice, but Russell and I stuck to the cause. We had a fire in our bellies, and it would take a lot more than a failed audition to put it out.

Tommy Wilkie came by one day with a fiddle, and I had to give it a try. The fingerboard on a mandolin is the same as the fingerboard on a fiddle, so I kinda had an idea where to put my fingers. It was when I applied the bow that the trouble started. How my parents ever put up with me, I'll never know. I made some of the most horrible noises on that fiddle you could ever imagine hearing.

Pat Thomas, one of the guys I went to school with, said that when I played the fiddle, it sounded like somebody stepped on a cat. It was that and worse as I squeaked and squawked my way through learning the basics. But as I said, I've never been short on tenacity. Before too long, I was playing a hoedown or two.

I never took a fiddle lesson and play totally by ear. When I started learning the fiddle, I learned all wrong. I hold the fiddle wrong. I hold the bow wrong and put too much pressure on it, which actually gives me the sound you hear on our records. It may not be proper, but as with so many things in life, it works for me.

The first money I ever made playing music was on a Saturday night when Russell Palmer and I were sitting around the local store with a guitar and fiddle, just hoping someone would ask us to play something. A car pulled up to the gas pump out front, and two couples got out and came into the store.

Noticing the instruments, one of the ladies said, "Play something." Well, Russell piped right up and said, "You got any money?" The lady reached into her purse and pulled out four dimes. That's twenty cents apiece. I wish I'd framed my two dimes.

Going to the Grand Ole Opry was a dream I'd had since I was a small child. It finally reached fruition in the summer of 1954, when Russell and me, along with a few of the local boys, chipped in for gas for a friend's car and took off for Nashville.

We knew nothing about the procedure or protocol for obtaining tickets

NEVER LOOK AT THE EMPTY SEATS

or show times and made no hotel reservations. We just piled in the car and, armed with a map and a whole lot of youthful fervor, embarked on the five hundred miles of mostly two-lane highways that led to Nashville.

The upshot was that after about three hours of standing in line outside the Ryman Auditorium, we did indeed get to see the *Grand Ole Opry*, all of it.

The *Opry* did two shows, turning the house in between to make room for the folks attending the second show. But instead of leaving, we found some empty seats and stayed around for the second show too.

The second show ended at midnight, and of course we had to go around the corner to the *Midnight Jamboree* at the Ernest Tubb Record Shop. We left Music City in the early morning hours, completely worn out but still inspired and buzzing in the afterglow.

The *Opry* was almost sensory overload for would-be pickers like Russell Palmer and me; we had experienced so much great music up close. But just the realization that at long last, after untold hours of listening, imagining, and dreaming, we had actually seen a live performance of the show of shows, the *Grand Ole Opry*—it was almost like a dream.

The next year we went back a little more prepared. We stayed at a hotel right next to the WSM Studios, where the live pre-*Opry* show took place, which we attended. Then, with reserved seat tickets in hand, we walked the few blocks to the Ryman for both *Grand Ole Opry* shows.

Downright sophistication.

One day when I was about sixteen, Joe Phillips showed up with some beer he had got ahold of somehow. I had never tasted any alcoholic beverage and sneaked off and downed my first beer. I didn't know what to expect, didn't know if I'd feel tipsy or sick or what. The truth is, I really didn't feel anything.

When I say I "sneaked off," I am serious, and for good reason. Drinking alcohol was very much frowned on by my mother, and I was grown before I would have as much as a glass of dinner wine around her.

We lived in a dry county, and alcoholic beverages were hard to come by. But this was to be the first of many covert cocktail hours.

Musically, things started looking up when Russell found out that he had a natural talent for a five-string banjo, adding another whole dimension to the music we played. We hooked up with a couple of other guys who were serious about picking.

Dave Hall played rhythm guitar and sang, and Ed Cooper sang and played the doghouse bass. For the first time, we really started to sound like a full-fledged band, complete with vocal harmonies.

We went to a lot of what was called "fiddler's conventions" in those days. "Fiddler's convention" was just another name for a talent show with small cash prizes for the best band, the best singer, and so on, with the biggest prize going to the best fiddler, which was decided by a panel of judges.

The local musicians took them pretty seriously and would show up in droves. So, when I won the very first two I ever competed in, it was a total surprise. And the dreams of one day making a living playing my music grew a little.

We bought a used one-speaker, one-mic sound system and started playing anywhere we could get anybody to listen. We also got our elusive radio show on WWGP in Sanford every Saturday afternoon. Another milestone, another small victory.

Shortly before graduation, I had an accident in the shop at school that could have easily changed the path of my life. In the first place, I'm not good with machinery, as I was to prove to myself many times during my life. And what happened to me was caused by a lack of concentration and trying to operate a piece of equipment I was not familiar with.

I was sawing a small piece of wood on a table saw and made the mistake of turning loose one end of it. When I did, the saw bucked and jerked my right hand across the blade, severing the ring finger at the base of the nail and sawing deep gashes in three of my other fingers.

The closest surgeons were in Sanford, about twelve miles away. Our principal, Mr. Clayton, hurriedly put me in his car, and we headed full tilt for the hospital in Lee County. When we arrived, we found that both qualified doctors were in surgery and would be there for a couple of hours.

My hand felt as if it was in a vice and somebody kept ratcheting it up tighter and tighter.

As bad as I am at remembering names, I can't even remember the name of the doctor who eventually treated my hand, but I will never forget the name of the angel of mercy who was in the emergency room that afternoon—Miss Ballard. She gave me a shot of belladonna, and pretty soon I was floating on a cloud and my mangled hand was floating right along with me.

After the doctor had amputated my ring finger below the first joint, stitched and bandaged and medicated me, Mr. Clayton took me home, and I had time to assess the damage to my fledgling music career.

The good news was that it was my right hand instead of my left, the left being the one I used on the neck of the instruments to form the notes and chords, the right being the one that held the bow or the pick. And as soon as I healed up, foregoing the possibility of a little different grip, I was going to be right back in business again. Had it been my left hand that took the injury, I'd have had to spend my life doing something besides playing a fiddle and you folks would probably never have heard of me.

But for the meantime, with the exception of having to eat with my left hand for a while, it would just be a major inconvenience.

Thank God.

CHAPTER 5

Finishing Up and Starting Over

Well, time marches on, and before any of us realized what was happening, it was time for the Goldston High School class of 1955 to don cap and gown. I had never given much thought to what I was going to do after I graduated. I knew what I wanted to do, but the opportunity simply didn't exist at that time.

When there are only twenty-two people in your class, graduation is a sober, lump-in-the-throat kind of affair. How do you suddenly say goodbye to people you have shared so much with? We marched down the aisle to the melancholy strains of "Pomp and Circumstance," picked up our diplomas, and walked out into a world we knew very little about.

A few in the class were headed for college, a couple for the military, some to run the family farm, and others, like me, to look for a job.

A couple of weeks after I finished high school, I started work at a capacitor factory in Sanford. Although I worked an eight-hour-a-day job five days a week, the nights and weekends were devoted to music.

My dream of someday being a full-fledged professional was just as much alive as ever. I knew where I wanted to go. I just didn't know how to get there yet.

In the mid-fifties, a new kind of music was sweeping the nation with the force of a runaway hurricane, and I wanted in on it. I started doing Little Richard songs at the fiddler's conventions and any place else we played. Now, I'll have to admit that "Tutti Frutti" done with bluegrass instrumentation was pretty strange. But the people just ate it up, and I knew I was on to something. I had discovered the power of rock and roll.

In the summer of 1955, a steel guitar player named Jerry Clark drifted through our part of the country. He was a professional who had played on the *Grand Ole Opry* with Little Jimmy Dickens, big stuff to guys who had never performed outside the Tarheel state. He was miles ahead of us musically, and when he agreed to play with us, we were ecstatic.

However, there was one problem. Jerry had a steel guitar but he didn't have an amplifier, which left him dead in the water. So, determined to make it work, I went down to Buchanan's Music Store in Sanford and cosigned for him to buy one on time and make monthly payments.

I wasn't too happy when Jerry drifted on out of town a few months later, leaving behind the amplifier and a bunch of unmade payments. Here I was, stuck with an amp, and I didn't even own an electric instrument. So I went back to Buchanan's and got a Gibson electric guitar.

It didn't take me long to realize what a big favor Jerry Clark had done for me by not paying for that amp. I was getting more and more into the new rock and roll sound, and that electric guitar went right along with me. Little did I know that the rockabilly era was just around the corner.

Our singer and rhythm guitar player, Dave Hall, moved out of town, and we replaced him with P. T. Wilkins, who also played guitar and was a terrific singer. We started playing some of the mainstream country songs, and with my formative efforts at rock, we began jelling as a band. We actually started getting paid modest sums for our efforts once in a while.

Things were proceeding quite nicely. I was making a living at my daytime job at the capacitor factory and working with the band doing our Saturday afternoon radio show and playing square dances, fiddler's conventions, and barbecue joints, where we'd set up in the parking lot and pass the hat.

CHAPTER 6

ANOTHER MOVE, AND THIS ONE HURT

Then Daddy changed jobs again, and the family moved back to Wilmington. It was one of the most painful of the many moves we had made over the years. I was nineteen years old, and some good things were just starting to happen for the band. After all the hard work, I'd be leaving it behind, not to mention the best friends I had in the world.

I wanted to stay, quit my daytime job, and give it a go with the music full time. But my parents said I was too young to strike out on my own, and they were probably right. Time has a way of turning disappointment into triumph, and that move was a necessary component in what was to happen to me during the next few years.

I had a day job waiting for me in Wilmington at Taylor Colquitt Creosoting Company. That was the same company Daddy was going to work for and where my maternal grandfather was a superintendent. But don't go getting any ideas about nepotism; it just wasn't that way. This was a job, not a patronage.

I was learning to be a timber inspector: inspecting, culling, and classifying poles, piling, and fence posts as they were brought onto the plant yard. The job involved a cant hook, a chain saw, and a whole lot of elbow grease.

I was training under Louis Frost, who years before had trained my daddy and knew ten times more about the job than I ever would. I was technically his boss, but I should have been working under him and was in every way but my title. Louis had one problem: he was black.

That's just how it was in those days. Civil rights legislation had been passed, but the perverse roots of segregation and discrimination hung stubbornly on in the Deep South. It would take many years and a lot of struggling before blacks gained much of anything from the newly passed laws.

I was born into a segregated Jim Crow society, and if you haven't lived through it, you couldn't possibly understand how it was.

The schools claimed to be "separate but equal," and at least the part about *separate* was true; *equal* was just a cruel lie. The black kids got the older school buses, the used books, the hand-me-downs, and the run-around. The white kids got the cream, and for some reason we all thought the black kids should be perfectly happy with whatever crumbs were thrown their way.

We never equated their emotions with ours. We thought they had a different set of values and priorities.

Every restaurant, every theater, every bus station, and every drinking fountain was designated black or white. There were three public bathrooms, white men's, white ladies', and colored. Sometimes there would be a sign in front of a business saying "White only." Black people were relegated to the back of the bus and special places on trains and were expected to use the back door when coming to a housekeeping job. They lived in their own shabby part of town referred to as "Niggertown."

I never went to school or church or sat in a movie theater with a single black person. It's hard for me to accept the fact that in my young life I was a part of a system that repressed a whole race of humans and that it came so naturally.

Although a lot of people would think that our attitudes were engendered by hate, that really wasn't it. Hate didn't enter into it. It was just an inbred sense of superiority that actually made you think you were created on a higher plane than black people. And it passed down through the generations like bad blood, indoctrinating children from the cradle until the conviction of racial superiority became as natural as walking.

It wasn't something you even thought about; it was just an automatic instinct that governed your actions in all situations, as if you were programmed.

There were devout Christians who could quote you chapter and verse of the Holy Bible who couldn't or wouldn't accept the fact that the

Scriptures said that God is no respecter of persons. Evidently, they thought that heaven must be segregated.

Looking back, it almost seems unreal. But it was real, all right; I lived through it.

I was working my day job and desperately trying to get something going musically. So far, all I had done was jam in somebody's living room. There just wasn't much going on at the time in Wilmington, North Carolina. Fraternal clubs like the Elks and Moose only had entertainment a few times a year, mostly on weekends or New Year's Eve, and the occasional school dance.

When the Sandy Brothers came to town and started their television show on WMFD TV, it caused quite a splash. WMFD was the only television station in southeastern coastal Carolina at the time, and people all over the area watched it.

The Sandy Brothers were head and shoulders above the rest of the country bands in the area, much more professional and polished. Leslie Sandy was a fine musician who had played with Bill Monroe and the Bluegrass Boys. He played fine guitar and was a good fiddle player. His brother Eldon played mandolin and brother Coolidge was on guitar. The same Jerry Clark who played steel guitar with the Misty Mountain Boys for a couple of months rounded out the band.

One Saturday night I went to the television studio to watch them do their show. One of the musicians didn't show up, and Leslie asked me if I wanted to fill in. Of course I wanted to fill in. The next day, I was amazed at the number of people who had seen me on *The Sandy Brothers Show*. I was learning about the power of the tube.

Jerry Clark left the band, and a piano player named Terue Davis took his place. I just kept hanging around, occasionally filling in on TV and going along on their road shows once in a while. I loved it. They weren't paying me anything much, but I didn't care. I was playing with the top band in the area.

As band members came and went, I did more and more with the Sandy Brothers. I started feeling I was important enough to become a full-time member and finally worked up the nerve to ask. I put the question to Leslie, but he wouldn't give me an answer right away. He told me he would talk it over with the rest of the guys and I should come by his place the next night and he'd let me know.

I went to Leslie's that night fully expecting to become a member of the band. After all, I played guitar and fiddle, sang, and could help out with the emceeing if needed. I had been loyal. I'd been there any time they'd needed me.

I drove up to Leslie's door, and he wasn't even home. He had left a note on the door telling me they wouldn't be needing my services anymore. I was bitterly disappointed, but I remember standing in Leslie Sandy's yard that night and thinking, *Before I'm finished, everybody in this state is going to know my name.* Little did I know, I was setting my sights way too low.

In the summer of 1956, I ran into Billy Shepard, a guitar player I had seen around town. He told me about a singer named Little Jill who had an offer for a six-night-a-week gig in Jacksonville, North Carolina. They were trying to put a band together, and was I interested?

Guess what my answer was.

CHAPTER 7

PAYING DUES ON THE INSTALLMENT PLAN

Jacksonville is about fifty miles from Wilmington and is the location of Camp Lejeune, home of the Second Marine Division. The gig would pay fifty dollars a week. It would require a round trip of one hundred miles a night, six times a week. This meant I'd be getting home after midnight, sleep a few hours, and go to my daytime job. So, what else was new? Bring it on.

You have to recognize opportunity, no matter how subtle the knock. Everything doesn't happen at once. One thing leads to another as the building blocks of your life start to take form. This was one of those times, and I just knew it.

We would be playing at Marvin's Western Bar four hours a night with a singer and a three-piece band. Little Jill was on vocals. Billy Shepard and I played guitars, and we had a drummer named Steve Kelly. It was the first band I played in with drums, and it really made me want to rock. Fueled by a bunch of hard-partying US Marines and copious amounts of Marvin's Old Mill Stream whiskey, we got pretty wild at times.

Little Jill, who actually hired us all, left the band, and Steve the drummer quit. We hired a drummer named Tommy Clemmons and a bass player named Norman Tyson and proceeded to rock Jacksonville.

We were actually hired as a country band, but things on the music scene were heating up. I was falling head over heels in love with rock and roll. I would just lose myself in the music at times, jumping around that little stage with my eyes closed, busting guitar strings, and singing "Be-Bop-a-Lula" for all I was worth. The US Marines just loved it.

They were a great audience. They were young, and many of them had just come out of boot camp at Paris Island. They were out to show the world how to party. Sometimes they'd get a little too exuberant, and it would result in fisticuffs. That's when the bouncers would move in. The last thing you wanted to do was cause trouble at a beer joint in Jacksonville, North Carolina, where the bouncer could well be a third-degree black belt karate expert or at least a talented street fighter.

We once had a bouncer who would put a sleeper hold on the rowdies and drag them out the door.

The only thing that was served at the bars in Jacksonville was 3.2 beer. The hard stuff had to be hidden in the back room and was illegal to even have in the place. But the legal drinking age was eighteen, and 3.2 percent beer was enough to get their motors revved. We all had a rocking good time.

I learned early on that I wanted to be an entertainer. Musicians come and go, but if you're able to entertain along with the music, there will always be a place for you. If you can make someone smile, it adds a lot to the show. It would be many years before I qualified as a real entertainer, but I was working on it.

For the first time in my life, I met people from all over the country. Marines from Boston, New York, California, Montana, Maryland, and all points in between came to Marvin's Western Bar to watch the chubby kid with the thick glasses get down.

The North Carolina ABC (Alcoholic Beverage Commission) slapped Marvin's Western Bar with a sixty-day suspension of license for some real or imagined infraction of the rules, and we were out of a job. But not for long. We moved across the street to a larger beer joint and a thirty-dollar-a-week-apiece raise.

The place was called S and M. I never knew what the letters stood for, but it was to be home to our band for a couple of years. The years 1956 and 1957 were intense periods of learning for me. I was onstage six nights a week, becoming more proficient on my guitar and finding what songs went over best in what order. I had stopped playing my fiddle. It just didn't fit into any of the music we were playing, and it would be a few years before I picked it up again.

I'd always wanted a Cadillac, and I finally got one. It was a black 1948 fastback with seven busted pistons. I had to get a bank loan to get it fixed. When I got it out of the shop and got it all polished up, it was a slick-looking piece of transportation.

I was getting up early six days a week for my daytime job, hurrying home every afternoon to shower, dress, and drive fifty miles. I would play four hours, drive back, and fall in bed exhausted after midnight.

I had no social life. On Sunday, my only day off from either job, I'd stay in bed all day. Sometimes I'd sleep until after dark Sunday night, when I'd get up and maybe go to a movie and then crawl back into bed until early Monday morning, when I'd start the whole thing over again.

Sometimes we'd play a service club on Camp Lejeune on Sunday afternoon. It was extra money and a lot of fun, but it meant working seven days a week. It was tough, but I was young and committed and jumped on any opportunity that presented itself.

My heart was in the music but not in my job at Taylor Colquitt. I was, for the first time in my life, making a living from my music. Actually, I was making more money from my playing job than I was from my day job. I had found something that I really wanted to devote my life to, and it had nothing to do with telephone poles and creosote.

It's funny how sometimes things come about as negatives and turn into positives. In the early summer of 1958, business had slowed down considerably at Taylor Colquitt; they were going through some layoffs. Guess who they were going to lay off in my department? My black co-worker Louis Frost, who knew ten times more about the job than I did or ever would.

The corporate decision was made on race alone, and it just wasn't right. In fact, as is the case with most of these kinds of decisions, it was downright bad business. I saw a chance to do Louis and myself a big favor. I said, "Lay me off. I've got another job."

So I left and Louis stayed, and a little piece of justice occurred because of my daddy. I had been on what was called straight time. In other words, I was paid a set amount regardless of what hours I put in. Louis and all of the other black employees were paid an hourly wage. If it rained or whatever and they couldn't work, they didn't get paid.

When I left, my daddy told his boss Mac Folger that Louis should take over the job I had left and be put on straight time. Mac Folger said, "Carl, we can't do that. We don't do it for any of our other colored employees."

Dad said, "Mac, let's do something right. I'm willing to stake my job on this."

The result was that Louis got the job, went on straight salary, and worked there until he retired many years later. I've always been proud of my daddy for having the courage to do the right thing.

Finally, and at last, I was exactly what I wanted to be, a full-time professional musician with no other means of income and no other ambitions that didn't pertain to music.

We had named the band "The Rockets" a year or so before. Though we were playing copy music, we started to develop a style of our own. Billy Shepard had a unique way of playing a boogie rhythm on the bass strings of his guitar. Norman Tyson had got rid of his big doghouse bass and got a Fender electric and amplifier that gave the music a thicker and hotter sound. Tommy Clemmons was on drums. I took care of vocals and lead guitar. We were young and rowdy and energetic, and it all came out in the music.

I bought an alto sax, learned a few finger positions, and added it to the show. I'd get up on the bar and walk around it blowing that horn and going through all kinds of contortions. It was actually pretty terrible, but with a driving rhythm section and a room of hard-partying US Marines, it was one of the high points of the night.

Then, for some reason that was never clear to me, Tommy Clemmons decided to join the army and we had to start looking for a new drummer.

In those days, rock music was fairly new, and most of the drummers old enough to play in a place that served alcohol had come out of jazz or big band dance music. It was tough finding a drummer who would just play the back beat and simple cymbal rhythms the music required.

There was a kid in Wilmington I had known since he was four or five years old. Even at that age he would take a pair of drumsticks and beat out a rhythm on anything you held in front of him. His name was Tony Hinnant. He was a teenager now, and he had gone on to play in the New Hanover County High School marching band and various combos around town.

When I approached him, he really wanted the job. The trouble was that he was only seventeen years old and had a year of school left. We decided that since he'd soon be eighteen, we'd just take a chance on him being underage. It was almost summertime, and we'd worry about the new school year when it started. In the meantime, Tony would finish out his junior year going to Jacksonville with us six nights a week and hope that the ABC guys wouldn't ask for his ID until he turned eighteen.

We bought plaid dinner jackets, tuxedo pants, cummerbunds, and bow ties that we would occasionally wear onstage. And we were packing 'em in.

I think we were the ones who got the closed-door policy instituted at the S and M.

In the summertime, the front door to the club would stay open and the music would pour out into the street, letting any and all know there was a live band. It would stay open until you couldn't pack another customer into the place.

I remember one night, when we were peeling the paint off the walls with our decibel level, a gentleman from some civic group or some such who was having a meeting down the street came to the S and M and asked Smitty, the club owner, to close the door. He said that the music was interfering with their meeting.

The closed-door policy stayed in force thereafter.

CHAPTER 8

Sometimes Fate Just Walks Right through the Door

It was a night in the summer of 1958, and The Rockets were at the top of our game when a very strange-looking person staggered into our lives.

His name was Bud Morris. He was as drunk as Cootie Brown, and what he was doing in Jacksonville, North Carolina, I'll never know. But there he was in the S and M bar, telling me how great The Rockets were and how we were wasting our incredible talent in a jerkwater town like Jacksonville. Due to his vast experience in show business, he knew just what we needed to do. The first thing was to get the heck out of Dodge, and he was the man who could facilitate such a move.

I was no stranger to such talk. More than once I had an inebriated US Marine or civilian tell me how well connected he was and how he could point the way to fame and fortune for The Rockets, only to disappear back into the woodwork, taking his fabulous connections with him.

Bud was staying at a small hotel next door. Somehow he convinced me to come by his room after work and let him tell me what great things he could do for the band. I don't know why I even went. As I said, I'd been approached by bogus blowhards before, but even as drunk as he was, there was just something different about this one.

I sat and talked with him for a while, and even in his snockered condition, it was apparent that he was no stranger to show business. He had a brother named Rod Morris I had heard of who was a Capitol recording artist, and I had to admit two things. He was really taken with our band,

and he did know a lot about the business, which I knew next to nothing about at the time.

I listened for a while and said goodnight, figuring I'd seen the last of Mr. Bud Morris. Little did I know that he would play a meaningful part in my career for years to come and would turn out to be one of the most colorful and resourceful characters I ever met.

Bud was a rambler and an alcoholic. But even at his most inebriated he never had a hair out of place, and his suit was always pressed.

When he started sobering up, he found himself hungover and broke. So he went to the local chapter of AA to find some temporary work to help him get back on his feet. The only thing he knew how to do was something related to show business. So the local AA guy called Smitty, our boss, and asked him if he had anything his broke AA brother could do to make a couple of bucks.

Well, Smitty, being the good-hearted fellow that he was, told them to send him on down, that he'd find something for him to do. It turned out that he would be the master of ceremonies for the band each night, which was kind of weird, to say the least. All we did at that time was flood the place with loud rock music for forty-five minutes, tell the US Marine audience we were going to take a fifteen-minute break, and come back and do it again.

Add Bud Morris, and it went something like this. Bud, all dressed up in suit and tie, would step to the mic and say something like, "Good evening, ladies and gentlemen. We welcome you to the S and M Lounge for an evening of fun and entertainment. We thank you for coming and know that you will enjoy our show. Now, to get things underway, here is The Rockets and their rendition of the Chuck Berry classic 'Johnny B. Goode.'"

He made a few attempts at comedy, but it fell pretty flat on a room full of young US Marines. But it became evident that this was not his first encounter with an audience. As I talked more with him, I found out that he did indeed have a lot of experience in show business, and he had been around the block with traveling variety shows and big bands.

He never lost his fascination with The Rockets. And in a few weeks when he drifted on, he promised he would call when he landed on his feet. I paid no attention to him and thought I'd finally heard the last of him.

We went back to our job, learning new material and rocking our way through four hours, six nights a week.

One night when I came offstage I had a phone call, and when I picked up the phone, I heard the unmistakable gravelly voice of Bud Morris. He was sober, and he was in Richmond, Virginia. He had gotten us an audition on the *Old Dominion Barn Dance*, a show patterned after the *Grand Ole Opry*. It was performed live on Saturday nights from the stage of the Virginia Theater and broadcast over WRVA, a fifty-thousand-watt powerhouse of a radio station.

He hadn't asked; he'd just done it. But he was so persuasive that I agreed to come to Richmond on a Sunday soon and audition for the *Old Dominion Barn Dance*.

So, after the last set on a given Saturday night, we packed up. Fortified with a fifth of bourbon and a case of beer, we set out for Richmond, Virginia, about three hundred miles away. Norman stayed sober and drove, and Tony wasn't much of a drinker. But Billy Shepard and I put a serious dent into our stash of alcohol, and we arrived in Richmond at about daylight on Sunday morning totally sloshed. We got rooms at some fleabag hotel Bud was staying at and slept a few, a very few, hours.

The audition was set for noon. When Bud woke us up to get ready, Billy and I were still walking loop-legged and hungover. After a shower and some coffee, we got dressed and went to the Virginia Theater, where Mr. Bert Repine, the manager of the *Old Dominion Barn Dance*, was waiting to hear us.

We went in, set up, and played a couple of lackluster tunes. During about the third or fourth song, the music clicked in. The sweat started popping out, and we were rocking that empty theater like it was sold out.

Mr. Repine was impressed and asked if we could come back and perform on a Saturday night in the not-too-distant future. He also asked if we'd be willing to play behind a girl singer he was managing named Janis Martin, who was signed to RCA Records and had already had a medium rock hit with a song called "Ooby Dooby."

Of course we were agreeable and set a date to return to Richmond. We said goodbye to Bud Morris and headed back to Jacksonville to explain to Smitty why we'd be needing a Saturday night off soon.

A few weeks later we headed for Richmond, sans bourbon and beer, to let the world outside coastal Carolina hear The Rockets for the first time.

In addition to playing the *Old Dominion Barn Dance* on Saturday night, Mr. Bert Repine had arranged an audition for us on Sunday up the road at Rose's Casino in North Beach, Maryland. The club, with slot machine gambling on the shores of the Chesapeake Bay, was a weekend summer retreat for people from the Washington and Baltimore areas.

The acts featured on the *Barn Dance* that Saturday night were the bluegrass group Don Reno and Red Smiley and Janis Martin and The Rockets. We had the only electric instruments on the whole show, and I don't believe the *Old Dominion Barn Dance* had ever seen anything like us.

When we hit the stage that night, the band was wearing loud plaid dinner jackets, and I was dressed in a fire-engine-red tuxedo. We did a couple of songs with Janis Martin and went into our own part of the show.

I really got into the music that night. It was our first show in front of a crowd outside of North Carolina, and I guess you could say we were showing off. I jumped all over the stage, slinging the expensive, radio-quality microphone down and jerking it back up by the cord, which was giving the engineers anxiety attacks. We rocked that crowd's socks off. I'm not bragging. I'm simply stating a fact. It was a stellar night.

We finished the evening with congratulations all around and admonitions from the engineering department that if we ever came back to take it a little easier on their microphones.

Flushed with the success of that appearance, we headed out to see what the good people of North Beach, Maryland, would think about The Rockets.

Rose's Casino was owned by Mr. Joe Rose, an astute businessman and an old-timer in the entertainment business. The club was on a choice corner across the street from a prime swimming area, and the streets were loaded as we took the stage. Soon it was the jumpingest joint on the beach.

You have to remember that rock and roll was in its infancy and not that many bands had caught on, and our little four-piece rockabilly band smoked the place. It was such a thrill to have people react to our music the way they did that weekend at the *Old Dominion Barn Dance* and Rose's Casino. We headed back to Jacksonville in a state of near euphoria.

We went back to our six-night-a-week gig at the S and M feeling pretty good about ourselves. Shortly after we got back, I got a call from Bud Morris, who had moved from Richmond, Virginia, to North Beach, Maryland. He was working as a bartender at Rose's Casino and had an offer for The Rockets to come up and play there for two weeks.

How could we turn down an offer like that? Our boss, Smitty, good fellow that he was, agreed to let us off for the two weeks.

Taking a job as a bartender is a bad idea for an alcoholic. When we got to North Beach, Bud was on a bender, sloppy drunk, and looking terrible. Tiny Jenkins, who was in charge of the entertainment, literally ran him off the property. I felt so sorry for him, the pitiful look in his eyes. The heartbreak of alcoholism really came home to me. But I hadn't heard the last of Mr. Bud Morris.

Through the week, it was just The Rockets and a guitar player/singer single named Cowboy Doug. But on the weekends there were two bands at Rose's, and we alternated sets. The other band was country. On Saturday and Sunday we started in the early afternoon and continued until closing time. It made for a long day, but we were breaking new ground and packing the place every weekend, which made up for any fatigue we might have felt.

The venue had agreed to provide lodging, which was a two-story house across the street with some beds, no air conditioning, and a cold-water shower. But it was handy and right on the beach. It was pretty primitive, but our work and social calendars had got so full that we didn't complain.

We had done excellent business and made some new fans and had a fun two weeks. When I went in to get paid after our last night, I thanked Mr. Rose for having us and told him goodbye.

"Where are you going?" he asked.

"We're going home, Mr. Rose. Our two weeks are up."

"You can't do that," he said. "I've got a union contract with a two-week option, and I'm picking it up."

The musicians' union provided contract forms that you just had to fill in the blanks and sign. I hadn't been a member very long and didn't understand about options and such. But here I was in the sweet dilemma of being such a smashing success on our first foray into the outside entertainment world that I had to call my employer and friend Jewel Smith in Jacksonville and tell him The Rockets would not be opening back at the S and M on Monday night.

Besides that, I was so homesick that I was about ready to cry and needed to get back to Carolina and see my family. Being away from home for extended periods of time was a new experience for me. But I was soon to become very accustomed to it.

I figured that if we were going to have to come back for two weeks, we may as well spend the summer, so I worked out a deal with Mr. Rose. We worked seven nights one week and five nights the next week. That way, we would get two nights off and go home every couple of weeks to charge our batteries.

Besides being in charge of booking the entertainment for Rose's Casino's summer season, Tiny Jenkins was a booking agent who had a lot of contacts in the Washington area. He assured us we could get work in D.C. when the summer beach season was over.

The band was starting to make a name for itself in the area, but we had one very serious problem. Our drummer, Tony Hinnant, still had one year of high school left, and the time for him to start the school year was fast approaching. Nobody, including him, wanted Tony to leave the band. I decided to talk to his father and see if he would give his permission for Tony to finish his senior year by taking correspondence courses. I was afraid I'd be disappointed with the result.

Tony Senior was a drummer himself and, as it turned out, very sympathetic to his son's desire to be a full-time professional musician. He agreed on the condition that Tony would take correspondence courses and get his diploma. Even though our intentions were sincere and honorable at the time, it never happened.

Tony was only eighteen years old, a good-looking kid, and a flashy drummer who quickly earned a reputation for turning the crowd on with his drum solos. Word was getting around. One day a long, tall, lanky character named Dave showed up at North Beach and said, "Where is this eighteen-year-old drummer who is going to make me break my drum sticks?"

Dave was a drummer in the Washington, D.C., area, and as I said, the band was gaining a reputation. That night he sat on the side of the stage, and when Tony launched into one of his solos, Dave literally tried to break a pair of drumsticks over his leg.

We spent the summer amid sunburns and slot machines, summer girlfriends, lessons learned, and the thrill of making a living playing our music. When the summer ended, Norman Tyson moved his family up from North Carolina. Tony, Billy, and I got an apartment together in D.C., and Tiny Jenkins booked The Rockets into the Famous Bar and Grill on New York Avenue in Washington, D.C.

Washington had a lot of clubs, and once you broke into the circuit, there were plenty of places to work. We joined a nucleus of other bands that moved from club to club, playing six nights a week and staying for two weeks or longer. Once we stayed at the Dixie Pig in Bladensburg, Maryland, for a whole year.

As I said, Norman Tyson was married, but Tony, Billy, and I were footloose and fancy-free. We rented apartments and all chipped in to pay the rent, which for some reason or another was always a few days late. We didn't fit in too well at the apartment complexes. We didn't get off work until 2:00 a.m., and we'd sleep the biggest part of the day. Our leisure time didn't start until the wee small hours of the morning, when most apartment dwellers were fast asleep. The well-attended parties we threw were boisterous, to say the least. They would sometimes end up with a visit from the D.C. police, answering a call from a justifiably irate neighbor who lived over, under, or across from us.

Needless to say, we had several addresses in those early years. We got together with a couple of other guys and rented a three-story house that turned into the party capital of the nation's capital. When the rest of the town was fast asleep, things were just getting started at our place, until we defaulted on the rent and were asked to leave and moved on to be a thorn in another neighborhood's side.

We ran into a terrific eighteen-year-old sax player named Paul King. He joined the band, adding a new musical diversity to our sound and broadening the range of material we played.

In those days we played a lot of Little Richard, Fats Domino, and Lloyd Price. Sax instrumentals like "Honky Tonk" and "Smokie Part Two" were hot dance pieces, so Paul's tenor sax fit right in.

We were staying anywhere from two to four weeks in the clubs on our circuit and had a solid following. We usually worked six nights a week with Monday night off and were just as apt to show up and jam with another band on our off nights.

We rehearsed often and kept up with the new music that fit into our repertoire. We dressed in loud dinner jackets and tuxedo pants, a pretty on-the-ball little outfit, and had no problem staying steadily employed.

But The Rockets' horizons were getting ready to expand by about three thousand miles.

CHAPTER 9

BLAST FROM THE PAST

In 1958 I got a call from the amazing Bud Morris. Remember, I told you how he kept popping up in my life. He had gotten married and was living in Riverside, California. He was flying to Washington to talk me into taking the band to California.

I met Bud at National Airport. As soon as he hit the ground, he started his sales pitch about how we could have the state of California at our feet if we would only go out there and show those people how wonderful we were. He proposed booking us on a string of one-nighters and wanted us to be there shortly after the first of the year, which was only a couple of months away.

I had never been west of the Mississippi River and was itching to see what the rest of the country looked like. "Hey, y'all, let's go to the left coast!!!"

Our trip would be in February and last about a month, so we just couldn't leave all of our D.C. friends without a loud, rowdy farewell party. I'm sure the month we were gone was a relief to the people who lived in our apartment complex.

I had traded in my Cadillac for a 1956 Ford station wagon. We painted the name of the band, The Rockets, on the side, loaded up, and headed for California. We had a luggage rack on top where most of the instruments and luggage rode. The rack piled high and with a tarp tied over it, we looked like fugitives from *The Grapes of Wrath* coming down the highway.

In those days the interstate system was practically nonexistent. We took what was called the "Rebel Route" through North and South Carolina,

Georgia, Alabama, Mississippi, Louisiana, Texas, and New Mexico, finishing on Route 66 through Arizona to California.

When we were playing in Jacksonville, I had made friends with a drummer named Bill Belcher, a US Marine stationed at Camp Lejeune. Bill was from Texas, and when his hitch was up, he had moved back. But he had stayed in touch. Since we were going through Fort Worth, we broke the trip up for a couple of days and stopped to see him, which turned out to be one of the best career moves I ever made.

We traveled straight through, switching off drivers, and got to Fort Worth early in the morning. After a lot of effort, we found Bill Belcher's house, said our hellos, met his wife, Nita, and his son, Kyle, and went and checked into a motel.

After sleeping for a while, we went back to Bill's house, where his wife had made a humongous pot of the best chili I ever tasted. Needless to say, we acquitted ourselves admirably at the table.

That night Bill showed us around town and told us about a friend of his who was in the music business. He said he'd like to bring him by the motel and introduce us to him the next day.

I happened to look out of my motel room window the next morning and saw Bill Belcher with some guy in tow, headed our way. I had a blank pistol with me, and when they got close to the room I stepped out, leveled the pistol at them, and started firing blanks. Both of them almost jumped off the second floor walkway before Bill recognized me.

Don Johnston was a struggling songwriter and record producer. And, much like I had been a couple of years before, he was doing everything he could to cut the apron strings of his day job and make it full-time in the music business. His ambition and work ethic knew no bounds, and he was determined that Fort Worth, Texas, wasn't going to hold him for long.

He was aggressive and confident. After a night on the town, he asked me if I'd like to take the band into the recording studio and cut something. I jumped at the opportunity.

The only problem was that we didn't have anything to record, which was not a deterrent to Don at all. He said, "We'll just write something." We moved all the band instruments into Don's mother's house and set to work.

Don's mother, Diane, was a songwriter signed to Mellin Music

Publishers in New York. She had written quite a few songs herself, including a Western favorite called "Miles and Miles of Texas," which was recorded by Bob Wills and His Texas Playboys and in later years by Asleep at the Wheel. She welcomed us with open arms, made sandwiches for us, and was a great encouragement and a pleasure to be around. It started a friendship, and I stayed in touch with her until she passed away a few years ago.

We started kicking around ideas, and after many hours and a lot of hard work, we came up with a slick little sax and guitar instrumental. The next night we moved the instruments into a recording studio, where the five of us, with Bill Belcher adding an extra snare drum, started a process that would last until daylight the next morning. When we finally got it finished and listened to the playback, we all agreed that "Jaguar" sounded like something that would play on the radio along with the Duane Eddie and Johnny and the Hurricanes instrumentals that were so popular at the time.

Don would send the tape to New York to Mellin Music, who would shop it to the record labels, a common practice in those days. Independent producers would make records and sell or lease them to the record labels. Some of the big hits of the 1950s and 1960s had happened that way.

Well, this was all very exciting, but we had gigs to play one thousand five hundred miles away in California. Don promised to call when he got word of the record companies' reactions to "Jaguar." We said our goodbyes and headed across the west Texas plains, still zinging in the glow of our very first real recording session.

Seeing the western United States for the very first time was a moving experience for a bunch of kids who had never been very far west of Charlotte, North Carolina. We watched the prairies turn into high desert and then to a barren landscape of sand and sagebrush as we drove straight to California. We got to Riverside on a late Saturday afternoon.

Bud Morris had been sober for quite a while and married a really nice lady. He was at the top of his game and as good as his word, and we went to work Sunday night. We played one-nighters in Barstow, Victorville, Pasadena, and all around southern California. We'd never seen highways with so many lanes and so many people driving so fast.

On one of our nights off, Bud took us to Las Vegas. We spent the biggest part of the night in the lounge in the Sahara Hotel listening to Louis

Prima and Keely Smith with Sam Butera and the Witnesses, who were one of our very favorite bands. We even got to meet Louis Prima. What a night!

Louis Prima and Keely Smith were the hottest lounge act in Las Vegas. Their show was fast paced and entertaining and made a profound impression on our whole band. We added quite a few of their numbers to our repertoire.

Bud also took us to Tijuana, Mexico, on one of our nights off. It was my very first trip into a foreign country. All we had to do was cross the border to realize just how blessed we were to live in the United States.

One Sunday afternoon we were playing at a club in Mojave. The dance floor was jammed and the band was cooking when two California ABC officers walked in and spotted Tony and Paul, who were both under the age to be in a bar in California. They wrote them up and took them to city hall to book them.

Of course they were terrified. Bud had to post bond before they would turn them loose. One of the officers was a real hard case in spite of all of our pleadings about being from out of state and that it wouldn't happen again. Tony and Paul were going to have to go to court, necessitating obtaining legal representation and making a return trip to California to face the charges in the future.

As it turned out, they had to do neither. The agent who wrote up the arrest papers wrote down the wrong law number, which meant they were charged with something they hadn't done. After we got back to the East Coast, they actually sent affidavits releasing the agent from liability. Tony and Paul could have sued the State of California, but they signed the affidavits and sent them back, glad to have it behind them.

In the meantime, it severely curbed the number of venues available to us in California, limiting us to places that had significant food service or didn't serve alcohol at all. But Bud found us enough work to get us through the rest of the tour.

Don Johnston called me and said that the instrumental we recorded with him in Fort Worth had been picked up by Epic Records, and we needed a B side before they could release the record. Well, that was just about the greatest news I could have gotten. We changed the name of the band from The Rockets to The Jaguars in honor of what we hoped would be our first hit record.

We were scheduled to open back at the Dixie Pig in Bladensburg, Maryland, after we finished our California run. So we headed out a couple of days early to go through Fort Worth and cut another side for "Jaguar" that we called "Exit Six."

The only bad part about our stop in Fort Worth was that we got the news about the plane crash that had taken the lives of Buddy Holly, Ritchie Valens, and J. P. "The Big Bopper" Richardson. You can't help but wonder where Buddy Holly would have taken his music if he had lived a few more decades.

It was February 9, 1959.

CHAPTER 10

MIDNIGHT MADNESS AND WILD OATS

We returned to The Dixie Pig to find ourselves billed as The Jaguars, "Just returned from the West Coast."

The Dixie Pig was a big old honkytonk where the blue-collar crowd came to party, dance, and sometimes fight. It had a nucleus of regulars that were fair but fearless when pushed. They brooked no foolishness, and if their dates told you that they didn't want to dance with you, it was wise not to ask again. But the rowdy bunch at The Dixie Pig, who for some unknown reason called themselves The Dirt Buzzards, loved the band, and we loved them, and a good time was had by all.

We dove back into the club scene with a vengeance, knowing our new record would soon be released. If it took off, we were going to be in demand in a lot of places besides the D.C. area.

Up until now, we had not had a regular booking agent. I had handled getting most of our work, but if we were going to take a big step, we needed to play outside the limited area we'd been appearing in and we needed representation. So we signed with the Norman Joyce Agency in Philadelphia. This would significantly expand our territory since the Joyce Agency handled a lot of club bands and pretty much had the Eastern Seaboard covered. But home base was still the D.C. area.

When Epic released our long-awaited record, it took off like a house on fire, being added to radio playlists all over the country. The most popular Top 40 stations in the D.C. area added it in regular rotation, which at one station meant it played every two hours.

We did the local version of Dick Clark's *American Bandstand*, *The Milt Grant Show*, and played the hops and teenage dances. It looked like our first record was going to be a hit, and it was. It was what was called a "turntable hit," which means it got lots of airplay but did not sell through in the record stores.

Bobby Mellin, who had placed our Jaguar record, wanted some more music from us and sent Don Johnston to town to make it happen. It would entail writing songs, arranging and rehearsing, and recording them, all the while working until almost 2:00 a.m. in a nightclub six nights a week.

The only time available to do this was in the mornings. We'd work our five hours at the club, tear down the instruments, and go to our apartment and sleep a few hours. Then we would go to a rehearsal hall or a recording studio, set up the equipment, rehearse or record until the afternoon, tear down the instruments, go back to The Dixie Pig, set the instruments back up, play our sets, and start the whole thing all over again.

Musicians, especially young musicians, are nocturnal creatures who like to sleep most of the day, but that all came to a screeching halt when Don Johnston came to town. We got up early and worked all day and most of the night.

I learned a lot about life and about myself during those hard-working days in Washington. If you want something bad enough, you're willing to work a little harder and make some sacrifices. Those days helped to shape my work ethic and built toughness. You need plenty of both if you're going to make it in the music business.

We released a few more singles, and nothing significant happened. But the studio experience I gained was to be a plus for me in the years to come. Don Johnston, who later changed his name to Bob Johnston, was to become a whole chapter in my life.

When we added a terrific trombone player named Robbie Robinson, it gave us a bigger sound and some decent three-part vocal harmony and enabled us to explore new musical horizons. We started leaning more and more toward a jazzy sound we called "Rockhouse," which was a grooving, shuffling, highly arranged type of music. It was much more polished and sophisticated than the raw driving sound we had become known for.

Actually, it was musical self-indulgence and worked for a while, but it would turn out to be a mistake in the long run.

Jazz had been king in the Washington area. Legendary names like guitarist Charlie Byrd and saxophonist Vi Burnside called Washington home base. Jazz played on the radio, and there were lots of combos playing the clubs around town. But insofar as being the dominant music around D.C., in the late 1950s jazz was in its death throes. It was being pushed out of the way by Elvis, Fats Domino, Little Richard, Carl Perkins, Jerry Lee, and the copy bands that played their songs.

We had come to town a four-piece band of wet-behind-the-ears kids who pushed it to the red line every time we got onstage. Now we were a six-piece band wearing black tuxedos, playing Frank Sinatra and the Four Freshmen, and trying to sound like some Miles Davis offshoot. I would soon learn my lesson that self-indulgence in the music business is a dangerous thing, especially when you're supposed to be playing dance music and the hits of the day in clubs that hire you for that reason and that reason alone.

I don't blame anybody for following their own creativity and their own musical tastes, playing whatever genre or style of music they want to. But there's a good chance you're going to end up sitting in your living room playing by yourself.

I was not a jazz musician. I was a Carolina boy with Southern roots, germinated in country, and one of the first passengers when the rock and roll train rolled through town.

And here I was trying to play music that I really didn't care that much about for no other reason than trying to be cool and trying to impress the out-of-work musicians who frequented the clubs and talked about Miles, Bags, and Kenton.

I was soon to learn some much-needed lessons in more ways than one.

CHAPTER 11

BURNED FINGERS AND BURNED BRIDGES

In 1961 I met and started dating a girl named Lee. She was fun to be with, and we started going steady, if you could define hanging out with a musician who had one night a week off as going steady.

She started talking about getting married right off the bat. I had never thought too much about marriage. I guess I just assumed that one day I would, but I was only twenty-four years old, and I had a lot I wanted to do in my life. That's why I can't figure out why I let myself get talked into it, but I did.

We tied the knot at my parents' house in Wilmington, went to Myrtle Beach for a couple of days, and lived in marital bliss all of two weeks before I realized I had made the biggest mistake of my life. We just didn't get along. She was always threatening to leave, and we came right to the edge of going our separate ways a few times. I'm old-fashioned about marriage and was determined to give it my best shot, but it was taking a toll on me. I have always hated arguing and dissension, and when you have it at home, you never get away from it. I kept hoping that things would get better, but I think I knew in my heart that they never would.

Robbie Robinson, our trombone player, stayed with us for about a year and then gave up the itinerant life to marry a wonderful girl named Barbara, whom he is still married to.

Tony and Billy married two great ladies named Sandy and Jan. Everybody in the band seemed happily married except me.

Paul King, our sax player, left the band to go with another outfit, and I hired a guy who played in bands around the D.C. area. His name was Adrian Swicegood, but for obvious reasons he went by the nickname Switchy, and we continued to play the club circuit.

Due to changing the style of music we played, we lost some of our popularity. We just weren't playing what the people wanted to hear, and I learned a hard lesson about dancing with the one who brung you.

Dissatisfaction and restlessness started creeping into the band. Norman moved his family back to Wilmington. Tony and Switchy went with other bands. Billy quit the music business and went back to doing the sheet-metal work he did before he became a full-time musician.

I formed a new band with a drummer from Wilmington named Ronnie Piner, a bass player named Boogie Nolan, and a sax player named John McGraw. We started doing one-nighters with Dick Obitts' Capitol Talent Agency, and things started getting hard. We had to drive long distances, set up the equipment, play until late at night, tear down, and drive back. I probably could have handled it if things had been good at home, but they weren't. The combination was getting to me. For better or for worse, I needed a change.

A singer named Barry Darvell needed a band to take on the road, and his first stop was Indianapolis. I got back together with my old drummer and sax player, Tony Hinnant and Paul King, added a bass player, rehearsed a few times, and got ready to go to Indy.

Lee and I gave up our apartment, sold our furniture, and took off with Barry Darvell in one last attempt to save our ailing marriage. We had no home base or permanent address. We had a car and what we could pack in it, and that was it.

Our first gig was for two weeks in the Tiki Ho Lounge at the Antlers Hotel in Indianapolis, and the next engagement was in Virginia Beach, but a hurricane got there before we did and badly damaged the club. Here I was, broke, out of work, and without any immediate prospect of finding any.

I called my daddy, and he sent me some money. Lee and I headed west, not really knowing where we were going, just looking for a place where we could fit in. We made a dartboard decision and headed for Denver, Colorado. We didn't have the money to stay in motels, and Lee couldn't drive, so when I'd get sleepy I'd find a place to pull over and sleep for a while and drive on. We ate cold-cut sandwiches and just kept moving west. When we got to Denver, we were so broke that we couldn't even get a place to stay.

I took what meager possessions we had left to a pawn shop. We got a room in a cheap motel and started looking for work. Lee didn't have a problem. Due to her secretarial experience, she got on with Manpower, the temporary employment agency. But with me, it was different. I couldn't even get anybody to listen to me play. I tried but couldn't find anybody who needed a guitar player in all of Denver.

I took a job separating metal at a junkyard, the only thing I've done that was not music-related between 1958 and the present day. It was a real low point in my life, not because I'm too good to work in a junkyard but because I was spinning my wheels, not doing what I had devoted my life to. But, looking back, it was probably a good lesson for me to learn.

I was desperate to get back to my music. After five weeks of working at Sam Barter's junkyard, I contacted my old drummer friend Bill Belcher, who had moved his family to El Paso, Texas. He was working days at a used car lot. He said to come on down, and we'd put a band together and get something going.

Since Lee could get a temporary job through Manpower just about anywhere and it seemed that things had slightly improved between us, we packed up and headed for El Paso, traveling on expired car tags.

A Colorado highway patrolman noticed and pulled us over. I told him our new tags were waiting for us in El Paso, which was an out-and-out lie. But he let us go.

The tags weren't the only thing expired on the car. I hadn't made a payment since we'd left D.C. and would never make another one. I would leave the car parked on the street and it would be picked up and repossessed, and they didn't even know where I was. That was one of the many things I did during that period of my life that I'm certainly not proud of.

CHAPTER 12

New Beginnings or Last Stand

Bill Belcher's family had grown; now in addition to his son, Kyle, they had a daughter, Lisa. When Lee and I moved in with him and Nita, they had a full house. In the daytime Bill was working at a used car lot, and at night we went pub crawling, looking for work and for musicians to play in the band we intended to put together.

We got a young bass player named Joe Johnson and a sax player named Jimmy Arceneaux. With Bill on drums and me on guitar, we started picking up a few gigs and building a local reputation.

Lee went back to work for Manpower, and we scraped up enough money to get a two-room apartment for fifteen dollars a week. But we were back to having serious problems again. All we did was argue, and I hated it. Things were coming apart at the seams, and the cheap wine and Mexican rum we consumed so much of weren't helping things. We were both drinking way too much.

One night during one of our frequent marital spats, I went across the border to Juarez and partied all night. I got up with a couple of Mexican guys who were about as looped as I was, and we were walking down the street being loud and boisterous and got picked up by the Juarez cops and hauled off to jail.

I was so out of it that I lay down in the cell they put me in and went to sleep until I was woken up early the next morning. I was put in the small claustrophobic back of a van and hauled over to the big jail, which is actually a prison with a holding cell for wayward Gringos, who they figure will eventually be bailed out.

As I sobered up, it started dawning on me what a mess I was in. I was in jail in a foreign country, where American due process doesn't apply, completely at the mercy of a judicial system that could make up the laws as it went along if it wanted to.

Nobody knew where I was. But in those days, when somebody didn't show up around El Paso, the first place the streetwise people checked was the Juarez jail, known for picking up Gringos for any trumped-up charge it could come up with to collect the bail money.

This is what happened, and some folks came over and bailed me out later in the morning. I went back across the border with my tail tucked and a strong resolve to stay out of Juarez, which worked for all of about three days before I started going back again, with a weather eye out for anybody wearing a badge.

The band was starting to pick up speed. We called ourselves The Jesters. At first we worked two or three nights a week, but a guy named Bill Barnes, stationed in the army at Fort Bliss, started booking us, and we got busy.

It seemed like the better things went for the band, the worse they got on the home front. I had no peace, and after a long and tedious night of fussing and arguing, at about three o'clock in the morning, I walked out of the apartment. I just couldn't take anymore. I didn't even know where I was going, but I just had to get away from that woman. It wasn't that I didn't love her; I just couldn't live with her. It was killing that part of me that had always been happy.

This time there would be no reconciliation. A few weeks later, we made it official with a Mexican divorce.

I started sharing a room with our booker, Bill Barnes, whose marriage was also on the rocks. I dove into my newfound bachelorhood with a vengeance. Most nights after work I was across the Rio Grande in Juarez, Mexico, boozing and carousing around. In those days it cost two cents to cross to the Mexican side and one cent to come back to the American side. I have been so broke after a night in Juarez that I had to borrow a penny to get back to the United States. Then I'd have to walk a couple of miles back to the place where I was staying.

One morning I woke up with a cop shaking me, not even realizing that the sun had come up and that people were walking all around me. I had fallen asleep on a bench in front of the El Paso Public Library.

We were working hard, and I was living even harder. It was a wild, unprincipled, and irresponsible time in my life. I slept the biggest part of the day, partied all night, and spent every cent I could get my hands on.

During the week we worked lounges and sometimes the service clubs at Fort Bliss and Biggs Air Force Base, but the weekends were a killer. They started with a Friday afternoon jam session at a funky joint called Chaplains on South El Paso Street, a few blocks from the Mexican border. Then we had the Friday night gig. Saturday started with an early afternoon television show at a used car lot, and then we had the Saturday night gig. We didn't have roadies; we humped our own equipment. I once walked several blocks carrying a Fender Twin amplifier because I didn't have the money for cab fare.

During the week the schedule let up a bit, but the partying stayed hot and heavy. Waking up with a hangover got to be par for the course. It was enough to wear down even a feisty twenty-five-year-old.

We started taking Preludin, a Mexican amphetamine you could buy over the counter at the drugstores in Juarez. I don't know what it had in it, but after a weekend of popping Preludin, you felt as if all the insulation had been stripped off your nerves and you were just about to explode.

The folks Bill Barnes and I were renting our room from moved across town and took over a bigger rooming house. We moved with them, getting a two-room apartment in the bargain. In that same apartment building lived a dark-eyed young Mexican lady named Sylvia Delores Socorro Ordonez. I felt an attraction to her, and she felt the same about me, so we started dating. We really enjoyed each other's company, and it may have turned into something. But I was not in the frame of mind for any serious stuff.

One morning I was coming out of Juarez after a night of being up to no good and tripped on a streetcar track, hitting my mouth on a rail. I was so loaded at the time that I didn't feel much pain until I woke up a few hours later to discover that I'd cracked my two front teeth beyond repair. I had to go back to Juarez, where a Mexican dentist dug the roots out. I went around with my two front teeth missing until I got the money to have another Mexican dentist make a partial for me.

For some reason I peroxided my hair, and it turned gray blonde. I had broken my regular glasses and wore thick prescription shades. With my two front teeth missing, I must have been a weird sight. I was living a wild, undisciplined life, living for the moment, with little thought for the consequences. I was out of control, burning the candle at both ends, and only the love of our merciful God kept me from disintegrating.

My mother and dad drove out to El Paso to visit me. When my mother first saw me, she started crying. I had changed so much since the last time she'd seen me that it really upset her. The first words she said to me were, "I'm taking you home with me." Of course I didn't leave with them. After staying a few days, they headed back to North Carolina, not feeling too good about their only son.

But I did start having second thoughts about the life I was living. I actually started staying home some nights after work, drinking less, and reevaluating my situation. I had to admit that although I thought I was having the time of my life in El Paso, I was actually slowly killing myself. I had put all my dreams of being somebody in the music business on hold, treading water, letting the world pass me by while I partied my life away on the Mexican border. After some honest soul searching, I came to the conclusion that if I stayed there, I would never accomplish any of the things I had set out to do.

I loved being in El Paso. I loved the band I was playing with. I had a girlfriend I really cared for and had forged some strong friendships. But something was missing in my life. I had had my fling. I had gotten out of a bad marriage and sown enough wild oats for any two people. I knew if I stayed there, it would be one beer joint and one party after another as the years rolled relentlessly by and the elusive bird of opportunity flew away.

I grew up a lot during that period of reflection. I made a hard decision. I was going to go back to the East Coast and get back in the race. I called my old booking agent Dick Obitts. He had gone into business with another agent named Bill Sizemore and was operating an agency called Capitol Talent out of an office in Baltimore. The icing on the cake was that they had a full-fledged recording studio. Dick wanted me to come back and write songs and produce records. Bingo!

It sounded like the ideal situation, or at least a good place to start. A few days before Christmas, I played my last gig in El Paso and said goodbye to Sylvia Delores Socorro Ordonez and all of my friends. I headed east, riding with Bill Barnes, who was driving back to the Washington area to spend Christmas with his family and would drop me off in Wilmington to spend Christmas with mine.

Then I was getting back into the game!

CHAPTER 13

Just a Stop Along the Way

When I got to North Carolina, I called Bob Johnston, who was now a staff writer for Hill & Range music and living in Nashville. He said he'd pay my airfare to Nashville and on to Baltimore if I wanted to come through town and spend a couple of days writing songs with him. I enthusiastically took him up on it.

Bob's wife is a beautiful and gracious lady named Joy. I really enjoyed the time I spent with them, but Bob believed in hard work. We spent endless hours putting words and music together, and one of the songs we wrote during those days in Nashville was to be the biggest thing to happen in the early days of my career.

I flew into Baltimore around noon on New Year's Eve of 1962. I had just come from the land of mild winters and was dressed accordingly. There was snow on the ground, and when I set my guitar and suitcase down to put my ungloved hands in my pockets, a frigid wind came along and started blowing my luggage down the icy sidewalk. The thought *What am I doing here?* occurred to me as I picked up my stuff and headed on out to find the Capitol Talent offices.

One of the bands that the agency booked had a New Year's Eve gig that night and was short a guitar player. So I worked on my first night in town and filled in with the band for a few weeks while they found a regular player.

Dick Obitts had arranged for me to share a small apartment with one of the local musicians, and I began a new phase of my life as a songwriter, record producer, and musician.

I wrote and cut quite a bit of music in Baltimore, and although I didn't produce any hits, I gained a lot of practical studio savvy and learned a lot about making records. It gave me the opportunity to hone my songwriting skills, which was to become a bigger and bigger part of my life. But as much as I loved writing and the studio, I quickly discovered that my heart was really onstage, playing music and entertaining people.

For some reason I would deviate from this realization several times in my career but always end up back at the same place.

I needed to put together a band and go back on the road. A local drummer named Buddy Davis wanted to sign on, and a guitar player named Ward Darby had just come to town and was looking for a job. He called a sax player he knew in Pittsburgh named Bill Vickers, who was interested and flew to Baltimore to join up. I switched from guitar to bass, and we had a slick little four-piece band.

We didn't have much rehearsal time because we started playing gigs right after Bill Vickers, who went by the name of Vic Catalano, got to town. But the audiences didn't know it because we were able to improvise on songs we all knew and play them together without rehearsal.

You could tell if a musician had put a lot of time in with club bands because there was a nucleus of songs that every club musician had to know. They were what the people wanted to hear and dance to. Everybody knew "Honky Tonk" and "Johnny B. Goode," the Elvis catalog, ballads like "In the Still of the Night," and the time-tested, standard R&B dance tunes. So, basically, all we had to work on were the latest tunes.

Clint Butram, an old friend of mine who was an apartment mate from my wild, single days in D.C., got in touch with me. He was living in Tulsa, Oklahoma, and said he thought the town was ripe for a good band and offered us a two-week booking at a club called the Fondalite. It sounded good to me, so we finished up the gigs we already had booked and headed west.

The Fondalite Club was situated at 11th and Denver and was already a popular night spot with the local bands it featured, and when The Jaguars hit town, we were like a breath of fresh air. Now that we were settled in one spot for a couple of weeks, we were able to catch up on rehearsals and learn the new popular tunes.

Some songs were so popular with the crowds that we had to play them three or four times a night. The Righteous Brothers' song "You've Lost That Lovin' Feelin'" was one of the most-requested songs we ever played.

Tulsa loved us, and we loved Tulsa and struck up a long and successful relationship with the Fondalite Club and Jerry Osborn, the owner. When we left town, it was with a promise to come back in the near future.

And return we did, on a regular basis from 1963 through 1966. We played there and at the Hi Ho Club in Wichita, Kansas, so often that we severed ties with the booking agency in Baltimore. Although we were living out of a suitcase, we considered Tulsa home.

I flew back to Nashville in 1963 to do some more writing with Bob Johnston. We knew that Elvis was recording at RCA studios, but what we didn't know was that he was recording a song called "It Hurts Me," the song we had written together in 1962. When we found out the next morning, it was like living in a wonderful Technicolor dream. Elvis Presley was the biggest artist on the planet, and to have him do a song I had cowritten was almost past imagining. Colonel Parker took half of the writers' royalties for Elvis when he hadn't written a note of it. But that didn't dampen my spirits at all; I was going to have my name on an Elvis Presley record!

I just couldn't wait for "It Hurts Me" to be released. Later in the year it came out on the flipside of a movie song called "Kissin' Cousins," but both sides of Elvis songs were hits in those days. My euphoria was short-lived when I found out that my name was not on the label, which turned out to be a clerical error. The second run of records included a very relieved "C. Daniels" in the writers' credits.

As great as it was being a cowriter on an Elvis Presley song, something much more wonderful was about to happen to me.

CHAPTER 14

TONIGHT I MET THE GIRL OF MY DREAMS, FOR REAL

One night during a break at the Fondalite Club, I stopped by a table to say hello to a girl my drummer Buddy was dating, and sitting at the table with her was a curvy little blonde. Her name was Hazel, and she was some kind of foxy. I was smitten and asked her to dance, which was probably the worst first impression I could have made on her since I'm just about the worst dancer in the Western world. But she didn't seem to mind my two left feet, and we hit it off.

That night a new and wonderful chapter began in my life, and I soon fell into a kind of love I didn't even know existed. The whole world seemed different; I wanted to be with her all the time. When I was away from Tulsa, I couldn't wait to get back to her, and the most incredible thing about it was that she felt the same way about me.

I'll never forget the day I told Hazel I loved her. It was on a beautiful Sunday afternoon on the top of a Ferris wheel at Mohawk Park in Tulsa that I told her how I felt about her. She said she felt the same, and when we got off that Ferris wheel, we knew we wanted to spend the rest of our lives together.

The only night I didn't have to work was Sunday, and on September 20, 1964, we were married by a justice of the peace. Our honeymoon consisted of one night in my room at the Reeder Hotel because I had to be back to work at the Fondalite Club that Monday. It was to be long, arduous years before I was able to give her a real honeymoon. But, thank God, I've been blessed to take her places we could have only dreamed about on that Sunday morning in Tulsa, Oklahoma.

Hazel has been the one stable thing in my life. No matter what else was going on, even if the world was falling in on me, she has always been there loving me, supporting me, and telling me that as long as we were together everything would be all right. She has given me the reason and encouragement to climb some very tall mountains and go through some very low valleys. She has stuck it out with me through cheap motels, cars that wouldn't start, used furniture, repossessions, mountainous debt, too many bills and too little money, and my being away from home for long periods of time.

There is nothing I wouldn't do for her, up to and including laying down my life. She is the glue that has held me together, the tether that has kept me from going off the deep end so many times and in so many ways. She is my anchor, my port in life's storms, and there is absolutely no way I could have accomplished what I have without her by my side.

For the first time in my life, I was truly fulfilled. I was happily married and the band was drawing crowds.

Then, businesswise, things started falling apart.

CHAPTER 15

THE SHOW NOT ONLY MUST
BUT WILL GO ON

We had a booking in Orlando, Florida, and when we got ready to leave town our drummer, Buddy Davis, informed me that he would not be going with us. No notice, no nothing. Buddy had gotten into a bad relationship that was just about to drive him crazy. He was confused and hurt, and I could sympathize with him. But that didn't change the fact that the band was opening at the La Flame Club in Orlando and I was leaving town without a drummer and little idea of where to find one on such short notice.

There was nothing else to do but pack up and head for Florida. I made phone calls to everybody I could think of, but nobody I wanted was available. By the time we got to Orlando, we were desperate and frantically put out the word that we needed a drummer right away, and a guy named Salty Loveland showed up. We quickly rehearsed enough tunes to get us through a couple of sets and went to work.

We had no sooner gotten the drummer replaced when Ward Darby, the guitar player, left the band. One night he was there, the next night he wasn't. I was stuck again.

I would like to interject something here, a little advice for all you aspiring band leaders, from a lesson I learned the hard way.

Both Buddy Davis and Ward Darby had threatened to leave the band before, and I had talked them out of it. That was a big mistake. If a musician threatens to quit, he is going to quit at some time in the future and possibly leave you in a lurch. I've developed a policy over the years. When an employee says anything about leaving my organization, if the word "quit" comes out of his mouth, he has given notice. He is gone, and I will replace him the next day if possible. I'll give him severance pay if he gives me notice, but I want him out of my outfit as soon as possible.

There is nothing to be gained by having a disillusioned employee hanging around. It causes dissension and affects the other band members. No matter how good a musician plays, he's not worth the hassle. And there's not a musician in the world who can't be replaced.

So don't bring your personal troubles to work with you one night and tell me you're going to quit because you'll wake up the next morning unemployed, and I'm not going to change my mind: you're out of here. There is no one in my band that can't be replaced except me.

I switched back from bass to guitar. That solved one problem but left me short on the bottom end of the band. I now needed a bass player.

There was another musician staying in the same motel as we were. He was an organ player who not only played the organ keyboard with his hands but played the bass pedals with his feet, and on top of that, he could sing. I'd see him from time to time around the motel, and he didn't seem to be working a lot. I asked him to come by and talk to me.

He was fresh out of Massachusetts and spoke with the "pahked the cah at the bah" New England accent. His name was William Joel DiGregorio, known professionally as Little Joe Roman, and in years to come, he would acquire the permanent nickname of Taz.

He had a great singing voice and did the James Brown, Wilson Pickett–type songs that were so popular with the dance crowd in the 1960s. And a new voice and an organ would give us a sound we'd never had.

I hired him on the spot and went into intense rehearsals to catch our new players up with the existing repertoire.

Some months before coming to Florida I had bought an old used school bus, pulled the seats out of it, and put in a couple of bunks and a couch. There was plenty of room for the instruments, and it was a great way to travel when it didn't break down, which it did frequently.

I hate old vehicles. I've driven so many pieces of junk, breaking down, not starting, blowing tires and engines, and keeping me broke trying to keep them running. I wanted a new vehicle. I've had enough worn-out, worrisome automotive garbage. I wanted a speedometer with zeros on it. But, there again, it would take me many years to learn that lesson and many more to acquire the resources to do anything about it.

CHAPTER 16

Happiness Comes in Swaddling Clothes

One of the very greatest blessings of my life occurred at Hillcrest Medical Center in Tulsa, Oklahoma, on April 28, 1965, when our one and only son was born. We had planned on naming him Charles Edward after me, but since Hazel's dad and my dad both had a William in their names, we decided to make everybody happy and name him Charles William.

I needed to do something nice for Hazel's family. An itinerant musician of meager means and questionable stability had taken away their baby daughter, and they didn't really understand what I did for a living and why I had to leave their daughter alone so much.

Her parents, Dessie and R. D., had taken me right into the family, but I'm sure they still had some serious doubts about their youngest daughter's future. The arrival of Charles William Daniels smoothed out any rough edges and gave them a whole different opinion of their wandering son-in-law.

A few weeks after he was born, Hazel flew to Wilmington to let my parents meet their only grandchild, and we had two sets of proud grandparents.

By far the hardest thing about being a professional road musician is being away from your family. It was hard enough before, but when my son was born it became doubly hard. When Little Charlie was about six months old, I was gone from home for sixteen weeks, and when I finally walked through the door and picked him up, he started crying. He didn't know who I was, and that hurt.

I have wept bitter tears because I missed my family so much. And it's no easier on the family. I missed my son's first steps, his first words, grammar school plays, and high school football games.

There is a price to be paid for following the path I chose. When I hear people nowadays say that I've had it easy because I've been able to chase my dreams, I think, *You don't have any idea.* I would advise anybody considering a career as a traveling musician to stop and weigh the cost before you take the leap, especially if you have a family.

In my case I was driven by something that I can't even put a name on. It just seemed there was something inside me that had to find a way to get out, something better, something higher, something unique and special, and something that I had to pursue. I felt that I had not touched my potential, that there were songs I hadn't written, musical heights I hadn't explored, and dreams I hadn't even dreamed yet. I knew that until I had exhausted every avenue open to me to accomplish whatever it was I was looking for, I would never be complete.

I realized early in my quest that there is no set of maps that can chart your course for you. There is only trial and error, growing some thick skin, getting up one more time than you get knocked down, and never ever giving up. And that requires some sacrifices.

You work while everybody else plays. You travel while everybody else sleeps. You miss family birthdays and anniversaries, and your kids grow and change while you're gone.

Yes, there's a price to be paid. I've seen strong men come apart on the road. What the public sees is the gilded tip of a very large iceberg. And that's as it should be. It's up to us who pursue the dream to cowboy up and walk onstage night after night as if we don't have a care in the world. When it gets to the point that you can't do that, it's time to go home and look for another profession.

Hazel understood this, and as my son grew older, he did too. I tried to make up for my long absences by maximizing my off time with my family, spending every minute I could with them.

Shortly after Little Charlie was born, our sax player Vic left the band. We were down to a trio and decided to stay that way. It was Salty Loveland on drums, Taz on organ, and me on guitar, and we were versatile and tight.

One of the finest female vocalists around in the 1960s was a pretty young black lady from Louisville named Ruby Winters. She could belt out a funky R&B tune or just melt you with a ballad, and when she came to work with us, it added to the musical and also the entertainment capabilities of the band.

Our club circuit had expanded, and in 1966 we went up to spend five weeks entertaining the troops at the air base in Thule, Greenland. It was the most isolated place I've ever been—on the edge of the polar ice cap, without a single tree or even a sprig of grass, nothing but ice and desolation as far as the eye could see.

There were no women there except for a few nurses and the female entertainers, especially none as pretty and as talented as Ruby Winters, who attained superstar status immediately. For the five weeks we were there, Ruby was the undisputed queen of Thule Air Base.

We were there with two other bands. There were three service clubs on the base—officers, noncoms, and enlisted men—and we alternated between them, playing a different one each night.

It's hard to even imagine the amount of alcohol consumed by the airmen, the civilian technical representatives, and the Danes who worked on the base. Denmark owns Greenland, and the Danes pride themselves as being able to hold their alcohol as well as anybody on the planet.

Guess it's that Viking blood.

I was sitting in the bar at the enlisted men's club one afternoon when this Danish guy walked in complaining that, although he had consumed copious amounts of alcohol, he hadn't been able to get drunk. I hadn't had any trouble and asked why he didn't try one of the high-powered specialty drinks the bartenders in Thule prided themselves on that were potent enough to stun an elephant.

He replied, "Have you ever seen a Dane drink?" As a matter of fact, I had seen quite a number of them staggering around the base, but out of regard for our host country, I didn't reply to his flippant put down.

There was this young American kid standing, or rather leaning, on the bar. He was already snockered, but nevertheless he alluded to how he could drink this Dane under the bar that was holding him up, eliciting a condescending scoff from the Dane. The kid was so drunk already that I figured if you hit him on the rear end with a rotten apple, he'd fall on the floor.

Well, one thing led to another, and it was agreed that there would be an American/Danish drinking contest, with each contestant consuming equal amounts of potent libations until one of them passed out or admitted defeat.

The first round went down rather smoothly, although the American kid appeared to get drunker and drunker while the Dane retained a smooth and debonair demeanor. By the time the second round was served up and consumed, the American kid looked like he had a weight on his head, his speech slurred and incoherent, while the Dane looked as if he'd had a glass of dinner wine.

They ordered the third round amid partisan concerns about our boy being able to hold up his end of the bargain. I was watching the American kid, who was in grave danger of toppling off his barstool, when I heard somebody holler, "Look at that Dane!" I did in time to watch him slowly slump to the barroom floor, out cold.

The American kid still had half his lethal concoction in his glass. He raised it to the ceiling, bellowed, "Here's to the King and Queen of Denmark," downed the rest of his liquid hangover, and joined the Dane on the floor. Of course, the Americans were ecstatic.

I saw glaciers, icebergs, huge Arctic rabbits, black Arctic foxes, and a polar bear in the wild in Greenland. I rode on a genuine Eskimo dog sled and saw a lot of sights I'll never forget. It was my first trip to a foreign military base, and I learned about the loneliness and sacrifice our armed forces make to keep America free.

In the days before satellite technology, bases like Thule were our first line of defense. Right across the North Pole from Russia, they monitored the Russian military in the air on huge radar screens. If the Soviets had shot a missile toward the United States, the troops at Thule would have been able to tell where it was shot from, its trajectory, and how fast it was moving. Then they would spread the word, and the counterattack would begin.

It was rumored that there was a nuclear armed flight that constantly flew in the skies close to Thule that was ready to drop its load on Russia if the big one ever started. It was a highly strategic and state-of-the-art base at the time, and I'm glad I got to see it in full operation.

Bases like Thule have largely been replaced by satellite surveillance and other technological advances. But looking back, it's frightening to think that the United States could have been moved to the edge of nuclear war by a blip on a radar screen. It took dedicated and responsible people to make split-second decisions to avert a catastrophe.

Thule was a hoot, but when our five weeks were over, we were all ready to see our families. I headed for Wilmington, where Hazel and Charlie were visiting my parents, stayed a couple of days, and pulled out for Toledo, Ohio, with my wife and baby in tow.

They would stay with me for a week or so. Then Hazel would go to Newport, Kentucky, to set up the apartment we had rented there, which would be our home for a year or so.

CHAPTER 17

OH THE JOYS OF LIVING THE HONKYTONK LIFE

It was a grinding, demanding kind of life playing the club circuit. It was six nights a week, five hours a night, and you played whatever the people wanted to hear. Some of the club owners were great people, and some of them were never satisfied. I got so tired of hearing, "You guys play too loud." But the truth was, we probably did.

We worked them all, the slick lounges with low lights and intimate dance floors, the honkytonks and skull orchards where the air always smelled like cigarette smoke and stale beer, where macho young predators roamed the shadows looking for a dance or a fight, whichever came first. We played the military bases, the roadhouses, and the occasional dance. We took on all comers and tried to give them their money's worth, no matter where and no matter what.

Being away from home for long periods of time is a lonesome experience that constantly pulls on your heartstrings in the most ordinary of circumstances, but when it started getting close to Christmas, the feelings intensified. When the carols started playing on the radio, the decorations started coming out, and the Christmas shows started on television, it really got tough. "Rudolph the Red-Nosed Reindeer" could make me so homesick, I was almost reduced to tears.

I would always be at home for at least a couple of days for Christmas, especially after I had a family. Hook, crook, drought, or flood, I was going to find a way to be with Hazel and Little Charlie on Christmas.

In the days before I was married, I spent Christmas Day in Wichita,

Kansas, at a movie with a couple of other musicians who couldn't make it home for Christmas. I never wanted to do that again.

Bill Sizemore, who I knew from the Capitol Talent Agency days in Baltimore, had gone on his own and opened a new agency in Newport, Kentucky, right across the river from Cincinnati, and offered me a partnership. That meant I could help out at the agency office, play gigs in the area, and spend more time at home with my wife and son. So, I broke up the band and moved my family into an apartment in Newport.

Tony Twist, an organ player from Tulsa, came to town, and we started a guitar and organ duo and got a long-term gig in a Holiday Inn lounge in Lexington, making the 150-mile round trip six nights a week. I had more family time than I'd had since Little Charlie had been born.

I had only been in Newport for a few months when I got a call from my old friend Bob Johnston. Bob had done well for himself in the past few years. He had gone to work for Columbia Records and produced highly successful albums by Bob Dylan, Simon and Garfunkel, and others. Columbia had given him the job as head of A&R operations in Nashville, replacing the legendary Don Law, who was retiring. Not only would Bob continue to produce artists, he would be in charge of Columbia Record's Nashville operation.

When he asked me if I'd like to move down there and try to get something going, I heard the subtle hand of opportunity knocking. It would basically mean starting over again, moving the family, and making a living in one of the most musically competitive towns in the country. But I had always wanted to live in Nashville, and it just felt right. It took Hazel all of five seconds to agree that it was a good move, so I started making arrangements to move to Music City, USA.

CHAPTER 18

Music City, Here I Come

Bob Johnston cosigned a thousand-dollar loan for me to move my family to Nashville and even let us rent a house he owned at a price we could afford. After paying my bills and buying a guitar I needed, I hit town on April 13, 1967, with a twenty-dollar bill, the clutch out on my car, and a busted water pipe in the house we were moving into.

I took everything of value we had left, got on a city bus, and went to a pawn shop in downtown Nashville. We had a baby to feed.

Cars were always a problem in those days. The first new car we managed to buy got repossessed, and I bought an old Opal from Tony Twist. By making regular trips to a local mechanic shop, it got us through for a while.

We wouldn't have made it in those early days in Nashville if it hadn't been for the generosity and friendship of Bob Johnston. He loaned me money and used me on recording sessions when he could. If there's a human I owe a lot to professionally, it's Bob. He'll always have a place in my heart.

I got a job on the weekends with a band in Lexington, Kentucky, and drove up on Friday afternoon, worked Friday and Saturday nights, and got home early on Sunday. Hazel said she could hear that old Opal coming from blocks away on a quiet Sunday morning. But it was a welcome sound because Daddy was coming home with money to buy groceries for another week.

As I said, Bob would use me on recording sessions when he could, but I didn't fit too well on Nashville sessions of that day. I was different. All of the Nashville pickers played like they were in a recording studio, and I played like I was slamming away in a beer joint. I was the proverbial square peg and just didn't fit the gentile sounds of country music in the 1960s.

I did whatever I could to make a living for my family, playing occasional recording sessions, filling in for club musicians, and driving to Lexington, Kentucky, every weekend to play my regular Friday and Saturday night gigs.

Christmas of 1967 was rolling around, and no matter what our financial situation, Santa was going to come to see Little Charlie. Hazel put toys in layaway, and we paid for them in increments and picked them up at Christmas.

Hazel and I were not going to exchange gifts that Christmas. But I had a chance to make some extra money playing a Saturday afternoon jam session with another band in Lexington and used the money to buy a small electric train for Little Charlie and a bowling ball for Hazel.

She had joined a bowling league but didn't have the money to buy her own ball. The surprise and happiness on her face when she saw it Christmas morning made all the extra work I'd done to get it seem trivial. To this day if you asked her what her favorite Christmas present of all time was, she'd tell you that sparkly green bowling ball I gave her in 1967.

A club owner I knew named Frank Duncan opened a new place called the Houndstooth on White Bridge Road in Nashville and offered me a job. It meant I would have a steady gig and wouldn't have to drive to Lexington, Kentucky, every weekend. So, I took him up on it.

Frank already had a dance band; he wanted somebody to entertain his clientele. There was a strange law in Nashville at the time: although the club could serve liquor until 2:00 a.m. on Sunday, people had to stop dancing at midnight. It was just one of those archaic laws that had not been stricken from the books for some reason or another and put a serious crimp in one of the biggest club nights of the week. At midnight when the dancing stopped, people would start leaving.

That's when I went into my act. I did impersonations, comedy bits, and a show-stopping version of "Malaguena" on my guitar, anything to keep the paying customers from walking out the door, and it worked.

I got up one morning in February 1968 coughing and with my chest and head full of congestion. After a several-decades-long period of denial and excuse making, I had to come face-to-face with the fact that what was actually wrong with me was caused by the out-of-control cigarette habit I had had for all of my adult life.

My nicotine dependency was so critical that if I got up during the night for one reason or another, I would have to have a cigarette before I went back to bed.

Any cold or bronchial infection I developed was exacerbated by my habit so that every bout would stretch into weeks of coughing and feeling fluey to the point that I basically kept a cold all winter long.

This particular morning when I got up, I felt so rotten and so stuffed up that I finally stepped over the line and admitted that my four-to-five-pack-a-day smoking habit was the cause of my misery. In a rush of honesty and enthusiasm, I blurted out, "I will never smoke another cigarette."

At about ten o'clock in the morning, as my lungs loosened up and my breathing got easier, the intense craving began, and I sincerely regretted making that promise. But a vow is a vow, and with nine packs of cigarettes left in a carton, I stuck to my guns.

For about two or three weeks, I almost tore the pockets out of my shirts trying to locate the cigarette I so badly craved, and then it was over. I have neither smoked nor craved a cigarette since.

Praise God!

CHAPTER 19

Opportunity Knock, Knock, Knocking on My Front Door

I had been at the Houndstooth for almost a year when Bob Dylan came to town to record another album with Bob Johnston and the Nashville pickers. I was and still am a big Dylan fan and admirer, so I asked Bob Johnston if there was any way he could let me play on just one session.

Sessions in Nashville are scheduled so you can fit four into a day: 10:00 a.m., 2:00 p.m., 6:00 p.m., and 10:00 p.m. As it happened, the guitar player they had scheduled for the 6:00 p.m. session couldn't make it and wouldn't show up until the 10:00 p.m. session, so Bob fit me in for 6:00 p.m.

I was the hungriest musician in the studio. I hung on every note that Bob Dylan sang and played on his guitar and did my best to interpret his music with feeling and passion. When the session was over, I was packing up my guitars to head to my club gig, and Bob Dylan asked Bob Johnston, "Where is Charlie going?" Bob told him I was leaving and that he had another guitar player coming in.

Then Bob Dylan said nine little words that would affect my life from that moment on. He said, "I don't want another guitar player. I want him."

And there it was. After all the put downs, condescension, and snide remarks, after all the times I'd driven to the hill above my house and shook my fist at Nashville and said, "You will not beat me." After all that rejection, none other than the legendary Bob Dylan was saying that I might be worth something after all. It's bits of encouragement like that that keep you going. Once in a while something just lights you up and you say, "Yeah, I can do this."

Needless to say, I called the Houndstooth and told them I wouldn't be coming in that night.

The album turned out to be *Nashville Skyline*, and I went on to play on two more Bob Dylan albums, *Self Portrait* and *New Morning*. Since Dylan always listed the names of his recording musicians in his album credits, some people started noticing my name and I started to get some public recognition.

Bob Johnston quit the corporate side of Columbia, went on his own as an independent producer, and continued to add meaningful artists to his roster. One of the first things Bob had done when he came to town was record the first number-one hit Marty Robbins had had in a while, a song called "Carmella," which helped him establish his bona fides in Music City.

Then he took Flatt and Scruggs to new levels of sales and brought Leonard Cohen to town for his *Songs from a Room* album. To top it all off, he recorded Johnny Cash's blockbuster album *Live at Folsom Prison*, and the floodgate opened.

Johnny Cash was bigger than life in the music industry and in person. Since I worked with Bob Johnston, I had the opportunity to run into Johnny a couple of times. He was unfailingly nice to me every time I saw him. He had no reason to be except that it was just the kind of man he was, and it meant so much to me. I'll always honor his memory.

After Flatt and Scruggs broke up, I played on some Earl Scruggs records. When he formed the Earl Scruggs Revue, he asked me to play with them. Earl's sons Gary and Randy were young and talented, and we had a great time together.

The first time I ever played on the *Grand Ole Opry* was with the Earl Scruggs Revue.

Nobody, and I mean nobody, played a five-string banjo like Earl. Guys came along who played faster and flashier, but nobody had the touch and the soul of Earl Scruggs. He was one of a kind.

Earl called me in late 1969 and told me he had made a decision to attend a peace rally to be held on the Mall in Washington with Peter, Paul, and Mary, Pete Seeger, Arlo Guthrie, and a bevy of politicians and public figures who were coming together to try to persuade the government to bring the troops home from Vietnam.

I know that decision had to be a tough one for Earl, as it could possibly have alienated a lot of his older, conservative fans who would misunderstand his motives. But Earl Scruggs was a man of principles and made up his mind based on those principles instead of his career.

I told Earl that of course I'd go with him, and on a cold November day we joined hundreds of thousands of other Americans on the big Mall in Washington to try to sway the Nixon White House to bring our troops home from Vietnam.

The problem with this and most of the other vast rallies of those days was that there were always fringe groups and troublemakers who showed up to grind their axes for everything from prison reform to evading the draft. But the massive crowds on the Mall in Washington that day had come for one reason: to bring our troops home from a war the politicians refused to let them win, and they got their point across.

My parents and grandparents came to spend a few days with us at our house in Nashville. Not being able to get tickets to the Saturday night *Grand Ole Opry*, Hazel took them to a Saturday afternoon performance, which the *Opry* was doing at that time to accommodate the overflow of folks who couldn't attend the Saturday night show. It featured some of the lesser lights, the up and comers, and other good artists, but not the top stars the *Opry* was known for.

My grandmother had listened to Roy Acuff ever since he had joined the *Opry* in 1938, and just before they left to go to the show, I remember her saying, "I don't reckon Roy Acuff will be there, will he?"

I said, "No, ma'am, he won't." But at the same time I was thinking, *Little lady, one of these days I'm going to take you to the Grand Ole Opry when Roy Acuff will be there.*

Some years later, I was able to take both of my grandparents backstage at the *Opry*, where my grandmother was able to meet Mr. Acuff, spend time, and take pictures with him.

That is one of the proudest nights of my life.

CHAPTER 20

The View from the Other Side of the Control Room Window

Bob Johnston was in demand and extremely busy and started giving me a weekly salary to be a kind of assistant and errand runner. I took things to Johnny Cash while he was doing his television show. I even picked up Bob's kids from school a couple of times.

We could never figure out how Bob Dylan's albums got bootlegged.

Spectators were not allowed in the studio when he recorded. At the end of each session, the tapes were locked away in a vault and mixes and copies were strictly controlled and carefully guarded.

I used to take a flight to New York for no other reason than to hand carry a copy of a mix of a Dylan album and personally put it into the hands of one of his people, for him to listen to and approve.

Yet with every precaution that was taken, somehow bootleg copies of Dylan's work would show up on the street.

One time I was in sole possession of an entire unmixed Bob Dylan album in several bulky eight-track tape boxes.

I was in New York and Bob Johnston didn't want to leave the tapes there, so he asked me to take them along with me and get them back to Nashville.

I was going to North Carolina to meet Hazel and Charlie Junior and spend a couple of days with my parents.

When I got to LaGuardia Airport—this was in the days before 9/11—they told me the boxes had to be run through the x-ray machine, which could erase part of the recording.

I told them it was the only copy of a new Bob Dylan album and that the only way I'd let it go through an X-ray machine was for the airline to assume the liability for any loss.

They backtracked pretty fast, and I was on my way, carrying my bulky load with me.

Even while doing these things, I was still playing on all the sessions I could, writing songs, and keeping my antenna out for anything that would take me another step up the slippery music business ladder.

Marty Robbins had been one of my favorite singers since he had come on the scene back in the 1950s, and working on a couple of his records was a real highlight for me. I remembering being in the studio playing guitar and hearing that magnificent voice singing, "My Woman, My Woman, My Wife."

For my money, Marty was one of the finest country music singers of all time and working on his records was an honor.

CHAPTER 21

BIRD ON A WIRE

When Bob Johnston brought Leonard Cohen to Nashville to record an album, I have to admit that I knew very little about him and was completely unfamiliar with his music.

Leonard was a totally different kind of artist than any I had ever worked with. His music was sensitive and haunting, and the imagery of his lyrics was abstract and poetic, like a Georgia O'Keeffe painting. Leonard was from Montreal and had already built an underground audience with his first album, *Suzanne*. He was best known in Europe and in his native Canada, where he was an unofficial poet laureate, but he was building a following among the college crowd in the United States.

When I first heard "Bird on a Wire," I didn't know what to think. Here was a truly unique artist, and his songs were so delicate that one out-of-place guitar lick could bend it out of shape. When you worked with Leonard, you had to listen closely and get in sync with what he was trying to convey. You had to interpret it in the same musical frame he was operating in. Sometimes it only called for a well-placed note or two, sparse but meaningful. I know that sounds philosophical and stilted, but so was Leonard's music. You needed to be in a certain frame of mind, and it was a challenging but satisfying experience.

After the popularity of "Bird on a Wire" and some of the other cuts on *Songs from a Room*, Leonard wanted to go on tour, and I was asked to be part of the backup band that would be called The Army. It was a different kind of band, mostly acoustical instruments with no drums. We needed to surround Leonard with delicate, genteel sounds. For a bang, slam, redline graduate of thirteen years of honkytonk and rock and roll, it would be a learning experience.

I had revived my interest in my fiddle and played it, mandolin, guitar, and bass. Bubba Fowler and Ron Cornelius played guitar, and Bob Johnston played harmonica and organ. We had two backup singers, Corlynn Hanney and Susan Musmanno, and with Leonard's gut-string guitar, it was the perfect backup group to match the complicated persona of Leonard Cohen and his unique and fragile music.

We played a few dates in the United States and embarked on a five-country European tour. Leonard and the rest of the band flew from Nashville to Holland, where we would open at the Concertgebouw in Amsterdam. Bob Johnston had to go through New York on business for a day and asked me to go with him. We would fly over and join the others the next day.

I was sitting around the hotel room in New York when Bob called and asked me if I'd like to come down to Columbia Studios and play bass on an impromptu recording session with Bob Dylan, George Harrison, and a studio drummer named Russ Kunkel. Of course I wanted to, and the four of us spent a relaxed and pleasant day just doing whatever song Dylan felt like doing. We cut old songs and new songs, none of which could be released by Columbia Records because George Harrison didn't have current working papers.

It was the neatest day and one of my all-time-favorite musical memories. Dylan even took requests that day. You could just name one of his songs, and he'd go into it.

George was a really nice little guy, friendly and conversational. It was right after Paul McCartney left the band, and he jokingly asked in his thick Liverpudlian accent, "Do you want to be a Beatle?"

He asked me who played steel guitar on Dylan's albums, and I told him it was Pete Drake. George was just about to go into the studio in London to record his *All Things Must Pass* album and said he'd like to have Pete come over and play on it. I got a contact number, gave it to Pete's office, and the rest is history. But that's not the end of the story; I'll get to it in a while.

The next night Bob and I caught a plane to Amsterdam and joined the rest of the band to start the tour. I was amazed at the popularity of Leonard Cohen in Europe. He sold out the Royal Albert Hall in London and the Olympia Theater in Paris, caused a near riot in Hamburg when he raised his arm in a misunderstood "Sieg Heil," and enchanted hundreds of thousands of people at two o'clock in the morning at the Isle of Wight Festival.

Earlier in the evening at the Isle of Wight, I stood in the wings of the stage watching Jimi Hendrix perform, having no idea that in about two weeks he would be dead.

Not long after I got back to Nashville, I got a call from Pete Drake's office to ask me to play on an album that Ringo Starr was coming to Nashville to do. It seemed that while Pete was in London playing on George Harrison's album, he had run into Ringo, who expressed a desire to do a country album. Pete told him to come on over to Nashville and get it done. If you look at the picture of the musicians on the back of Ringo's *Beaucoups of Blues* album, you'll see a young Charlie Daniels sprouting the beginnings of the beard I've worn ever since.

CHAPTER 22

YOUNGBLOOD AND NEW GROUND

The music business is wheels within wheels. One thing leads to another, and you never know when something mundane and ordinary is going to lead to something exciting.

Bob Johnston was hot and in demand. And when he was approached by a San Francisco group called The Youngbloods, he told them that he didn't have time to produce an album for them but had a friend in Nashville named Charlie Daniels who did.

The upshot was that The Youngbloods wanted to have a face-to-face meeting and talk it over, so I boarded a plane for Los Angeles, where the band was already at RCA studios, working on some tracks without a producer.

They were a three-piece band that sounded much bigger. Joe Bauer was the drummer, a guy known simply as Banana played guitar and key-boards, and one of the best singers I've ever worked with, Jesse Colin Young, handled most of the vocals and played bass. I hung out in the stu-dio with them for a while. We had lunch and talked, and they decided they wanted to work with me. I went back to Nashville as proud as a peacock. A few weeks later, I headed out to California to produce an album for The Youngbloods.

The first problem we faced was that the RCA studios in Hollywood were built to record movie soundtracks with a seventy-piece orchestra. They were so big that you could have played a game of touch football in them.

We built a room out of sound baffling in one end of the studio so that

The Youngbloods's three pieces wouldn't look like an island in a lake, and we started to work on a project called *Elephant Mountain*.

It became clear very early that there were two factions in the band. There was Jesse, and there was Joe and Banana. Most disagreements about sounds and mixing divided along those lines, which left me in the unenviable position of taking sides. That's why I'm opposed to a band not having a clear-cut leader; otherwise, you're floundering around and arguing and nitpicking every time there is a decision to be made.

When I came on board, the band was working on one of Jesse's songs called "Darkness, Darkness," which was to become my all-time favorite Youngbloods song. With Joe locked in on drums, Banana's smoking guitar, and Jesse's magnificent voice floating over the top, and with the addition of the fiddle work of a player they brought in from the band Kaleidoscope, it was an impressive piece of work.

We finished a few tracks and broke for Christmas. When we came back, we moved to a much smaller studio on Vine Street that suited the purposes of a three-piece band much better.

We started cutting a track for another one of Jesse's songs; it was a breezy piece called "Ride the Wind." It needed a light, airy treatment, and try as we might, we just couldn't get it to feel right. Finally, on the sixth day of tracking that one song, I pushed the talk-back button and said, "Gentlemen, I think we've got a track," and it was a good one.

In fact, the whole *Elephant Mountain* project was a fine piece of work and the first album I produced that made the Billboard charts.

The next project I worked on with The Youngbloods was a live album named after Jesse's "Ride the Wind" song and recorded at Fillmore West in San Francisco, Fillmore East in New York, and a pop festival in Baton Rouge, Louisiana. Something unique happened at all three venues.

Fillmore West was the first time I had ever heard Chicago. They were on the bill with The Youngbloods that weekend and nothing short of great. I was in the recording truck outside the venue. It was a Sunday night, and Bill Graham, who had just come in from New York, got onstage and said, "About three o'clock this morning, upstate New York found out about Santana." It was Woodstock weekend.

On a Saturday night at Fillmore East that featured The Youngbloods and Jefferson Airplane, Bill Graham got ticked off at the opening act, a group who called themselves the New York Rock Ensemble, and fired them on the spot, leaving the show an act short. Jack Casady and Jorma Kaukonen, the bass player and guitar player for the Airplane, brought in a couple of guys and took the spot, the advent of Hot Tuna.

In those days, a pop festival was a three- or four-day event featuring maybe twenty or so bands. The one we recorded live in Baton Rouge was no exception, with the Grateful Dead, Jefferson Airplane, Chicago, Tyrannosaurus Rex, and of course The Youngbloods, among others.

Most of the bands were staying at the same motel, and it was shortly after the *Easy Rider* movie came out. You talk about a nervous bunch, sitting right there in the Deep South with all that long hair and those weird-looking clothes. It was as if danger lurked around every corner, and somebody was going to show up and have a mass lynching.

Being from the South, I thought their attitude was funny, and it got me thinking along the lines that led to the song "Uneasy Rider." Wheels within wheels.

Working with The Youngbloods was my first venture into the San Francisco rock scene but was not to be my last. Jerry Corbitt had been a member of The Youngbloods until he opted out for a solo career, and he was ready to make his first album for Capitol and was looking for the right producer. After Jerry had a conversation with Jesse Colin Young, who gave me good grades on The Youngbloods's project, he contacted me about working with him.

A deal was struck, and I was on my way back to California, this time to help Jerry Corbitt make his first solo album in, of all places, crazy Berkeley.

CHAPTER 23

What Goes Around Comes Around

Berkeley was not your typical middle-American city in the early 1970s. Just about every far-left radical organization had a presence on the West Coast. It was a mecca for fringe groups and oddballs, and there were some pretty far-out people walking the streets, some of them truly committed to one cause or another but a lot of them just along for the ride.

One morning on the way to the studio, I stopped at a drugstore for something. There was this dingy little guy with tangled rat's-nest hair trying to buy a bottle of cheap wine but he was short a dime. Somebody in line behind him paid the ten cents for him, and he bellowed, "Thank you, brother, the revolution will be won on ripple."

Now, what kind of revolution was going to be won by a man who couldn't even find his way to a shower and was out buying a bottle of rotgut at ten o'clock in the morning? Certainly not one that I'd want anything to do with. That was a problem with the hippie movement. Some of the people involved had ideas and causes, although some of them were seriously misguided, but most of them were just clones who grew their hair out and came to the Bay Area to get high and participate in the free love movement.

The album I produced for Jerry Corbitt was not successful sales-wise, but I had made a lifelong friend, and as a result of our relationship, something would happen that would change the course of my career.

Jerry and I met Jerry's manager, Donald Rubin, in Los Angeles and went by Capitol Records to play some rough mixes of the music we were working on for the record company executives. At the end of the meeting, Donald said, "Charlie, why don't you play some of your songs." I picked up a guitar and played some of my music, and a really nice gentleman named Carl Ingerman signed me to Capitol Records on the spot. I walked in a record producer and walked out a recording artist.

It was a time for some serious soul searching. I could make an album for Capitol and continue to pursue being a record producer, songwriter, and session musician. Or I could get back in the game, put a band together, and go out whole hog to try to make it to the top of the charts and the big concert circuit. One would mean a fairly settled life; I would be at home most of the time. The other would mean going back on the road, playing whatever venues we could get into, opening shows for anybody who would have us, and building a new following from the ground up, entering an implacable world where the competition is unrelenting and you only get so many chances to shine before you're banished back to the bush leagues.

I had tried. I had worked hard and established a toehold and had a chance at a future in the behind-the-scenes end of the music business. But to be honest, it could never compare with the thrill of walking on stage in front of a crowd of people and turning them on with a live performance.

In the end, I had to follow my heart and admit that I'd never be completely happy until I had proven to myself and everybody else that I had some world-class music in me and the guts and tenacity to meet the competition head on and breathe the rarified air of sweet success in the business that I loved so very much.

I was thirty-four years old and starting all over again, going up against guys ten years younger and ten times better looking than me, but none of them could possibly want to make it more than I did. As the old Southern saying went, I was "eat up with it." I determined that if I had to work harder than anybody else, I was going to make my mark on the music world as a recording and concert artist.

I waded into making that first album for Capitol, using some of my favorite Nashville pickers: Karl Himmel on drums, Bob Wilson on piano, and Tim Drummond on bass. Jerry Corbitt and I had really clicked while I was producing his album, so I asked him to produce mine.

The album was simply titled *Charlie Daniels* and had some good songs; the players were exceptional, the arrangements were catchy, and the performances were solid. But there was one thing missing, and it was a glaring and important one. The vocals were all over the place, with no originality, reminiscent of the many artists who had influenced me during my years on the nightclub circuit.

In the world of copy bands, where I had spent the first thirteen years of my career, the closer you sounded to the artists whose music you were playing, the more popular you became and the bigger crowds you could attract to the clubs you worked in.

My first attempts at developing my own vocal style were a hodgepodge of pilfered licks that my voice naturally fell into when interpreting a song of one style or another. My original music covered a wide range of genres.

I put a new band together. Taz DiGregorio had spent two years in the army since we'd last worked together. He was working with a club band playing copy music and was ready to come on board and help create some original stuff. The bass player, Earl Grigsby, was from Kentucky, and the drummer, Jeffrey Myer, was from California.

I signed a management and publishing deal with Donald Rubin and his partner, Charles Koppelman, and we were ready to hit the road.

In the early 1970s there were lots of clubs around the country that featured bands who were promoting their albums, trying to build a following, and establish airplay in the area. The biggest concentration of these venues was in San Francisco, Oakland, Berkeley, and the dozens of small towns that make up the Bay Area. It was a tacit requirement to play these venues if you were trying to break a record. With my newly formed band, we hooked up a U-Haul trailer on the back of my car and headed that way.

On the way we stopped in El Paso and picked up my old friend Bill Belcher, who would be our roadie and road manager.

Lewis Perles, who worked the West Coast for Koppelman-Rubin, booked us in several of the venues around the Bay Area. We sweated it out night after night in the clubs, trying to make a dent in the crazy and highly competitive left-coast music scene. The band got tighter, and the people who came to see us play got into the music. But it became evident that my first album was not going to be a hit, and Capitol Records dropped me like a hot potato.

One thing I got out of the deal was that the advance from Capitol Records had gone into a down payment for a house we built in Wilson

County, Tennessee, and we moved in just in time for Little Charlie to start first grade at Lakeview Elementary School, away from the hassles of a big-city educational system.

In the meantime, Donald Rubin and Charles Koppelman were looking for a new record deal for me. They found one with Kama Sutra, a label run by a human dynamo named Neil Bogart and a truly nice gentleman named Art Kass.

Donald and Charles wanted us to come to New York and record in the late Jimi Hendrix's Electric Lady Studios with one of their associates, Gary Myers, producing. They rented us a big three-story house in Hampton Bays, Long Island, for the band to live and rehearse in.

It was wintertime, and the area was practically deserted. We left our instruments set up and worked on our music any time of the day or night we wanted to. After a few days of putting the finishing touches on the arrangements, we began driving into the heart of Manhattan five days a week to record our first album for Kama Sutra.

Te John, Grease, & Wolfman was released in 1972. Again, there was good material, the musicians played great, and the arrangements were inventive, but I still hadn't really found myself vocally. It was better but not there yet.

We headed back to California and more showroom gigs and radio promotions, and this time we made a little more headway. Sometimes we appeared alone, and other times we opened for Elvin Bishop, Mike Bloomfield, Stoneground, and others.

If there was ever a music junkie, it was Jerry Garcia. When he was not on the road with the Grateful Dead, he would put together combos and play the same venues we were playing. Jerry was a down-to-earth, nice guy, and I liked him a lot.

Elvin Bishop was a mainstay in the Bay Area in the early 1970s, and he always kept a top-notch outfit. He had a great sense of humor and was always fun to be around. Our paths would cross many times through the years.

We signed with a couple of different booking agencies, trying to find one that could deliver meaningful work. We needed the kind of shows where we could get in front of lots of people and play our music, opening for headliners and influential listening clubs. But that's what everybody at our level was trying to do, and the competition for those kind of gigs was fierce. It took effort from the booking agency and support from the record company to make it happen.

I've always ascribed to the theory that if you can't get what you want, take what you can get and make what you want out of it, and we tried to make the best situation we could out of whatever we were presented with. If there were only twenty people in the place, you played for those twenty people. If what you do pleases them, they'll be back and probably bring somebody else with them. And it snowballs. That's how you build a following.

Bring your "A" game every night, and never look at the empty seats.

CHAPTER 24

GEARING UP FOR THE LONG RUN

Jeffrey Myer left the band to join Jesse Colin Young, who quit The Youngbloods to start a solo career. I always liked the two-drummer sound of The Allman Brothers Band and decided to give it a try. I met a gentle, long-haired kid in California named Freddie Edwards and was still looking for one more drummer when Buddy Davis called, the same Buddy Davis who had left me in a lurch in Tulsa back in 1964. I was leery about hiring Buddy after he had left me without notice, but he wanted the job so badly that I gave it to him.

It was 1973 and time to go back into the recording studio and cut another album. I decided to produce this one myself. We moved our gear into a studio in Nashville and started work on *Honey in the Rock*, which contained our very first bona fide hit, a novelty song called "Uneasy Rider," and it was back on the road to try to capitalize on it.

Earl Grigsby, our bass player, came to me and said that for deep personal reasons he felt that he had to leave the band. We parted friends and remained so until Earl passed away a few years ago.

We used interim bass player Ted Reynolds, and Billy Cox, Jimi Hendrix's old bass player, worked with us for a while, but things were kind of unsettled in the band, and it was pretty obvious that we would soon be making some changes.

Buddy Davis, the drummer, quit, confirming my theory of not hiring people twice. I replaced him with a Nashville drummer, Gary Allen. I also hired a guitar player from Nashville named Barry Barnes and a bass player from the eastern shore of Maryland named Mark Fitzgerald. We were whole again, well-rehearsed, hot and ready to go, and around Nashville we were coming to be known as The CDB.

In the winter of 1973, the East Coast got hit with the biggest snowstorm in its history, crippling the Mid-Atlantic Seaboard. I got a call from Wade Conklin, our local Kama Sutra promotion man, telling me that the opening act for the Quicksilver Messenger Service show, scheduled for Nashville that night, had gotten weathered in on the East Coast and the promoter, Joe Sullivan, was looking for a replacement. Would I be interested?

Of course we were interested. I got the band together, and we went down to War Memorial Auditorium and played a smoking set of CDB music, and the crowd just loved it.

I went out of town that weekend, and when I came back I had several messages from the promoter, Joe Sullivan, on my answering machine. I called him back, and we set up a meeting where he told me that he wanted to go into artist management and had been looking for a band with star potential. After seeing us at the Quicksilver show, he felt we were what he was looking for. He was very enthusiastic and convincing.

Well, there sure wasn't anything super exciting going on in my career at the moment, and I thought that Joe Sullivan, with all of his genuine enthusiasm, might be just what we needed. But I had one problem. I was still signed with Donald Rubin. That didn't even faze Joe; he said he would work something out with Donald.

A few days later when Joe went to New York to meet with Donald Rubin, I flew up to meet with Kama Sutra about promoting our new *Honey in the Rock* album. I found out to my delight that our single "Uneasy Rider" was taking off all over the country.

There is nothing in the world like watching a hit record happen, especially in the days when most of the radio stations were locally owned, operated, and programmed. When the program directors for the individual stations decided for themselves which records to play, they would then start making noise in the smaller markets and work their way through to the biggest stations. "Uneasy Rider" was doing just that, and I was flying high until I received some heartbreaking news.

At noon on April 13, 1973, my mother called and told me that my dad had died suddenly from a heart attack. I couldn't believe it; he was only fifty-six years old. I had to hang up the phone and get myself together before I could even continue the conversation. When I regained my composure, I called back and told her that we'd be there as soon as possible.

Hazel, Little Charlie, and myself were all devastated as we caught a flight for Wilmington. I made the funeral arrangements. There would be a service in Wilmington, and then Dad's body would be driven to Elizabethtown, where there would be a graveside service and internment at the Daniel family cemetery near the old home place in Bladen County.

Even after the funeral it seemed so unreal; he had died so suddenly and unexpectedly. There were loose ends to be tied up, and I went around Wilmington settling my daddy's last earthly affairs.

When you lose a parent, it's unlike any other experience you'll ever go through. When you realize that the person whose face you saw from your cradle is gone, never to be a part of your earthly life again, there's a sense of heavy loss, and then there's always the guilty feelings.

Why didn't I go see him more often?

Why didn't I call him more often?

What could I have done to make life better for the one who took me hunting and to football games, the one who taught me so many lessons about life and about values and work ethic, who encouraged me in pursuing a career in music? It was so ironic; now I was on my way to having my first hit record, and my dad didn't live to see it. The *Honey in the Rock* album was on his turntable when he died, and had he lived just another few weeks, he would have been some kind of proud as "Uneasy Rider" climbed the charts.

I picked out a headstone for Daddy and wrote the epitaph. The inscription, nestled among a garland of pine boughs, reads, "Tall whispering long leaf pine trees play his song." He had spent his life among the trees, and it only seemed proper for him to be remembered that way.

A couple of days after the funeral, Joe Sullivan, who indeed had worked out a deal with Donald Rubin to take over our management, called and asked me to go back to work. At first I was a little insulted to be asked to start working again so soon after burying my father, but it turned out to be a good thing to get back in the race. It helped ease the pain.

About the time I signed with Joe Sullivan, a brilliant young lady named

Pat Halverson came to work in his office and played a big role in my career for many years to come.

Pat was just one of those people who had a knack for anticipating trouble and dealing with it before it happened. She was always working ahead of the curve: a problem solver, and a quick study, learning about the internal workings of a traveling band and becoming a part of our day-to-day operations. She was also good for a quick plane reservation or whatever it took to help us get to the next gig.

Pat was my first introduction to a truly capable office person who left no loose ends and organized everything that came across her desk into practical increments. She was resourceful and tenacious and played a major role in my management team and would set the bar for those to follow.

I joined the band in Atlanta for a week-long stand at a place called Richards. It was one of those listening rooms where the up-and-coming bands played and attracted a young, hip crowd. It was a good place to start building a fan base in Atlanta. Of course, you needed airplay to have a hit record, but a fan base was the foundation of a successful career.

We would play Richards many times over the years. Atlanta is a major market with a number of meaningful radio stations in the city and surrounding area. In the daytime I'd hook up with our local Kama Sutra promotion man and we'd work the stations, doing live interviews and hanging out with the on-air personalities, which was a vital part of promotion in the days when stations did their own programming and playlists.

That was basically standard procedure in whatever market we were playing. And in those days, at some of the more progressive album stations, I'd take along a guitar and play songs on the air for an hour or more.

It was a wonderful time for music. If you had a good record, you could get it played on its own merit.

Neil Bogart, the head of Kama Sutra records, was a man capable of thinking outside the box. He was bright and innovative and responsible for the very first video I ever remember when he did one for our "Uneasy Rider" song. We didn't call it a video. It was in the days before MTV, and there were few places to expose it, but Neil had the idea and whatever Neil wanted, Neil usually got.

CHAPTER 25

A Long Road and a Little Wheel

U neasy Rider" is the story of a long-haired hippie traveling through Mississippi who has a flat tire, gets himself into a tough situation in a redneck bar, and gets out of it by using his brain. We acted out the story in a joint in Nashville, complete with a hotrod Chevy and a character named Old Green Teeth.

We had no idea that what we were doing would become a major promotion tool in a few years when MTV would create a whole twenty-four-hour-a-day channel for nothing but videos.

The single climbed to the top ten in charts across the nation. We sold a lot of singles, but the *Honey in the Rock* album only experienced moderate sales. "Uneasy Rider" was a novelty song, and although very successful, it was not the kind of song that made people want to hear the rest of the album it was on.

In the heyday of AOR, or album-oriented radio, and in the days before the national consultants muddied the waters, if the station liked an album enough, it would play as many as two or three cuts, which gave the listeners more of an idea of what the band was about, motivating sales.

What we needed was a solid hit album, and I was constantly working on material that would help us reach that point. I still wasn't happy with the way I was singing, but I was working on that too.

Our record label leased two Ford vans for us to travel to concerts and promote our records. We also needed support personnel, and I hired a young man named Jesse Greg to be our roadie and road manager. He did everything from drive the van to collect our money at the end of an evening's performance. In addition I hired a kid from Nashville named

David Corlew to help out, and we would soon add Leo Kiserow to help with the equipment and mix our sound.

I've always had a special bond with my road crew. They work harder and put in more hours than anybody in the outfit. They are the first ones to get to the venue and the last ones to leave, humping tons of equipment around the country, constantly setting it up and tearing it down, sometimes sleeping a few hours and making an early stage call while the band is still asleep at the hotel.

As we added personnel and gear, the vans got too small, and we needed a larger form of transportation. After shopping around for something we could afford, we settled for a 1950s vintage Scenicruiser double-decker bus that had already been driven five million miles by the Greyhound Bus Co. and then been bought by Tommy Overstreet and customized with bunks and couches.

We christened it Uneasy Rider, which turned out to be a most appropriate name.

We got the Uneasy Rider on a Sunday afternoon and were completely taken with it. No more sleeping on the hot floor of a van and switching off drivers in the middle of the night. We had bunks, a bathroom, and our very own full-time driver, and all of the band equipment fit in the bays underneath.

We headed for Cleveland, where our driver, Jimmy Klein, bumped into a shuttle van at the Holiday Inn where we were staying, earning him the nickname Crash Klein on his first trip.

CDB has played more dates with The Marshall Tucker Band than any other act we've ever worked with. In 1974 and 1975 we were constantly on the road together. Their debut album was a smash, and they were in demand all over the country.

We hit it off right from the start and really enjoyed working together. The original band was Toy Caldwell on lead guitar, his brother Tommy on bass, George McCorkle on rhythm guitar, Paul Riddle on drums, Jerry Eubanks on sax and flute, and Doug Gray on vocals. They could flat honk, and they tore the crowd up every night.

Our shows would end in a gigantic jam, with both bands onstage blowing the roof off the venue, to the delight of the fans. We'd have three drummers onstage at one time, and we kicked out all the stops. To this day, no two bands I've ever heard could rival the jams MTB and CDB had back in the day.

Promoters weren't paying us very well for the dates we were doing with Tucker. We were a great addition to the show, and the crowds really got off on us, but we'd only had one hit single and our marquee value was not too high.

One night Tommy Caldwell came into our dressing room and wanted to know why we weren't staying in the same motel the Tucker band was staying in. I had to tell him that the truth of the matter was that we simply couldn't afford it. Tommy reached down in his boot, pulled out a thousand dollars in cash, and handed it to me and said, "Pay it back when you can, and if you can't, don't worry about it. But from now on, I want to see y'all at the same motels as us."

That was typical; both Tommy and Toy were generous and loyal friends, and I loved them both. By the way, we did pay the loan back. I hear a lot about bonding these days; for us it came as natural as falling off a log. The Tucker boys were family to us.

My road manager, Jesse Greg, leaving was no surprise. Some people are just not cut out for the rigors of the road, especially when a band is going through the process of building a name. It's a tough row to hoe, and only the most dedicated stick it out. You've got to take it like it comes on the road; whatever the situation is, you've got to cowboy up and conquer it. If it means crawling out of your bunk on an icy night when the bus breaks down in the middle of nowhere, flagging down a ride, and finding a mechanic or renting cars and a U-Haul to get the band to the next show, you've got to rise to the occasion. Everybody didn't have that in them, but I thought I knew somebody who did.

I promoted David Corlew to road manager and hired Sonny Mattheny and Gene Key to work with the road crew, and shortly afterward Michael "Mule" Sanderson and Wayne "Skinny" Smith came with us. Gene and Sonny would soon leave, but when Roger Campbell joined us, we had a road crew that would basically stay intact for years.

When The Marshall Tucker Band went into the Capricorn Studios in Macon to make a new album called *A New Life*, they called and asked if

I'd come down and play fiddle on a couple of cuts. I played on "Blue Ridge Mountain Sky," and when I heard the track to "24 Hours at a Time," I nearly flipped. What a great piece of music!

Tucker's producer was a laidback good ol' boy from Alabama named Paul Hornsby. I met him when I worked on Tucker's records and liked his style. He'd done a great job with Marshall Tucker's records. CDB could sure use some help with our records. I liked the thought of working at Capricorn Studios, and I thought perhaps Paul Hornsby was just what we needed.

CHAPTER 26

RED HOT CHICKEN AND THE
ADVENT OF THE VOLUNTEER JAM

Macon, Georgia, was the mecca of what was becoming known as Southern Rock in those days. The Capricorn label had two of the hottest bands in the country with The Allman Brothers Band and The Marshall Tucker Band. The studio was state of the art, and the recording engineers were young and hip and capable.

The city of Macon was Southern to the core, with restaurants ranging from genuine home cooking at Momma Lowe's to the continental menu and extensive wine list of Le Bistro. And where else could you get a Nehi peach soda and a barbecue sandwich at two in the morning?

There was one place that didn't even open until midnight, and they served one dish, Red Hot Chicken. It sure lived up to its name. La Carousel also had light bread and beer. Not having a beer license didn't bother Hidges, the owner, at all; he'd sell you as many Pabst Blue Ribbon tallboys as you wanted to cool your burning palate.

Eating Red Hot Chicken would have been torture if it didn't taste so good.

We found a perfect place to stay at an old 1930s-style motel called the Courtesy Court. The owners, Jimmy and Dot Hammock, treated us like family. We were set in a comfort zone and ready to cut a record.

I put a lot of thought and effort into writing the songs and rehearsing the band. I also made my mind up that this time when I was ready to do vocals, I'd just open my mouth and let whatever was there come out naturally, without any coaxing from the ghosts of the past from my club years. Good, bad, or indifferent, this time I was determined to sound like whoever I was and nobody else. We loaded into Capricorn Studios and went to work.

On this album I wanted to include two live cuts recorded in front of an audience, so we scheduled a show at the twenty-two-hundred-seat War Memorial Auditorium in Nashville. When it sold out in advance, WKDF, the local album rock station, wanted to broadcast it live. My manager, Joe Sullivan, came up with the name Volunteer Jam, which of course referred to the Volunteer State of Tennessee, never realizing it was a name that would be heard around the world.

The first Volunteer Jam was supposed to be a one-time event. I casually invited some buddies to drop by for a jam, and three of the Tucker boys and Dickey Betts from The Allman Brothers Band came that night. Both bands were red hot in the Nashville area. When I surprised the crowd by introducing them, the roof almost came off the place, and it became evident that we were onto something special.

The show took on a life of its own, a special kind of excitement you can't create. It just has to happen naturally. Due to the live radio broadcast and word of mouth by the twenty-two hundred people who had attended, it was the most talked-about show of the year. It became evident that we should plan on doing another Volunteer Jam the next year.

The 1975 version would sell out thirteen thousand seats at Murphy Center in Murfreesboro, Tennessee. But we'll go more in depth about the Volunteer Jam a little later on.

We went back to Macon and recorded and mixed the album in thirteen days. All that was left to do was come up with an album title and get the packaging designed.

The cover art was done by a very talented visual artist named Flournoy Holmes. When I first saw it, I loved it. It fit so perfectly into what the music on the album was about. Flournoy had nailed it. Now I had to come up with a killer album title.

Sometimes that's one of the most difficult parts of the process. I agonized and walked the floor as the deadline approached, thinking of and rejecting ideas. All at once out of the blue, it came to me.

Fire on the Mountain!

Thank You, Lord!

We finally had the whole package, and we knew it. It was by far the best production, the best selection of songs, the best cover art, and the best instrumental performances. Finally and at last, I was happy with the way I had handled the vocals. No fluff. No flourish. No impersonations. Just me, organic and unadorned, and, for better or worse, my own natural vocal sound.

It was obvious even before *Fire on the Mountain* was released that it was special. Our new producer, Paul Hornsby, and the folks at Capricorn Studios had lived up to all expectations.

The two live cuts, "No Place to Go" and "Orange Blossom Special," were hot. There were blazing guitar songs like "Caballo Diablo" and fiddle on "The South's Gonna Do It Again." Dickey Betts's classic dobro solo on "Long Haired Country Boy" was nothing short of brilliant.

What we needed was a blockbuster at radio. The kind of response that would lead them to play two or three cuts off of our new album. So, Wade Conklin, our local Kama Sutra promotion man, had a prerelease listening party for some of the Nashville radio folks. When I saw the reaction of Ron Huntsman, the program director of WKDA, our local album station, I started dreaming about a big record.

Everything was positive, including the reaction of the promotion department and label executives at Kama Sutra in New York. The only thing left was to put it on the street and see what John Q. Public thought of it.

When *Fire on the Mountain* was released, a Kama Sutra promotion man, Bill Able, and me took off flying across the country on an extensive promotion tour. Stopping at major-market radio stations across the nation, it soon became obvious that this was going to be by far the most successful album CDB had ever recorded. At many of the stations, the individual disc jockeys played whatever records they wanted to on their air shift, and at others, the program directors added music at their own discretion. They were liking some of the cuts on our new album, with "Long Haired Country Boy" and "The South's Gonna Do It Again" getting a lot of attention.

Pop radio stations had only played the hits up until the 1960s. The industry standard was that when you had cut enough hits to make up an album, they'd release one. AM stations were the successful ones, with FM stations relegated to playing mostly elevator music or the classics. FM sounded better, but you couldn't take it with you or play it in your car. But that was all about to change with the advent of FM car radios and the radical programming idea of a guy named Tom Donahue at KSAN FM in San Francisco. He started playing album cuts by some of the more progressive rock bands. The Bay Area went crazy over it, and soon the idea spread across the country. Album-oriented radio was born, and FM stations started pulling large audiences and selling records.

These stations were our bread and butter, and they were playing *Fire on the Mountain*.

Even more importantly, the album started walking out of the record stores and showing up on the charts. CDB still had a lot to prove, but we finally had a foot in the door.

I ended a successful promotion tour in Los Angeles and joined the band in Tucson, Arizona, for a live broadcast and got really busy. I was playing shows with the band at night and going around to radio stations in the daytime, sometimes flying ahead of the band to a new market to work the record before the show. I was hitting it hard.

And loving every minute of it.

CHAPTER 27

ALWAYS WORKS OUT FOR THE BEST

I don't think Barry Barnes, Gary Allen, or Mark Fitzgerald were ever completely happy in the band. They had their own ideas about how things should be run and the music we should be playing. They all left to start their own band, and I needed a guitar player, drummer, and bass player *muy pronto*. As it turned out, the changes only made the band better.

The last thing you want in a band are dissatisfied musicians, and I had three of them. Even though they constituted half of the band, I knew that the sooner I could replace them all, the better off we'd be. I set about the task immediately.

The only musician I ever hired sight unseen and without ever hearing him play was a bass player from Holt, Alabama, named Charlie Hayward. I called our record producer, Paul Hornsby, and asked him if he knew of a good bass player, and he recommended Charlie. I called him, and he said he was interested. We were playing in Tuscaloosa with Lynyrd Skynyrd a few nights later, and Charlie got on the bus and left with us. He's been here ever since, for more than forty years now.

We hired a drummer from Maryland named Don Murray, who walked onstage with us, without any rehearsal, and performed the set as if he'd been playing with us for years.

Another piece of the musical machine in place and clicking.

What we needed now was a well-rounded, red-hot, Dixie-fried guitar player, and I thought I knew where to find one.

Tommy Crain was a local Nashville guitar player who I'd been hearing about for a while. When I asked him if he'd like to work with us, he came out on the road, and we broke in all three new players at the same time. It only took a few shows for me to realize that I had the best band I'd ever had. Freddy Edwards and Don Murray on drums, Charlie Hayward on bass, Taz on keyboards, and Tommy Crain and me on guitars, and of course me doubling on fiddle.

I had used the fiddle in a limited sort of way on some earlier albums, but on *Fire on the Mountain* we stuck it right out front with a couple of showcase tunes, and when I listen to it I realize that a lot of my fiddle playing style started right there.

The heart of any band is the rhythm section. If you haven't got it covered there, all is for naught. No matter how good your singers and soloists are, if the drummer and bass player are not locked in, it's like building a house on a rotten foundation.

Don Murray and Freddy Edwards laid down the beat, and nobody I ever played with locks in on a bass guitar like Charlie Hayward. His playing over the years has become an intricate part of the sound this band has developed. He's solid as a rock onstage and off.

Taz DiGregorio was the best singer I ever had in the band. He had a great set of pipes and a soulful feeling for the bluesy stuff, while his keyboard playing was innovative and energetic. He came up with some of the signature licks and dynamic rhythms that we used so much in the formative years.

Tommy Crain's guitar playing was a couple of cuts above anybody I had ever played with, and playing beside him inspired me to greater heights. We had some memorable nights together, pushing each other higher and higher, with the rhythm section in high gear. We were lighting up stages all over the country and getting the reputation for being a hot band.

For the first time we were developing a musical personality, a consistency of style, and an identifiable sound that separated us from other bands. The sound of a band is always the sum total of the players, with each member contributing his or her individual musical talents. We had found a combination that worked for us, and it felt good. That feeling went spilling off the stage every night, blazing new trails and making new fans as we went.

There were weekly network TV shows that featured up-and-coming bands, shows like *Midnight Special* and *Don Kirshner's Rock Concert*. An appearance on these shows meant mass exposure and could cut a lot of corners in breaking a musical act, and we started getting calls to play them.

The first time we were invited to play *Midnight Special*, they told us to be there at 7:00 a.m. We thought that seemed a little early for a Los Angeles TV show to start taping. But that's what we were told, and a few minutes before 7:00 a.m., the Uneasy Rider was sitting at the front gate of the NBC Television Studios in Burbank, California.

The guard at the gate didn't know anything about a band from Tennessee in a vintage Scenicruiser being at the gate of NBC Television at such an early hour. He didn't have our name on the list to come in at all, so we pulled over to the side and waited.

Sometime later in the day, an employee of the show arrived and informed the guard that the boys from Tennessee were indeed supposed to be there that day. But he didn't know why we had arrived so early since the show didn't tape until the afternoon.

The upshot is that we did go through the gate, we did do the show, and we did inform the *Midnight Special* folks that we were country boys. Unlike a lot of the rock and roll acts they were used to dealing with, if told to be there at 7:00 a.m., we would be there at 7:00 a.m., and we would be on time no matter when it was. And, should there be a next time, we would appreciate a more timely stage call.

There were next times, many more next times. We played *Midnight Special* several times over the years.

CHAPTER 28

DEMISE OF THE UNEASY RIDER: NEW RIDES

Things were going really well for the CDB, except for our transportation. The old Uneasy Rider, after rolling on the Greyhound line for around five million miles before it passed into our hands, was truly on its last leg. We could hardly get past the city limit sign before it would break down. Plus, with the addition of several new road crew members, it was starting to get crowded.

It was a bold step and a lot of debt to go into, but we ordered two brand-new MCI buses. And we bought a box truck that we promptly dubbed the Gray Ghost. The only problem was that until we took delivery on the new buses, we were stuck with the Uneasy Rider. It seemed like the old girl was taking revenge by breaking down even more often, a frustrating experience to say the least.

To add insult to injury, I got behind the wheel one night and drove around the parking lot of a truck stop. I scraped into a hinge on the back of an eighteen-wheeler and tore the side of the bus open. We went down the road in our embarrassing wreck with a big rip on the side and the insulation showing through until we got it covered with a piece of sheet metal. But we still looked like a rolling junkyard.

We were jumping around all over the place trying to play in front of as many people as we could. Shelley Grafman, the program director for KSHE, the big rocker in St. Louis, invited us to play at a listener-appreciation event called the *KSHE Kite Fly*. We were immediately exposed to fifty thousand people. It gave the band a lot of credibility in St. Louis, which turned out to be one of our biggest markets over the years.

KSHE was king of St. Louis rock radio in those days, and the *Kite*

Fly was the beginning of a decades-long relationship with the station and friendship with Shelley Grafman and his family.

On July 4, 1975, we were asked to open for the Rolling Stones in Memphis. I still run into people who remember the music we played that afternoon.

When we finished at the Rolling Stones show, we caught a plane for Austin to play at Willie Nelson's picnic. I can't come up with a better description of the music The Charlie Daniels Band plays. A rock show one afternoon and a country show the next night. We don't fall into any one genre of music. We've always been all over the board, and just when somebody thinks they've got us figured out, we do something different.

That's just my musical personality. I guess I was exposed to so many types of music in my formative days that when I write original stuff, it bleeds into my creative process and comes out in a variety of styles, sometimes within the confines of one song.

I'm constantly asked what kind of music CDB plays, and I always say American music. We play country, bluegrass, gospel, rock, blues, and jazz—the genres of music that America gave the world. It's just our style. We don't follow trends or fads. We just follow our own hearts and musical instincts, and it's worked out pretty well so far.

We needed a road accountant to handle the financial side of touring. Things were happening fast. David Corlew couldn't handle demands of being road manager and the additional job of handling all the finances and the paperwork that went along with it. We hired a sharp young man fresh out of college named Robert Stewart to help ease the load.

We shared a tradition with The Marshall Tucker Band. When anybody in the band or crew had a birthday, we hit them in the face with a pie. Everybody got it, me included, and it just so happened that Robert Stewart's first day with us was also his birthday. We were on a plane flying to Austin, and American Airlines served little individual pies for lunch. I welcomed him to the CDB with a face full of pie, much to his and the stewardess's surprise; it was probably the first time she had ever seen it happen.

With the success of *Fire on the Mountain*, we were in demand as an opening act. For a while we bounced back and forth across the country between a Joe Walsh tour and a Lynyrd Skynyrd tour. We did that all the way to California. Then we joined Skynyrd full-time for what they were calling The Torture Tour. We worked our way back to their hometown of Jacksonville, Florida, where the tour would end.

It was a grueling schedule, but we were performing in front of a lot of people and that's what we needed.

I hit it off with Ronnie Van Zant from the first time I met him in 1974. We spent a lot of hours together in hotel rooms and buses and became good friends in the process. Ronnie used to call me the King of Dixie, a title I certainly didn't deserve, but I was honored that he would think about me in that way.

In 1974 I got my birthday pie, or actually pies, in the face in Utica, New York. I was sitting in the Holiday Inn lounge when someone from the hotel came in and told me I had an overseas call at the front desk. I couldn't imagine who'd be calling me and was pleasantly surprised to hear Ronnie's voice calling from the United Kingdom, where the band was touring.

I thought he had called to wish me a happy birthday, but that wasn't the reason at all. He said, "Charlie, I've got a question for you. You know that big Rebel flag we have onstage behind us? Well, last night it fell on the floor, and we took it out in the alley and burned it. Now, you're the King of Dixie, and I just want to know, do you think we should go onstage without that flag?"

I think Ronnie was just homesick and wanted to hear a friendly voice from back home.

The last two nights of the tour were in Atlanta and Jacksonville. Atlanta was a huge Skynyrd market, and the Omni was completely sold out. After the show in Atlanta, Ronnie wanted me to go with him to a club called Hotlanta, where his brother Donnie was playing with a new band. You could see the pride on Ronnie's face as he watched his little brother light the place up with a band that was soon to go on to bigger and better things when they became known as 38 Special.

The next night in Jacksonville was the final date of The Torture Tour and the much-anticipated homecoming of Lynyrd Skynyrd. The Jacksonville Coliseum was packed to the rafters with diehard hometown fans. Family and longtime friends were in attendance, and they gave Ronnie the key to the city. It was shaping up to be a total triumph for the Skynyrd boys.

Just before we went out to do our set, Ronnie walked into our dressing room and presented me with a highly polished, vintage National steel-p guitar. It's one of my most treasured possessions to this day.

We did our set and the crowd really got into it, but we were just the appetizer; the main course was coming up next, and they had one thing on their minds. They came to see their hometown heroes, and the place was pulsing with energy. We finished our show, the stage was set, and the crowd was supercharged with excitement. The evening was ready to go pedal to the metal when the problems started.

We waited and waited. The crowd started getting restless, and it was apparent that something was wrong. I went to Skynyrd's dressing room to check it out and found Ronnie bent over a garbage can with a violent case of dry heaves. What a horrible time to get sick, with a sold-out hometown crowd out front, waiting for the band to take the stage.

Sidney Drashin, the promoter, asked me to go onstage and do a couple of tunes with the rest of the band in hopes that Ronnie would soon feel well enough to go on. Of course I was glad to help out and went onstage with Gary and Allen and the rest of the guys. We jammed a few songs, but the crowd had come to see Skynyrd. It was not Skynyrd without Ronnie Van Zant. They were getting impatient, and a rock and roll crowd with an attitude is a dangerous thing.

I've got to hand it to Ronnie, as sick as he was, he managed to come onstage and join the band for "Free Bird." He tried to explain the situation, telling the crowd that the band would redo the show even if he personally had to foot the bill. But by that time, the crowd had reached the point of rowdiness, with the few troublemakers that are always in every crowd egging the situation on. They started throwing things and tearing up the venue, and there was a near riot.

I felt so sorry for my friends. What should have been one of the greatest nights of their career had, through no fault of their own, turned into a nightmare. It was a sad way to end a highly successful tour. Ronnie Van Zant would never again have the chance to take the stage of the Jacksonville Coliseum.

The years of 1974 and 1975 were to be some of the most intense periods of touring we would ever experience. We were constantly on the road. Even at Christmastime we would come home for a few days and leave Christmas night to go back on tour.

It takes a good woman to keep the home fires burning while the man of the house is gone two hundred and fifty days a year. Hazel was a rock, and she still is. Without her and Little Charlie's constant love and understanding, I would never have made it. They were the only two people in the world I would have given my career up for. But they never asked. Instead, they encouraged me, taking as much pleasure in every increment of success as I did. They have been such a blessing and still are.

I remember the day the Uneasy Rider finally breathed her last. We were touring in the Southeast. We played Monroe, Louisiana, and were headed for Ruston, Louisiana. I was behind the wheel when it stopped again. I got my stuff and got off the bus. I told Robert Stewart to find a phone and call Joe Sullivan and tell him I had just gotten off the Uneasy Rider for the last time. I would never get back on it again. We leased a bus until we got our new ones.

Soon it was time to make another album. We headed back to Macon and Capricorn Studios with Paul Hornsby, a batch of new songs, and three new band members. This one was to be called *Nightrider*. It didn't enjoy the immediate success of *Fire on the Mountain*, which went on to sell more than four million records over the years. But it still had some good songs, sold well, and was another step in the right direction.

At Volunteer Jam 2, Art Kass and Wade Conklin from our record label presented us with our very first gold album for *Fire on the Mountain*. The guest list in 1975 was Buckeye, Chuck Leavell, Roni Stoneman, Mylon LeFevre, and Alvin Lee, and it was the first and only appearance of the entire original Marshall Tucker Band. We had the cameras rolling that night, and Volunteer Jam 2 would turn into a full-length documentary movie.

In addition, there have been several television documentaries and live albums. The Jam was broadcast around the world on the Voice of America. That was back in the Cold War days. It was an awesome experience to be standing on a stage in Nashville and know that you're talking to people imprisoned behind the Iron Curtain, not to mention most of the rest of the planet.

I don't know why the phrase came into my mind, but one night onstage at one of the early Jams I said, "Ain't it good to be alive and be in Tennessee." I had no idea that it would become part of the Lexicon of the Volunteer State I love so much, even quoted from the pulpit on at least one instance.

In 1976 it seemed that we had gone about as far as we could go with Kama Sutra records. Neil Bogart had left the company to form the Casablanca label, taking some of the personnel and a lot of the energy with him. With the success of *Fire on the Mountain*, we had attracted the attention of some of the major players and felt it was time to take advantage of the situation while we had the chance. We let it be known through our music business attorney Eric Kronfeld that we were available and would entertain any and all offers from any major record companies who saw fit to bid for our services.

We were to find out that there were several.

CHAPTER 29

DECISIONS, DECISIONS

We had bites from two major labels right off the bat: CBS and MCA. They were both serious about signing the band and were anxious to see us in concert.

We were playing a concert in Houston one night and Dallas the next. It was arranged for the CBS folks to see us in Houston and the MCA folks in Dallas. I had gone to Stelzig's Western Store in Houston to get some new shirts and things when I got a call. "Charlie, there's a whole bunch of CBS people here waiting to see you." I hurried back to the hotel to indeed find a room full of CBS folks waiting to see me. They came out in full strength, including Walter Yetnikoff the president, Jim Jefferies the national promotion man, and a slew of functionaries and executives and VIPs. But the one who really impressed me was a vibrant ball of fire named Ron Alexenburg, who was the head of Epic records.

They emphasized the availability of the executives to the artists and promotion and distribution advantages. Ron Alexenburg was excited and really anxious to sign the band, and his excitement only increased when he saw us live at the Sam Houston Coliseum that night.

The next night in Dallas, Mike Maitland and Mike Cook from MCA came to see the band. They, too, were impressed and eager to offer us a deal. MCA had done a great job with Lynyrd Skynyrd and was a solid company that understood promoting our kind of music. We talked to Jimmy Bowen at MGM in Los Angeles and the folks at Atlantic Records in New York. After comparing notes, we felt it would be either CBS or MCA. We had identical offers from both labels, and it was now down to the process of splitting hairs.

Joe Sullivan, David Corlew, and me flew to New York to meet with CBS and then to Los Angeles to meet with MCA. We spent a day with each, observing their operations firsthand before getting down to the tough decision of which one of the two we wanted to sign with. Since they had made us identical offers, it came down to which one would do the best job promoting and selling our records.

CBS corporate headquarters in New York is in an impressive skyscraper called Black Rock. When I showed up on the thirteenth floor among all the suits that morning in a Western hat and cowboy boots, I'm sure a lot of folks didn't quite know what to make of us. But we were warmly treated and soon getting educated on the internal workings of Epic Records.

It was so different from what we'd been used to at Kama Sutra, actually a David and Goliath situation. Kama Sutra was a small, independent label with a small promotion staff. It was distributed by independent distributors and had little international clout. CBS was the biggest record company in the world, with their own distributors, massive coast-to-coast promotion staffs, and offices in cities around the world. It seemed they had a department for everything.

One of the highlights of my visit to Black Rock was running into music business legend John Hammond, the man who discovered Bessie Smith, Benny Goodman, Bob Dylan, Bruce Springsteen, and Stevie Ray Vaughan, among others. I treasure the few minutes I was able to spend with him.

MCA also had its own building in Los Angeles, and its operation was also impressive. Each company had its own particular perks and advantages. Both really wanted to sign the CDB. The money both were guaranteeing was the same. The number of albums we would record for both was the same. Both were mammoth record companies with international operations. Now it was time for me to make a decision about who I wanted to sign with. Others could advise, make recommendations, and express opinions. But when it came right down to it, I was the only one who could make the decision.

Us and our lawyer, Eric Kronfeld, were in Los Angeles. We had seen both operations, and now it was time to make a choice. We met at Eric's hotel, and everybody was waiting for me to state my preference. This was the biggest business decision I had ever made in my life. If the CDB was to go onward and upward, we needed to have successful records. Who was more capable of delivering them? CBS or MCA? I walked outside by myself to make the decision.

No matter what else I considered about the two record companies, I could not get away from the energy and excitement of Ron Alexenburg. I walked back into Eric's hotel room and told everybody that it would be CBS, or more specifically, Epic Records and Ron Alexenburg.

Remembering what had been said about the accessibility of CBS executives to the artists, I had Eric call the president of CBS, Walter Yetnikoff, in New York, where it was about 2:00 a.m. We got him out of bed so I could personally tell him that he'd just signed himself an artist.

We were super excited about making our first album for Epic Records, and they were super excited about getting it. We went back to Macon to get together with Paul Hornsby. We recorded the songs we had written and rehearsed for an album that would eventually be called *Saddle Tramp*.

The title song "Saddle Tramp" started out as an instrumental. We had planned to leave it that way until one night I had an idea for a lyric. We put the two together, and it turned out to be one of the most durable and favorite jam tunes in our repertoire. We still play it onstage to this day.

The record started with a snappy fiddle tune called "Dixie on My Mind." There was a ballad called "It's My Life," Tommy Crain's "Cumberland Mountain Number Nine," and a few others. We were ready to deliver our very first Epic album.

We knew nothing about the protocol of working with a major record company. We approached *Saddle Tramp* the same way we had approached every other album we had ever recorded. We wrote the songs, recorded them, got somebody to design an album cover, wrote the liner notes, and turned the whole thing in. We bypassed the A&R department, the art department, the artist development department, and all the rest that make up the bureaucracy of a big record company. We stepped on toes we didn't know even existed.

As time passed, we learned to operate within the system a little better by working, to our advantage I might add, with the different entities that made up the Epic apparatus. But one thing was strictly off-limits: nobody told me what music to record. At that time, nobody at the label wanted to. That would come much later.

Saddle Tramp was released on March 29, 1976. From that point on, I didn't have time to do anything except play concerts and do record promotions. Where we had had a handful of promotion men at Kama Sutra, Epic had a staff from coast to coast. Sometimes they would be waiting for me when our bus got to town in the morning. We'd spend the day visiting radio stations, and they'd get me back to the hotel in time to get ready for the show that night.

We were opening shows for The Allman Brothers Band, Lynyrd Skynyrd, and The Marshall Tucker Band. We did a coast-to-coast tour with Eric Clapton and were doing one-offs, opening shows for all kinds of acts.

It was an exciting time in my career, but it was also a demanding period. Between the concerts and promotion schedule, I was constantly on the move. But this was what I wanted, and I threw myself into it. It was paying off.

Our whole family had gotten into horseback riding and spent a lot of my limited time at home riding horses. We had to board them because we didn't have a place to keep them. We started looking around for a place in the country to build a home and a barn and some acreage to ride our horses on.

Hazel looked hard but to no avail. She had one more place to look at, so when I came home for a few days, we went to check it out. When we came through the front gate, the first thing we saw was a big pond between two hills. We knew if the back hill was flat enough to build a house on, we had found our dream spot. We walked to the top of the hill and found it to be ideal. A short while later, we closed the deal for just more than fifty acres of land and started to build a small horse barn right away.

We named the front hill Sugar Hill and the back hill High Lonesome. There were two pine trees side by side on Sugar Hill, and we called the place Twin Pines. Over the years, it has evolved into a two-story log home and a big barn where we raise quarter horses and cattle. It's where I want to spend the rest of my life. In fact, when I leave Tennessee, I want to go to heaven. It's the only other place I'd rather live than Twin Pines.

But I'm getting a little ahead of myself. Don Murray, one of our drummers, decided he'd had enough of the road. We replaced him with a fine player from California named Jim Marshall without missing a lick.

It's amazing, but every move I've made with having musicians leave and choosing another one to take his place has turned out to be a good one, and Jim Marshall was no exception. He was a fine player and was to go on to play on some of our most successful records.

Saddle Tramp was well received on the radio and would eventually go on to be a gold album for us.

We went back to Macon and Paul Hornsby to make an album titled *High Lonesome*. It was released on November 5, 1976, and sold well, but it didn't immediately reach the coveted gold status of five hundred thousand. We were doing well, making a good living even if we weren't exactly a household name, touring hard and turning on the concert crowds we played for.

We went back into the studio to do another album we would call *Midnight Wind*. The recording itself went well, but this was to be my first run in with the bureaucratic side of Epic Records. When I turned in our concept for an album cover, the art department balked. I asked them to come up with something better, and they basically came up with a pile of junk. I approved what was probably the worst cover we've ever had so we could get the record out on time.

It went against the grain, but we needed to get the record out. We had a tour planned.

CHAPTER 30

It Was October in St. Louis Town When We Heard That the Free Bird Had Fell to the Ground

M*idnight Wind* was released on October 7, 1977. Our tour would open at Kiel Theater in St. Louis on October 20. We had added Ben Smathers and The Stoney Mountain Cloggers square dancers from the *Grand Ole Opry* to spice up the fiddle tunes at the end of the set. We were locked and loaded and ready for a great fall tour.

The St. Louis show was sold out in advance, and we were in a fine old mood as we sat in the dressing room warming up and getting ready to go on. Just a few minutes before time to head for the stage, someone, I don't remember who, came in the dressing room and said that he had heard a rumor that Lynyrd Skynyrd's plane had crashed and there had been fatalities.

To be truthful, I didn't believe it. I thought it was just a cruel rock-and-roll rumor that somebody had started. But I went down to the stage level and found my friend Shelley Grafman, the program director of KSHE radio station, and asked him to check it out for me. I went back to the dressing room, called the band together, and told them what I'd heard. We had a few moments of silent prayer before we went to the stage to start the show.

Right before we walked onstage, we received the awful news. Yes, there had been a plane crash. Yes, there had been fatalities. But nobody knew how many or who until the notification of the next of kin. I called the band together and shared the news with them. I told them that if that had been us in the plane crash, we wouldn't want Skynyrd to blow a show over us, and that Skynyrd wouldn't want us to blow a show over them. We were going to go onstage and do our show.

What a strange feeling it was walking on the stage of Kiel Auditorium that night. We were pretty torn up. I remember that Tommy Crain was on the verge of tears. He said, "Charlie, I don't know what to do." I said, "I know what we're going to do. We're going to go on that stage and play these folks some music." They had bought tickets and deserved the best we had. God willing, we were going to give it to them.

And we did. I don't know how long we played that night; I only wish I had a recording of the set. We jammed and stretched out. We took solace the only way we knew how, in the music that bound us and all of our brothers together. We didn't mention anything about the tragedy to the crowd that night. Even after the show was over, we still weren't able to find out who had been killed.

Ron Huntsman had resigned his radio job and was working full-time with us as our in-house promotion man. We were spending the night in St. Louis and flying out the next morning to start a promotion tour for the new *Midnight Wind* album. After we got back to our hotel, we called around well into the night, trying to find which of our friends we'd lost. But there was no news forthcoming until about two o'clock in the morning. We found out that Ronnie Van Zant had been killed, along with Steve and Cassie Gaines, Dean Kilpatrick, and the pilots of the plane. Some of the others were seriously hurt but alive.

I truly cared about all the people who had met such an untimely and tragic end that night, but Ronnie was my buddy. A cloud of depression settled over me and would linger until I took steps to do something about it.

I have a special feeling for those who, like me, travel the highways playing our music. We have a kind of kinship that goes deeper than friendship and, more than just being in the same business, a kind of fraternity bound together by the music we play and the late-night hours we share after the spotlight has faded. I would never share those hours with Ronnie again. My small world had been diminished by one and that was way too many.

We immediately started getting calls from radio stations wanting a quote about the tragedy and the death of Ronnie Van Zant, but I just wasn't ready to talk about it. I couldn't think of anything that would come close to expressing the depth of my feeling until I walked into a hotel room in Phoenix, took a piece of hotel stationery, and started writing. When I had finished, I felt that I'd done about all I could do and felt better.

> A brief candle; both ends burning
> A weary mile; a bus wheel turning
> A friend to share the lonely times
> A handshake and a sip of wine
> So say it loud and let it ring
> That we're all part of everything
> The present, future, and the past
> Fly on proud bird; you're free at last.

Writing this simple poem that we gave radio stations who asked for a comment somehow helped lift some of the depression I was feeling and gave me at least partial closure on the death of my friend. When I attended Ronnie's funeral, I sang "Peace in the Valley" and read the poem. I gave it to Ronnie's wife, Judy, and was deeply honored and moved when she had it carved into a bench that sits outside Ronnie's tomb.

The 1978 Volunteer Jam was truly special because it included a performance by the remaining members of Lynyrd Skynyrd, at least the ones who had healed enough to play. They played a few songs and went into an instrumental version of "Free Bird," hanging one of Ronnie's signature gambler's hats on a microphone. When some thoughtful spotlight operator hit it with a spotlight, it was one of those special, spontaneous moments that just happen sometimes.

CHAPTER 31

A Million Miles, A New Face, and the Devil Went Down to Georgia

We had done five albums at Capricorn Studios with Paul Hornsby and had been successful, but it was time to make a change. Sometimes a fresh approach can breathe new life into a project. After calling Paul and ending our arrangement as friends, I started looking around for a new producer I felt could help us reach the next level.

I have special requirements for someone who produces for the CDB. I don't work with tyrants or egomaniacs or know-it-alls. First of all, we are a six-piece band, and the sound of our instrumental music is an important part of the songs we record. We don't want to sound like anybody else; we just want to be us.

A producer has to understand that and, in essence, become another member of the band. Pooling his ideas with ours and working within the bounds of our sound and musicianship helps to bring out the best in not just me but all the players.

It was time for a monster album for the CDB. We had come close, had made great inroads, and had a concert following. We had forged relationships with radio stations across the country and just needed to come up with something that would make their request lines light up.

I talked to some producers. But there was nobody I felt could really get with the program, share in the excitement we generated when we played together, and help us record the blockbuster we needed. Somebody brought up John Boylan, a name I was not familiar with. He had a track record with Linda Ronstadt, Michael Murphey, and others. John worked in the West

Coast office of CBS, and when we went out to play the Forum at the end of a tour, John came by my hotel room. It was obvious he had done his homework.

He had listened to our records, offered some valid criticism, and said, "I'm an obstetric producer. I deliver your brainchild." I really liked this guy. I liked his honesty and his approach to working with a group, and I wanted to make a record with him. John would soon come to Nashville and check out studios. We would go into rehearsal mode and get ready to make a new album.

My approach to songwriting in those days was different from the way most people did it. I almost always started with a melody or a guitar riff. I would get together with the band and it would morph into a piece of music. We would write and arrange whole songs without as much as a title. I have been known to put the finishing touches on the lyrics right before I was getting ready to sing them in the studio.

It was standard procedure for me, but nobody had told John Boylan that. After we had played him the songs we were planning to record and asked him what he thought, I think he was a little bewildered that a lot of the songs had no lyrics. I assured him that the lyrics would be forthcoming and not to be concerned. On this premise, we moved our gear to Woodland Sound Studios in Nashville, John brought in a twenty-one-year-old genius engineer from Los Angeles named Paul Grupp, and we got ready to make a record.

John Boylan had written a really good song called "Behind Your Eyes" that everybody agreed had good airplay potential. We were moving right along cutting the tracks when we came to the glaring realization that we needed a fiddle song for the album. Why we hadn't come to this conclusion during the writing and rehearsal phase of the project, I just don't know. The decision was made to move the equipment into a rehearsal studio and write one.

I think that when you have a God-given talent to write songs, you tend to, maybe even subconsciously, catalog scraps and pieces of song ideas and pull them out at a time when you need them. I don't know where the phrase "The Devil Went Down to Georgia" came from or why it entered my mind that day in the rehearsal studio. I don't even know where the song idea came from. Possibly it was from a Stephen Vincent Benét poem called "The Mountain Whippoorwill" that I had read in literature class in high school. But when it started coming, it came in a gush. The band grabbed ahold, and when Taz came up with the signature keyboard lick behind the devil's fiddle part, we knew we were on to something.

You have to understand the chemistry that started bubbling when the six members of the band got together to create original music. I would throw an idea out, maybe a riff or a chord progression. Freddie and Jim would start trying out drumbeats. Charlie Hayward would experiment with some bass part, and Taz, Tommy, and I would slide in trying and rejecting parts until we found something that worked. Sometimes we'd just sit there and jam until something popped out at us. Sometimes we'd head off in a totally different direction from the original idea.

We'd spend hours and hours putting music together, and the fruits of our labor can be heard on the albums we recorded together. Surprisingly, "The Devil Went Down to Georgia" took a lot less time than a lot of the other songs on the album. We got our arrangement down, and I finished the lyrics. We moved the gear back into Woodland Sound and set to work to bring our new fiddle song to life.

The devil's fiddle part presented a challenge. We wanted a dark, ominous, intimidating sound and hit on the idea of multiple fiddles. Nowadays, that part would most likely be done electronically, but in 1979 we were basically on our own. I played seven different fiddle parts, one of them a specially rigged eight-string fiddle. Paul Grupp worked his magic and made the devil's fiddle solo just what we wanted it to be.

I had written the original lyrics with a line that went, "I done told you once, you son of a bitch," which I knew the album stations wouldn't have any trouble with. But just in case the song should break into the Top 40 area, we also did a "son of a gun" version.

We had written a song about the untimely deaths of Elvis Presley, Janis Joplin, and Ronnie Van Zant that we called "Reflections." We named the album *Million Mile Reflections*, which was a nod to both the song and the miles the band had traveled.

I wanted a unique cover. We used an artist's rendering of the band standing with our backs to an empty concert hall, with a highway leading out the back and disappearing in the distance.

I was happy with the cover, the band's performances, the songs we had written, Paul Grupp's engineering, and John Boylan's production. The music was a cross section of what the CDB is all about. It mixed genres and styles with all the controlled wildness that came out when we played together. I was happier with it than with any album we had ever done.

The first single release from *Million Mile Reflections* was "Behind Your Eyes," the song John Boylan had written. It did fairly well. Then we released "The Devil Went Down to Georgia," and things started popping. The song started climbing the charts on the album stations, with Top 40 and country soon falling in line. Soon the album was selling more and much faster than anything we'd ever released.

It crossed formats without a wrinkle. I heard about at least one gospel station playing it, the sanitized version, I'm sure.

Ron Huntsman made a special trip to one of our concerts to deliver the news in person that *Million Mile Reflections* had just gone platinum. A year after its release, it had sold more than two million copies and was still moving.

CHAPTER 32

URBAN COWBOY

In 1980 our office got a call from a movie production company that was shooting a film in Texas. They were interested in having us come out and appear in it as ourselves and play some of our songs.

They sent a script of a project they called *Urban Cowboy* starring John Travolta in the title role and newcomer Debra Winger in the female lead. The setting was at the world's biggest honkytonk, Gilley's in Pasadena, Texas. The story was about the ups and downs of a newly married redneck couple and their rowdy friends.

Well, all right! Let's go to Texas and shoot a movie!

You hear a lot of things about Hollywood people, and being a novice on a movie set, I had no idea what to expect. But my apprehensions were soon relieved when, shortly after arriving in the parking lot at Gilley's, John Travolta and Debra Winger both came out and spent some time on the bus with us.

The director, James Bridges, treated us with respect and was friendly and patient. Of course, Mickey Gilley and his crew showed us some good ol' Texas hospitality.

Pasadena, Texas, is as hot as blue blazes in September. Since the air conditioning at Gilley's interfered with the filming and had to be turned off, we sweated our way through take after take of our tunes. A shot from the front, tear down, and change the lighting. A shot from the left side, tear down, and change the lighting. And so on.

Movie making is repetitive and tedious from my point of view, and I didn't have to do anything but play my fiddle.

We went to the premier of *Urban Cowboy* in Houston. It was pretty neat when the first scenes opened with John Travolta driving to Houston in a pickup truck listening to the CDB's recording of "Texas" playing on the radio.

Urban Cowboy depicted the nightlife in a Texas honkytonk, complete with the two-step, fisticuffs, flirting, loving, leaving, separation, reconciliation, and even mechanical bull riding. It was obvious to everybody that Debra Winger was going to be a star. She played the part of a hard-living party gal to a T.

John Travolta did a great job of going from the fleet-footed, hip city slicker in *Saturday Night Fever* to the beer-drinking, snuff-dipping, two-fisted cowboy who worked at a refinery in the daytime and spent his nights hanging with the regulars at Gilley's.

I've been asked many times in interviews just what impact *Urban Cowboy* had on country music.

I think one of the most positive things that happened is that the popularity of John Travolta, especially among the younger people, somewhat legitimized a genre of music many of them had considered corny and unhip. Some of the crowd who had stood in line at Studio 54 headed over to the Lone Star Cafe, New York's first Texas-style honkytonk, to have a go at the two step.

People in large urban areas started wearing Western hats and cowboy boots, and new country music radio formats started popping up around the country.

Of course, part of this was fad. There are the camp followers who wear Stetsons one month and the next have orange hair and rings in their noses. But some people found out that the music they had always deemed to be a couple of cuts below their sophistication level had substance. It told stories, reflected everyday life, and could move the heart and the feet.

They came on board for Hank Jr. and in the process discovered Merle Haggard.

CHAPTER 33

Big Show, Big Crowds, Big Crew

In 1979 we prepared to do the biggest tour we'd ever done. We would be playing major venues, carrying sound and a custom light system, three tractor trailer rigs, and three buses. We were adding a horn section and three female backup singers from Los Angeles; we called them the LA Reflection Section. We also took Ben Smathers and the Stoney Mountain Cloggers, a *Grand Ole Opry* dance troupe. Altogether this added up to fifty people.

We needed someone to coordinate concert and backstage security. So we hired Rick Rentz, a former Green Beret who owned a concert security company in Connecticut, and he traveled with us full-time.

I needed an assistant to help arrange my schedule, handle meet and greets after the concerts, fly with me on the promotion tours, and handle the retail record-store appearances I was doing so much of, so I hired Bill Yarbrough, who we called Bill Bro, and he went everywhere with me.

As things got crazier and more hectic, we added Junior Rose as a second security man.

It made for a tremendous show, but looking back I can see that we fell into the same trap that a lot of young artists who taste real success for the first time do. We thought bigger was better. The entourage was indeed impressive coming down the road with three trucks and two of the buses all painted up with the band name. The show was an extravaganza. But what the people had heard and come to see was The Charlie Daniels Band. Everything else was just icing on the cake and a lot of extra expense.

I see young artists nowadays doing the same thing, adding stage settings, elaborate lighting systems, and extra personnel and vehicles. In many cases, they are totally unnecessary and super expensive, eating up the bottom line every time a wheel rolls over.

I'm all for expanding and enhancing the show, but I think there's a happy medium in between the things that actually improve a show and the point where the ego takes over and it becomes superfluous glitz.

Just one of the many lessons I learned and will pass on as I go along.

We were selling out big arenas and getting a lot of attention from the media. The *20/20* television show sent a crew out to travel with us for a few days and do a segment about life on the road with the CDB. We did *Austin City Limits*, *The Fall Guy*, and the network music shows that were so popular in those days.

The *Million Mile Reflections* tour continued hot and heavy through the end of 1979 with basically the same personnel. We did make some changes in the LA Reflection Section, one of the changes involving a young lady who replaced one of the backup singers in late 1979.

Her name was Carolyn Brand. Later on, in October 1983, her name was to change to Carolyn Corlew when she married my road manager and friend David Corlew.

Carolyn would go on to sing with the band until 1995, when she had to go home and put their daughter Taylor in school. She still comes and helps me out when we need another harmony voice.

We were in Los Angeles doing TV, and I got a call from George McCorkle of The Marshall Tucker Band telling me that Tommy Caldwell had been very seriously injured in an automobile accident. He was in a hospital in Spartanburg, South Carolina, and the outlook was grim. I stayed in touch with George and Paul Riddle as to Tommy's condition, hoping against hope as the news got worse and worse.

I loved Tommy like a brother and was saddened beyond words when George called to let me know he had passed away. It just didn't seem possible. I had just attended the funeral of the younger Caldwell brother, Tim, who had been killed in a car accident just one month before. I knew that Toy and Mr. and Mrs. Caldwell had to be devastated.

We cancelled our television schedule for a couple of days. Little Charlie was on the road with me, and the two of us, David Corlew, and Wayne Smith caught a plane to Spartanburg, South Carolina. I took solace in the only way I knew how, by writing a piece I called "To a Brother," and using it as a dedication on our next album.

TO A BROTHER

I guess we who take the highway are a different breed of men
With a special kind of feeling, for the ones that we call friend
It's an arm around your shoulder when the morning comes too soon
And a late night conversation in a thousand motel rooms
It's a flood in California and a snowstorm in St. Paul
And it takes a tough old soldier to keep going through it all
But we're so much less than human when we lose one of our own
Now there's one more empty saddle
This old cowboy has gone home.

Tommy Caldwell had been much more than a friend; he had been a supporter and a buddy. Toy and Tommy had been so close, brothers in every sense of the word. It would take super strength for Toy to go on with The Marshall Tucker Band without his brother beside him. But the Caldwell boys were made out of tough material, and Toy and the guys would keep on keeping on.

We went back to California to resume our television taping. While I was there, I did some vocal parts on a really unique concept album called *The Legend of Jesse James*, featuring Johnny Cash, Levon Helm, and Emmylou Harris. It was written by a brilliant young Englishman named Paul Kennerley. It was a fine piece of work, and I was honored to be a part of it.

By January 12, 1980, the Volunteer Jam had taken on a mystique and life of its own. The annual show that had started as a live recording session in 1974 had spawned television specials, a movie, and a couple of live albums. It had been broadcast across the United States and around the world and attracted fans from all over the nation who traveled to Nashville to be a part of it. There was one group who called themselves the Long Island Jam Delegation who drove down from New York every year to see the show. In 1980, we put twenty-five acts onstage in eight hours, which is a testament to the caliber and efficiency of the CDB road crew and office staff.

CHAPTER 34

Broken Arms and Grammys

On January 29, 1980, I was at home at Twin Pines Ranch with a crew of guys digging postholes for a new fence. I've never been good around machinery and should have stayed away from the posthole digger, which is an auger attached to the power drive on the back of a tractor. It turns around and drills holes in the ground. The first thing I knew, my right arm was wrapped up in the posthole auger and snapping bones like twigs.

I was on my knees with my arm tangled in the auger up to my shoulder. Another turn or two probably would have pulled my whole arm off. David Corlew was sitting at the controls and quickly switched the power off. But sometimes a diesel engine will jerk another turn even after the power is killed. I remember crying, "Help me, Lord," and He did. The engine shut down immediately.

They unwrapped my arm from the auger and rushed me to the hospital seven miles away in Lebanon, where I got a pain shot and was transferred to an ambulance and taken to Baptist Hospital in Nashville where Dr. Don Eyler had the operating room ready and a surgical team assembled. My terrified wife had hurried to Lebanon and rode in the ambulance with me.

Just before we went into the operating room, I told Dr. Eyler, "Just get me to where I can hold a guitar pick and a fiddle bow." But he wasn't making any promises.

My arm was badly broken in three places. The bone broke completely in two and was coming through the skin in two of them. Dr. Eyler worked on me for several hours, putting pins in my bones and closing the wounds. When he finished, he looked at me and said, "You're going to be all right."

Even in my highly sedated condition, the message got through. I would be able to play again when my arm healed. Thanks and glory be to our merciful God. There was no major muscle or nerve damage, just badly broken bones. In the liner notes of our next album, I gave thanks to God for saving my right arm.

They took me to a hospital room, and I lay there with a morphine drip, my arm hanging straight up, swollen as big as a football. I was drifting in and out of sleep, and during one of my out periods, the phone in the room rang. Little Charlie, who was fourteen at the time, answered it. It was President Jimmy Carter's office. They had called so President Carter could speak to me and see how I was doing. Little Charlie told them I was asleep and couldn't be disturbed. I don't know how the local TV stations found out about it, but they had a ball talking about Little Charlie refusing to let the president of the United States speak to his daddy because he was asleep. Mr. Carter was nice enough to call back again when I was awake.

I stayed in the hospital for a few days, and then Hazel took me home to experience one of the most frustrating periods of my life. I couldn't play my instruments, and we had to cancel the show dates we had on the books at one of the hottest periods of our career.

I was in pain, but the medicine they gave me for it made me feel crazy, so I avoided it as much as I could. I had a hospital bed in the bedroom and one in the basement where the big-screen television was. The Winter Olympics were on that year, and it provided some much-needed distraction and enjoyment, especially when the young American hockey team beat the Russians and won the gold medal. I almost jumped out of bed, arm and all.

The 1980 Grammy Awards were in February in Los Angeles. "The Devil Went Down to Georgia" was nominated. They wanted us to perform the song live on the show, but there was no way I could even hold a fiddle, much less play one. But I sure didn't want to miss out on playing our nominated song before millions of people on national television.

I didn't relish the long plane flight to Los Angeles, but I figured I could manage it, and a plan was devised. Buddy Spicher and Vassar Clements would join the band onstage and play the fiddle parts. I would stand there with my arm in a sling and sing. Vassar Clements and Buddy Spicher were two of the finest fiddle players on the planet. "The Devil Went Down to

Georgia" had probably never been performed with the precision it was played with that night.

Shortly after the performance, Johnny Cash and June Carter presented the Grammy for Best Country Single of the Year. When they called out our name, all the hassle of coming to Los Angeles with a broken arm was worth it. What an incredible night, to win a Grammy and have the great Johnny Cash and June Carter present it.

The Grammy was the first of many awards we would win in 1980. We won Touring Band of the Year at the Academy of Country Music Awards. We won Single of the Year and Performance Group of the Year and I won Instrumentalist of the Year at the Country Music Association Awards. We also won several others, including one from NARAS (National Academy of Recording Arts and Sciences).

It seemed like a lot longer, but I was only out of commission for four months. I was elated to get that sling off and get back to my instruments. My arms and fingers were as stiff as a board. I practiced scales on my guitar two hours a day to loosen up. I had done nothing but sit around for four months, and I was in horrible shape. As soon as I could, I started walking. I could only make it for about one hundred yards to start with, but I kept increasing the level of exercise. Soon I was jogging a couple of miles a day.

When you're young, you take your health and well-being for granted, but as you put on a few years or experience a near catastrophic accident like I had, it dawns on you that health, and life for that matter, can disappear in a hurry and you should make every effort to maintain it.

I learned a big lesson and have done some form of exercise on a regular basis ever since.

Another lesson I learned is that no matter what the exercise gurus and fad videos advise, pick a level of exercise you're comfortable with, something you can do every day. If you start doing something beyond your daily capabilities, you'll finally get worn out on it and quit. Consistency is the name of the game, and I believe that if you're breaking a sweat, walking, running, or whatever, and doing it on a regular basis, you'll benefit.

God is so good. He has saved me from catastrophe so many times. I know in my heart that He has blessed me so very much to bring me back from the brink of disaster and restore me to the career that I love so much.

CHAPTER 35

Just a Hill with Some Tall Trees Where a Creek Comes Bubbling By

No story of my life could ever be complete without including Twin Pines Ranch. It has been a major part of my life for the past forty years and, God willing, will be a major part of my life until He calls me home.

We bought the original piece of land in 1976 and eventually built our home in 1979. After living in apartments and in neighborhoods our whole married life, the secluded fifty acres looked like *Bonanza* to us.

There were open lanes and wooded trails to ride our horses on, a huge pond to fish in, plenty of safe places to fire our guns, and the privacy we wanted so much.

We were around thirty miles out of Music City, which was handy since at that time we were still making our records in Nashville studios, and the airport was even closer.

We built a small barn, moved our horses out, and spent as much time as we could riding.

It was becoming apparent that there was a lot of upkeep and maintenance, fencing, bush hogging, and so on. The horses had to be looked after, so we hired our next-door neighbor's son, a young man named Robbie Stem, to look after things.

An additional twenty acres joining our land came up for sale and we bought it, increasing our land holdings to seventy acres and expanding our pastures by several acres. The great thing was that it had a double-wide mobile home where our family could spend nights if we wanted to ride our horses for a weekend.

I started thinking about increasing our horse herd and making a commercial venture out of it. Before Robbie left to go to another job, he introduced me to Thurman Mullins, who was a ranger at nearby Cedars of Lebanon Park. Thurman was one of the most likable people I had ever met and one of the most knowledgeable about horses.

I approached him and asked him how he would feel about coming to work for me and starting a horse ranch, getting into buying, selling, and breeding.

This was a big decision for Thurman, as he was working for the State of Tennessee with job security and benefits. I couldn't offer him these things, but he loved working with horses and was pretty fed up with the bureaucratic side of his job and decided to give it a try.

We had just finished our new house on the ranch and were living there full-time. When Thurman agreed to sign on and start the horse business, we immediately started building a new barn with twelve stalls, automatic waterers, an oversized stall for our mares to foal in, a wash pad, a shop, and a ranch office.

Thurman gave the state his notice and came to work in September 1979 and began buying and trading horses. At first we leaned toward Tennessee Walkers, but after a short time it became apparent to us that there was a bigger demand for the quarter horses, a more down-to-earth and common breed that made a great pleasure ride or a "using horse," a common name for a ranch horse used for anything from roping to gathering cattle, so we headed in that direction.

Thurman decided we needed to upgrade our bloodline, so we began hauling some of our mares down to the Santa Gertrudis division of the King Ranch in Texas, which was standing some of the finest quarter horse stallions anywhere. We bred mares to the legendary Mr. San Peppy, Peppy San Badger, and Doc Holliday, among others.

It was obvious that we would need additional help, a top hand who was good with horses and the cattle we planned on getting into. He showed up one day in the person of Leroy Crawford, a brush-popping little cowboy from Mississippi who could rope with the best of 'em and put a handle on any horse that came through our barn.

Leroy is an excellent roper, and we purchased a small herd of Corriente steers and started learning to team rope. We had built a lighted arena along with the barn and added a return alley and a release chute, and when I'd come home off the road, the boys had a hard time getting the regular ranch work done because I kept them in the roping arena all the time.

The late 1970s and early 1980s were the heyday of the cutting horse, as it was also the heyday of the Texas oil business, and several well-heeled oil men got into the game. As the demand grew, the price of high-blooded cutting stock went through the ceiling. Unproven colts that had never had a saddle on their backs were selling for up to thirty thousand dollars, and the big-name cutting horse trainers had their barns full of top prospects.

The cutting horse business was red-hot and showed no sign of cooling off until the price of oil started dropping.

People who a few short months before were paying fifty thousand to a hundred thousand dollars or more for a competitive cutting horse were stuck with a barn full of stock they no longer wanted to feed, train, and haul. The rush to sell before the bottom dropped completely out was on.

Thurman had been in the market for a high-blooded stallion to stand at Twin Pines and had been talking to a gentleman from Texas who had exactly what we were looking for.

The only problem was that the price was astronomically out of our budget. But the calls persisted. The price kept coming down, and when the rancher asked us to make him an offer for the Stallion and thirty-eight other well-bred mares and geldings, Thurman told him that he didn't want to insult him by offering him what the ranch could afford to pay.

The gentleman kept insisting that Thurman make an offer, and when he did, thinking he'd probably be laughed at, the man said, "Come and get 'em."

What we figured was that the rancher wanted out. He wanted the expense of feeding and maintaining a sizable bunch of horses off his hands, but knowing how people gossip, he didn't want to sell cheap in his own backyard. But if he sold out of state to a reputable barn and the buyers kept the price a secret, it looked a lot better. All of a sudden, the horse herd at Twin Pines Ranch doubled in size and quadrupled in quality.

Several of the mares already had their register of merit in cutting, but we were not so interested in that aspect. What we wanted was good, solid quarter horses that could be trained for team roping or broke for pleasure, gentle horses the whole family could ride.

The boys began hauling the horses in and got busy turning them into what we needed.

But the horse that owned every heart at Twin Pines was a 14/3-hand stud horse we called King Bear. He was born on the ranch out of one of our mares and a California stallion named Sun Fritz and was the sweetest-tempered little guy you could ever hope to put a saddle on. When he turned three, Leroy started working with him. After he had been riding him for two months or so, I was at the barn one day when he had him saddled and he told me, "Get on him, Boss."

I said, "Leroy, you know I don't ride fresh horses."

He said, "Just get on him and ride him like you would old Freckles." Freckles was one of our using horses I rode a lot.

And Leroy was right. I crawled aboard, and he became one of my regular mounts.

King Bear was the standing stallion at Twin Pines until he got too old to breed and passed the torch to his own son. We called him Little Bear.

In January 7, 2011, Hazel and I were on vacation in Colorado when Thurman called and told me that the barn was on fire. Our barn was a thirty-year-old wooden structure and went up like kindling wood.

It was frustrating being fifteen hundred miles away and getting periodic reports on the phone as our barn burned to the ground. And with the wind blowing, we were concerned about our house, which was just up the hill.

The Gladeville Volunteer Fire Department showed up immediately. But we didn't have a hydrant anywhere close to the barn, and they had to continually haul water in from outside the ranch. The efforts of our neighbors kept the fire from spreading any farther; you can't beat country folks. Even our county sheriff, Terry Ashe, came out and helped watch over things.

After the fire was out, the damage was assessed. We had lost both tractors, the dually ranch pickup and stock trailer, which was hooked up and left in the barn loaded with a bull Thurman was delivering the next morning, all of our saddles and tack, and a lot of memorabilia that can never be replaced.

But the heartbreaking thing was that nine of our finest horses perished in the fire. All the other things we lost were material things, most of which could be replaced. But knowing that nine horses and a bull died in a barn fire they had no way of escaping from was depressing.

It really bothered me, but it bothered Thurman more than anything I had seen him face in the twenty-five years I'd known him. He kept thinking that if he had only been able to get there a few minutes earlier he could have saved some of the stock, but the truth is that once the fire started, with the wind blowing and the dryness of the wood, it was gone in a few minutes and getting there earlier would only have made the experience even more frustrating.

In one fell swoop we had lost a blood line we had worked with for more than twenty years, with no way to replace it. Little Bear had been in the barn that night. The next morning on a phone call, I told a very depressed Thurman Mullins that we'd start over, that we'd make a new beginning.

We went through the long process of the insurance investigation. The prognosis was that a squirrel or a raccoon had chewed into some electric wires and started the fire.

The burned scraps were removed, and our new barn began to rise. We got two new tractors and a dually pickup and trailer, ordered saddles and tack, and slowly replaced the replaceable things.

But the King Bear blood line was gone forever, or at least that's what we thought.

A few months after the barn fire, a friend of ours, Jerry Mansfield, called Thurman and told him that he'd located a son of Little Bear and was going to see that we got him.

He was a stud colt. And to the cowboys at Twin Pines Ranch, he was the most beautiful thing we'd ever laid our eyes on.

What else could we name him but New Beginnings?

Ain't God good?

CHAPTER 36

You Never Did Think that It Ever Would Happen Again

I t was 1980 and time to start writing for a new album. I went into it with both barrels blazing.

It's a funny thing about patriotism. I had seen it at its white-hot peak during World War II. It was at its lowest ebb in the latter days of the Vietnam War, when desecrating the flag, draft card burning, and disrespecting returning soldiers were commonplace. I had thought it was way past time to bring our troops home from a war the politicians refused to let them win, but flag burning and stoned-out hippies spitting on soldiers who had risked their lives for them made me angry, sick, and bewildered. I wondered if we'd ever pull together as one united people again.

In 1979, when the Iranians took over the American embassy in Tehran and held the staff hostage, parading them around like blindfolded sheep for the world media to see, I felt a creeping anger growing across the face of this nation. As the days dragged by and only an embarrassing, failed attempt was mounted to free the hostages, the frustration and animosity among the people grew. I started hearing things like, "We oughta bomb those idiots" and "We ought to go over there and take our people back." The phrase "You never did think that it ever would happen again" came into my mind. I wrote a song I called "In America."

I wanted to write a ghost story song but had a hard time coming up with a theme. I thought about old folk stories and Indian legends, but nothing appealed to me. Then I remembered a spooky old swamp in Bladen County, North Carolina, where we had coon hunted when I was a boy. The place was filled with thick undergrowth, vines and briars, and patches of marshy ground. Nobody actually lived there, and there were no alligators, but with the aid of my poetic license I wrote a song about it, "The Legend of Wooley Swamp."

I wrote a ballad about growing up in rural North Carolina and married it up with a piece of prose I had written years before. It turned into "Carolina (I Remember You)." Drawing on my days on the Mexican border, I wrote a song about a bullfighter and called it "El Toreador." I wrote a new fiddle tune called "Dance, Gypsy, Dance," a light little piece called "South Sea Song," and a rocker called "Money." With Tommy Crain's "Lonesome Boy from Dixie" and Taz's bluesy "No Potion for the Pain," we were ready to cut a record we would call *Full Moon*.

For some reason I can't recall, we recorded "In America" at the Record Factory in Los Angeles. I don't remember if it was logistical or if we had figured it was going to be a single and tried to get a jump on it to get it ready for release before the rest of the album, but it was the only song we recorded in Los Angeles; we did the rest in Nashville later.

A few days after we recorded it, we performed "In America" on the *Academy of Country Music Awards* television show. The next day Epic Records was getting calls from radio stations around the country wanting to know why they didn't have "In America." Even the local station in Wilmington called my mother wanting to know where Charlie's new record was.

America had had enough pushing and was ready to get behind a patriotic piece of music, and "In America" fit the bill. When it was released we immediately started getting major airplay. Then, when the *Full Moon* album was released, we were soon on our way to our second consecutive platinum record.

We set a blistering pace with our touring schedule and hit the road with a vengeance and a hot show. We were selling out big venues and playing a two-and-a-quarter-hour set of music, most nights doing three encores.

Something very special happened at the Volunteer Jam that year. I was onstage with the band and looked over to the wings of the stage, and standing there grinning like a possum was none other than one of my lifetime heroes, Roy Acuff, who had come out between shows at the *Grand Ole Opry*

Top to bottom, Left to Right:
Age 5, Carolina Beach
5th grade school picture, Goldston, NC
Mother, Dad, & me, circa 1940

Left to Right, Top to bottom:
Me & Hazel, 1964
Me, Little Charlie, & Hazel, Nashville 1968
Hazel, me, & Little Charlie in front of our house at Twin Pines, circa 1980
Little Charlie, me, & Hazel snowmobiling in the Rockies
Santa & Mrs. Claus
One of the greatest nights of my life introducing my grandmother to Roy Acuff

Counterclockwise from top left:
Shooting pictures for our *Saddle Tramp* album. L to R: Taz DiGregorio, Freddie Edwards, me, Don Murray, Charlie Hayward, Tommy Crain
With Mr. Acuff on the Opry
Presentation of our first Gold Album, Volunteer Jam II, 1975, Murphy Center, Murfreesboro, TN. L to R: Art Cass, Wade Conklin, Little Charlie, me
Bob Dylan, Fred Carter, me, Columbia Recording Studios, Nashville, TN, 1969
Taz DiGregorio: Jan. 8, 1944–Oct. 12, 2011
CDB on the set of *Urban Cowboy* with John Travolta. L to R: Taz DiGregorio, Freddie Edwards, me, John Travolta, Jim Marshall, Charlie Hayward

Left to Right, Top to bottom:
    Getting set to heel a steer on my horse, Buck
    Nothing like riding a good cutting horse
    Fun on a cutting horse
    Best houlihan loop I ever threw
    With ranch manager, Thurman Mullins

To my fri... Bill

Left to Right, Top to bottom:
With Reverend Billy Graham
Receiving my honorary doctor of
    letters degree from UNCW, 1996
Inserting a prayer into the Wailing
    Wall, Jerusalem
Sandstorm during our show in Al
    Asad, Iraq (photo by Dean Tubb)
David Corlew and me in Iraq
Camp Victory, Baghdad, Iraq, 2005

Left to Right, Top to bottom:
  With the best blues artist in the world, B.B. King
  With my friend Coach Phil Fulmer
  With Dale Earnhardt in Talladega, AL (photo by Dean Tubb)
  Jamming with Garth Brooks
  With Mickey Mantle
  Presenting a Quarterback Club Award to Peyton Manning

Left to Right, Top to bottom:

Willie and me

Bob Johnston—my mentor, my teacher, and above all, my friend

CDB office staff

 L to R: DeAnna Winn, Angela Wheeler, David Corlew, Paula Szeigis, Randy Owen,
 Charlie Daniels, Jr., Donna Copeland, J.B. Copeland, Carolyn Corlew, Bebe Evans

CDB road crew

 L to R: Bob Workman, Roger Campbell, Steve Morgan, Jimmy Burton, Jackie McClure,
 Jimmy Potts, Dean Tubb, Brian Madaris, Chris Potts

CDB at Country Music Hall of Fame (photo by Anna Webber/Getty Images for CMHOF & Museum)

Left to Right, Top to bottom:
    Russell Palmer playing a song with CDB at my induction into the Grand Ole Opry
    Acceptance speech at my induction into the Country Music Hall of Fame (photo by Jason Davis/
        Getty Images)
    Country Music Hall of Fame, 2016
    CDB present-day (photo by Erick Anderson)
        L to R: Chris Wormer, Ron Gannaway, me, Shannon Wickline, Charlie Hayward, Bruce Brown

because he knew it would thrill me to no end. I, of course, called him out onstage, and the crowd loved him. I couldn't believe it. Here was the King of Country Music, the superstar *Opry* legend I had listened to on our old Zenith radio before I'd even started school, standing on my stage, singing a song with my band on a Saturday night in Nashville, Tennessee. Mercy!

When you're doing something you love and the momentum keeps increasing, it seems that the world just spins a little faster, and the first thing I knew, it was 1981. Little Charlie had turned sixteen and was getting a driver's license. He had gotten his learner's permit at fifteen and a half, done a lot of supervised driving, and proven himself responsible and capable. So when he got his license on the day he turned sixteen, how could we refuse to let him drive to an all-night skating party in Mount Juliet?

He didn't drink, he'd been an obedient and thoughtful son, and we were sure he would be just fine. But when you think of your baby making his first solo flight, you can't help but be a little bit apprehensive. Of course, being the man of the house, I tried to approach it with a somewhat blasé attitude, thinking that this was really going to be hard on Hazel. Guess who laid awake until three o'clock in the morning while his wife slept like a baby? The creak of the front gate was the sweetest sound I'd ever heard, and I thanked God my son was home safe.

Of course, when kids get their driver's licenses, they discover a whole new kind of freedom. Then, of course, comes the dating and all of the other teenage interests, and the first thing you know they're spending a lot of time behind the steering wheel. I used to worry every time Charlie pulled out of the driveway. I soon learned that all I could do was ask God to protect him and leave it in His capable hands.

Charlie was, and still is, a very considerate kid. If he was out and about and was going to be more than a few minutes late, he would find a phone and call to let us know.

I wanted him to know what real work was, so he worked in the barn doing whatever needed to be done. He cleaned out a lot of stalls in his teenage years. I think that every kid should know what it's like to sweat, to pick up heavy loads, to do things that are not particularly pleasant but necessary, to know what it's like for a lot of people on this planet, and to feel an empathy for all working people.

Our children grow up so quickly, changing before our eyes, going from one phase to the next almost overnight, it seems. I enjoyed watching my son grow up and dreaded the day he would cut the apron strings, but for now he was living at home.

It was time to break some new ground. We got a call from our booking agency, saying that they'd been approached by Harrah's Casino in Lake Tahoe. Frank Sinatra had cancelled a week's engagement and Willie Nelson had agreed to fill some of the days, but they still had three open and wanted the CDB to fill it.

I was stunned. I had always thought of the Nevada casino circuit as being the private preserve of The Rat Pack, Tony Bennett, Barbra Streisand, and entertainers of that genre. Of course, I knew that Willie Nelson had broken into the scene in a big way, but Willie could match voices with any of those people and hold his own. We were a loud, raw Southern band that jammed and slammed our way through a show, and our crowds were anything but the suit-and-tie bunch.

Although we had the time and it would fit perfectly into our routing, I really had my doubts about taking the engagement. This was the main room of a famous casino, a stage that the legends of show business had performed on. We told our agency that all we knew how to do was play two CDB sets a night, no bells and whistles and no smoke and mirrors, just two hours of hardcore guitar and fiddle rocking out and taking no prisoners.

They said to come on, and we did. I flew in, and they sent a car to pick me up at the airport, and as I often do, I invited the driver to come to a show. He said, "I believe all your shows are sold out." I thought he surely must be mistaken, but when I got to Harrah's, Stu Carnell, the guy who booked the show, confirmed it. All six CDB shows were sold out in advance.

And that was not the only surprise I had waiting for me at Harrah's. The place where I would be staying was what they called the Star Suite, a lavish apartment that was part of two floors, with its own kitchen complete with personal cook, a fireplace, a movie screen that came down out of the ceiling, a fully stocked bar, and a bedroom that could have been straight off a movie set. Hazel flew in, and we enjoyed Harrah's hospitality to the fullest.

A two-hour-and-fifteen-minute show in a casino where the prime concern is to get everybody to the gaming tables is unheard of. But that's what we did, twice a night for three nights in a row.

We would play Harrah's properties in Tahoe, Reno, and Atlantic City many times over the years and did eventually cut our show to a more suitable length.

CHAPTER 37

Talk to Me Fiddle, Tell Me About the Time When You Came Across the Sea

Everybody agreed that it was time to do a foreign tour. We had been overseas a couple of times but had never had a record that had done as well as our latest ones, and "The Devil Went Down to Georgia" had been very successful in countries where English was not even spoken. The tour started out with a bang, with three packed-out nights in London.

Everything was going great until we flew into Paris to tape a television show. When we got to Paris, the truck from London with our equipment had been held up at the border because the French customs agents had gone on strike. When we got to the theater for our sound check and camera blocks, we found out that we would not be taping a television show but a radio show because the French camera operators' union had gone on strike.

We had rented a small bus to move us around Paris while we were there, and when we finished our sound check and went out to go back to the hotel, the bus was sitting on the street, locked, and the driver was nowhere to be found. We took cabs back to the hotel. He finally showed up in time to take us to the show that night.

The next morning we went to the airport to catch a plane to Bremen, Germany, only to find that the French air traffic controllers had gone on strike and our flight had been cancelled.

We didn't actually have to be in Bremen until the next night. Since the planes weren't flying, it was decided that we would go to the bus company, rent a bigger bus, and ride to Bremen, which was only eight hours away. Then we'd have it take us on to Amsterdam, the next date on the tour.

This all happened in the morning, and after our people spent all day trying to arrange for a bus, we pulled out of Paris about sundown with two bus drivers we named Slinky and Blinky. They spoke all of ten words of English and drove forty-five miles an hour all the way from Paris to Bremen, Germany, turning an eight-hour trip into a thirteen-hour trip.

Feeling that we would like to get to Amsterdam before the new year, our people called the bus company in Paris and told them that we would not be taking their bus to Amsterdam because their drivers drove like escargot herders. They assured us that they would talk to Slinky and Blinky and have them put the pedal to the metal if we would only keep the bus. Since Amsterdam was not too far away, we agreed.

Slinky and Blinky did step it up a bit, probably to 55 or so, but the speed limit on the autobahn is 125 miles per hour for cars, and it still seemed we were crawling. When we finally got to Holland, we had the bus drop us off at the television show location, and J. B. Copeland went to check in and drop our luggage off at the hotel in Amsterdam. Slinky and Blinky tried to make him get off the bus blocks away from the hotel with all the luggage, which J. B. refused to do. Our two French bus drivers were last seen driving away from the Amsterdam Marriott trying to maneuver the narrow streets of downtown Amsterdam. I hope they made it back to Paris.

Million Mile Reflections and *Full Moon* had taken the CDB to a whole new level internationally. The album went platinum in Canada, where we did a cross-country tour from the Maritimes to British Columbia. We played New Zealand and did a tour of Australia with the Little River Band and of course toured the United States constantly.

The concert we did in New Zealand, an outdoor show called the Mombasa Festival, was like walking back into the sixties, complete with brightly painted hippy vans and people who looked as if they'd just walked off Haight-Ashbury at the height of San Francisco's psychedelic period.

It was a pretty strange bill. I remember that Dizzy Gillespie was supposed to go on before us, but he was upset about his money or something and wasn't going to play. I said, "We'll go on, money or no money. We didn't come this far not to play our music."

Things can get out of hand at these kinds of affairs, and David Corlew decided Rick Rentz, our security man, may have needed some extra help and hired a couple of the Maoris, New Zealand's aborigines, who were supposedly doing security for the event. But when David offered them cash on the barrel head, they came aboard in a hurry.

We were getting ready to play our set, and all of a sudden Dizzy decided he wanted to play. We were all set up and ready to rock, so we didn't want to leave the stage. When the promoter tried to come onstage and get us off so Dizzy could come on, one of our Maori, a huge guy we called Mongo, wouldn't let him come onstage.

"But I'm the promoter!"

"I don't work for you; I work for him," Mongo said, pointing at David.

We played our set and rode off the property with our new Maori friends walking on each side of the car.

Then, off to the land down under to join the Little River Band for a tour of Australia.

The mecca of Australian country music is an outback town called Tamworth. It could be compared with Nashville in that the Australian Country Music Awards take place there every year, and as we were up for an award, I went to Tamworth to accept it.

Australia has its own brand of country music and its own stars. Slim Dusty has been referred to as the Australian Roy Acuff in that he was considered a pioneer of country music in Australia.

Smoky Dawson, another Australian star, has a river named after him.

I met both of these gentlemen and enjoyed a night of the Aussie's brand of country music. I would go back to Tamworth several years later and play on the *Australian Country Music Awards*.

The Little River Band is the only group we ever toured with for which I stayed around almost every night for their set after we did the opener. They had the best and tightest vocal harmony of any band I'd ever worked with and a very talented sound man mixing out front. They were as close to perfection as I've ever heard any band be, night after night.

I fell in love with Australia as we toured around the country, and I felt that the United States and Australia had a lot in common. The people are warm and fun loving, and their beloved Australia spans a continent, just as our United States does.

We are both relatively new countries compared to Europe and Asia. It had taken a hard and determined bunch of people to settle the untamed stretches of these two vast lands. And the Australian people have a sense of national pride and independence that I could identify with.

No matter how much we enjoy seeing new places and making new fans, it's always a blast when you clear customs and somebody says, "Welcome to the United States of America."

CARDBOARD CRITICS

When we released "In America" as a single there was some criticism—not a lot, but there was a little residue of anti-American sentiment among the left-wing press and aging hippie music critics, and such a flag waver was a little much for them. This was nothing new and nothing to be feared because I had had flak from the elitists in the press all of my career. The CDB was once named one of the five most worthless bands in rock and roll, along with the Grateful Dead and Rush, by a music critic who wrote for the *Baltimore Sun*. I've often wondered what ever happened to him.

For the most part I have had a wonderful relationship with the music media. But with some of the more self-diagnosed intellectuals, our music either goes over or under their heads, and they use every obscure word they learned in English class to tell the world how they feel about it.

A Canadian critic once described Leonard Cohen's music as "inane."

The dictionary defines *inane* as meaning "silly."[3] If anything is very silly or stupid, it is the critic's use of the word *inane* to describe the work of one of the most sensitive and poetic songwriters of our time.

The thing you have to remember is that music critics are nothing more than humans with opinions. Some of them who couldn't cut it in the performance end of the business have decided to take out their frustration on artists they don't consider their cerebral equals. I've had critics point out things that I knew went wrong in a show, and I don't mind it at all. But when someone fills up a column with superfluous and hurtful comments, I take offense. Many times I answer back in kind, sorta critique the critics, and they don't like it at all. Too bad. I have as much right to critique their work as they have to critique mine.

One of the most blatant flubs by a critic I've ever heard of was when one of the big-city critics covered a Buck Owens show. He wrote that he didn't know why Buck had to do that old Beatles song in his set. He was referring to "Act Naturally," which the Beatles released in 1965, a couple of years after Buck had a big hit with it in 1963. In fact, it was a Buck Owens classic.

As somebody so aptly put it, critics are like eunuchs. They can observe and assess, but they can never, ever participate.

"In America" was off and running, and the *Full Moon* album was walking out of record stores. With the release of our second single, "The Legend of Wooley Swamp," we were on our way to another big record.

CHAPTER 39

HIGH LONESOME, OUR LITTLE
PIECE OF TENNESSEE

In 1979 our family moved into a two-story log house at the top of a hill on Twin Pines Ranch. While nothing fancy, it was the homey sort of place that suited our family's taste. With a big stone fireplace and a screened-in upstairs porch with a good view of the big pond at the bottom of the hill and a patch of woods on each side, it was our dream house, and still is.

I love my professional life. I love entertaining and touring, being around people, and all the other facets that make up the life of a professional traveling musician. But my private life begins when I turn off the little two-lane road that runs past the entrance to Twin Pines Ranch.

That's the line of demarcation between Charlie Daniels public figure and Charlie Daniels private citizen.

I have tried to surround my family and myself with the things we enjoy. Over the years we have been blessed with many desires of our hearts. Due to the fact that the area we built in was basically undeveloped when we moved there, the land surrounding us was cheap. We bought several small tracts until Twin Pines Ranch was a little more than four hundred acres, with several ponds, a lighted roping arena, a swimming pool, a tennis court, a putting green, and a small shooting range where I'll sometimes pop off several hundred rounds in a day's time.

We live in a simple two-story split-log house with four porches and a swimming pool. The interior is decorated in a hodgepodge of my Western art and Hazel's antiques. We don't try to impress anybody but ourselves in the way we decorate our house. We just try to surround ourselves with the things that are pleasing to our eyes and would probably run an interior decorator slam up the wall, and we couldn't care less.

Our house is meant to be lived in, not impress, and we live in every inch of it. In the wintertime I crank up the fireplace and kick back. I keep a guitar and fiddle on stands beside my favorite chair. The table next to it is usually covered with the remnants of whatever project I'm working on—sheets of paper, computers, guitar picks, and other bits and pieces of my sloppy creative process.

There's a chair in the kitchen that Hazel calls my office, where I drop everything when I come in off the road—clothes, computers, books, belts, caps, mail, and periodicals I intend to read but probably never will. There may even be a box of ginger snaps. I don't want anybody to touch anything in my "office." Of course, Hazel usually lowers the boom when the chair gets so full you can't tell the color of the fabric and, despite my protest, moves things around.

I have my own personal cabinet in the entrance hall that resembles a miniature version of Fibber McGee's closet. When opened, there is perpetual danger of fomenting a small avalanche of knives, bullets, fishing lures, shoulder holsters, gun cleaning kits, bits and pieces of leather, sharpening tools, and all manner of my hoarded treasures.

I won't even go into what my personal drawer in the kitchen looks like.

To say I'm messy would be like calling Lake Pontchartrain a mud puddle. But my long-suffering wife loves me anyway, even if I do get salt all over the table when I eat, occasionally forget to completely shut the refrigerator door, and get toothpaste and shaving cream on the bathroom mirror.

Hazel is in charge of every room in our house except the den. My exclusive domain is filled with Western art, bronze sculptures, Kachina dolls, muzzle loaders and flintlocks on the wall, a tanned fox hide, a painted cow skull, handmade knives, and swords. It also has our best TV and is likely to be the loudest room in the house during the NFL season.

In mild weather Hazel and I like to sit on the upstairs screened-in porch and listen to the night critters praise their Maker. Once in a while we hear a whip-poor-will that always sounds a long way off. In the summer there's usually a big bullfrog sounding off down at the big pond and maybe the soft knicker of a horse or "Where's Momma?" call from one of this year's calves.

I can stay at Twin Pines Ranch for days on end and never go outside the gate and be perfectly happy. You could find me astride a horse, trying to fool one of the largemouth in the big pond, or in the back pasture sliding around in the mud on a four-wheeler.

About a quarter of a mile down the road as the crow flies is another two-story, split-log structure that houses the offices and recording studio of The Charlie Daniels Band, where a small dedicated group of people show up on a daily basis and run the day-to-day business, organizing tours, keeping the books, and doing publicity, publishing, and all the other activities involved in keeping the CDB rolling.

I love my employees and know their spouses, children, and, in some cases, grandchildren. Our organization is small but totally efficient, with no wasted effort or overlapping. Everybody has a job to do, and they do it well.

My philosophy for hiring an employee is first of all to hire somebody who is capable of doing the job. They must have a willingness to do whatever it takes to get the job done, regardless of the time and effort involved and, above all else, have a good attitude and honesty.

Then I believe in getting out of their way and letting them work. If they have a problem or a decision that requires my involvement, I am readily available. Otherwise, take the initiative and get it done.

The Twin Pines staff take care of the ranch. Thurman Mullins is the ranch manager and makes most of the decisions having to do with the sale and purchase of cattle and horses. He chooses which pastures are grazed and when and keeps a close eye on the place. He is apt to be at any part of the property at any time of the day or night and is the first one called in cases of a burglar alarm going off or any kind of problem concerning security at the ranch.

Leroy Crawford is top hand and can handle anything concerning a tractor or livestock, and he has a way with horses few people do. He can gentle a fresh colt, put a handle on him, and have him ready to ride in a few months.

Brud Spickard is the all-around handyman, lives at the front gate, and is very choosy about who is allowed through it.

Donna Copeland, J. B.'s wife, is Hazel's personal assistant and makes sure the house is taken care of when we are gone. She's a great organizer and does the extensive decorating at our house every Christmas. She does the major household shopping and handles a lot of details.

I tell people that my day-to-day life is run by three women. Three very strong-willed ladies, I might add. One, of course, is my wife, Hazel. Another is Paula Szeigis. And the other is Bebe Evans.

Of course, Hazel is my constant companion and figures into almost every decision I make.

Bebe and Paula know more about where I'm going to be and what I'm going to be doing in the near future than I do.

Bebe is in charge of the touring department. The show offers from promoters come through our booking agency and to her desk. She accepts them or doesn't accept them depending on a lot of elements like price, routing, scheduling, and so on.

If she accepts an offer, she plugs it into the system and it goes to the road manager, Jimmy Burton, to be advanced for all pertinent and practical information. The sound man, Bob Workman, and lighting director, Brian Maderis, check out electric power, sound, and light companies involved and all other technical considerations.

After Jimmy and Bob do their thing, there is another follow-up call from Bebe to make sure all the bases are covered. The date is passed on to Paula, who sets up radio and press interviews to publicize the concert. She also handles the mail-outs and publicity mats used in print ads and other visual publicity.

Paula sets up telephone interviews on a weekly basis. She also accompanies me on promotion trips to do publicity blitzes in major markets when we are working a new record, book, or some other project.

J. B. Copeland is office manager and handles anything to do with money, from processing the payroll to paying the bills. He does so with an efficiency that would make an IRS agent proud. He can lay his hand on any figures you need in a matter of minutes and documents every cent that comes through his hands.

Paula and Bebe are fierce guardians of my time and my safety. Both are completely convinced that I am not capable of catching an airplane alone or even driving myself thirty-five miles into Nashville for a doctor's appointment. When Hazel, Paula, and Bebe join forces, I just give in and do whatever they want. It ain't worth the effort to do otherwise.

After a concert date is accepted, vetted, advanced, and approved, it is passed on to our travel agent, Nick Gold. He finds accommodations in proximity of the venue that have ample parking for two forty-five-foot buses and a truck and a block of rooms available.

Angela Wheeler is the secretary for my manager, David Corlew. She also does the CDB itinerary and handles any number of odds and ends that pop up all the time.

DeAnna Winn directs phone calls and runs the Volunteers, the CDB fan club.

Randy Owen works with Charlie Jr. in the publishing end of things. And everybody helps everybody else if the need arises.

When a date is added to the books, an itinerary is published, leaving times established, equipment loaded on the truck, maps routed out, and the CDB rolls.

Jimmy Potts drives the equipment truck. His son Chris is the relief driver and merchandise manager, handling the sale of T-shirts, caps, CDs, and such.

The band and road crew ride on a bus named the Lady LaRue. It was named after my mother, who passed away several years ago. There are two drivers on the Lady LaRue. A daytime driver, Jackie McClure, and a nighttime driver, Steve Morgan, are necessary because of the miles they travel and the schedule they have to keep. They may deadhead from Nashville to San Francisco, stopping only for fuel and food.

The bus Hazel and I travel on has been driven for the last thirty years by Dean Tubb, who is like a second son to us. He comes from a prominent country music family; he is the youngest son of the great Ernest Tubb.

When Dean's son Evan was born in 1997, Hazel and I unofficially adopted him as our grandson. He became a part of our lives. He really is a grandson in every sense of the word and travels with us when he is out of school in the summertime.

And then, after Evan's mother, Meleia, remarried, she had a daughter named Alaya in 2008, and we unofficially adopted her too. We had never had a little girl in our lives, and we love our two adopted grandchildren and thoroughly enjoy spending time with them.

Jimmy Burton rides herd on the road operation. He is responsible for everything that happens before the band takes the stage, from leaving times, dressing room assignments, transportation for the crew and band, and making sure the show runs smoothly.

Roger Campbell handles my instruments and is my onstage roadie. We have worked together for so long that I can look at him and mouth a word and he knows what I'm talking about. He responds whether I've broken a string or just decided to do a song I need a different instrument to play.

Bob Workman is responsible for how the band sounds out front and takes his job seriously. He spends hours before the show adjusting the out-front sound and the onstage monitors.

Bryan Madaris, our lighting director, rounds out our small but efficient traveling unit. We usually log close to a hundred thousand miles a year and do in excess of a hundred shows a year.

We don't have unimportant people in our outfit. Everybody has a job to do, and at some time during the day or night, that job is the most important one in the bunch.

When we roll, the drivers are the most important. They drive through the midnight hours with a busload of sleeping people. Those lives are in the driver's hands. The same is true with the truck. If our equipment doesn't make it, we can't do the show.

When we hit town, the road crew becomes the most important faction, unloading and setting up our equipment, setting the lights, fine tuning the sound system, provisioning the dressing rooms, and having everything ready to go on time.

And here I'd like to say a word about refreshment riders. They are the part of the concert contract that deals with food and drink supplied by the promoter for the band and crew.

There was a time when a lot of food was put into the band's dressing room every night, such as deli and pastry trays, candy and desserts, finger foods, and a variety of beverages and condiments. Most of it was wasted every night, as the band didn't particularly care to eat before a show and were more into the after-show pizza they get every night than deli trays that have set for hours without refrigeration.

All I ask a promoter to do is to feed my road crew. They have to spend the day at the venue. If they provide the beverages we need to get us through the night, they can forget catering the dressing room with food that will be wasted.

I once knew of a manager who would include rare, expensive wines on the band's rider, which he took home for his private wine cellar. Try finding a bottle of Lafite Rothschild 1947 in a little town in Georgia.

Making promoters jump through hoops just because you can is ridiculous, and they don't forget it.

Our shows start on time.

Barring a technical glitch or a request from the promoter to let all the crowd get in and get settled, CDB shows start exactly when they're supposed to. If the ticket says eight o'clock, the show starts at eight o'clock.

There is usually very little plausible reason for a show to run late. I have no patience with bands who, for no other reason than sloppiness and ego, make the paying customers wait for a show to start.

Jimmy Burton is standing in the wings with my fiddle, and I ask him the same thing every night.

"Do we have any impediments?"

Meaning, is there anything between here and where I'm going onstage that will trip me up? The reason I do that is because one night going onstage I tripped on a cord and fractured my shoulder. I want to make sure the way is clear before I hustle onstage.

If there is an obstacle, he points it out and then keys his radio and says the same thing every night.

"Bob Workman, start that 'Tennessee Waltz.' Skin 'er back, it's showtime!"

Patti Page's timeless version of the "Tennessee Waltz" starts playing; it is followed by a short bombastic classical piece Chris Wormer and myself wrote called "Notte Pericolosa." Sean Hannity's recorded voice says, "From Mount Juliet, Tennessee, The Charlie Daniels Band!"

And then it's off to the races.

CHAPTER 40

HEART OF MY HEART, ROCK OF MY SOUL, YOU CHANGED MY LIFE WHEN YOU TOOK CONTROL

Up until now I have only mentioned my faith, but I have not gone into detail about what or how I believe.

I've been asked about my testimony many times and have never really formulated a cohesive response. The story goes through many phases and covers many years and is an ongoing part of my life.

I was raised in a Christian family, and from the time of my earliest remembrances I heard the phrase, "Jesus died for our sins." As I look back, I accepted it as fact, although I really had little comprehension of what it actually meant and how it applied to the salvation of my soul.

As with many young people of my day, I figured that the path to salvation lay along the road of righteousness. Being good enough and not sinning was the only way to gain eternal life. In essence, you had to live an almost perfect life, and once you made your profession of faith, you could lose your salvation by sinning.

I went to all kinds of churches in my youth. Both sides of my family had been Methodists. But when I reached adolescence, I branched out and went to services ranging from dignified Presbyterian to spirit-filled Holiness where the sermons were fire and brimstone and the congregants spoke in tongues.

But of all the churches I went to, I can't ever remember anybody ever explaining in full to me how Jesus' sacrifice on the cross applied to my personal salvation, why it was necessary, or how it paid for my sins.

So, I was still of the opinion that it had to do with my performance rather than what Jesus Christ had done on the cross two thousand years ago. I had to prove myself worthy. Any sin I committed could remove all the good I had ever tried to do and cancel out my salvation, whatever I perceived it to be.

The impossibility of living a totally sin-free life didn't really register in my young mind. Doubt and confusion set in, reinforced by the strict doctrine of the church I was going to at the time. That church frowned on women cutting their hair, on going to movies, and the wearing of makeup and jewelry, and they had zero tolerance for alcohol and tobacco. It basically favored a cloistered lifestyle away from the wiles of the world and the temptations of society.

If you asked about the liberal consumption of wine in the Bible, the stock answer was that it was not the kind of wine that would lead to inebriation. It was some form of mild grape drink that was only referred to as wine. It is a bogus answer because there are accounts in the Bible of people getting inebriated from consuming too much wine.

And if drinking wine was a sin, why would Jesus change water into wine?

Now, I am not promoting the use of alcohol and certainly not condoning overindulgence. But as Paul said in 1 Corinthians 6:12, "Everything is permissible for me; but not all things are helpful" (AMPC). Overindulgence in many things is bad for you, and good sense and moderation in all things is the answer.

But to twist the Scripture to make a theological point that suits your purposes or supports your dogma could open a whole plethora of questions to someone seeking clarity and truth.

I know that there is a lot of symbolism and mystery in the Bible, but it is my belief that most of the Scripture can and should be taken literally.

When it says that the whale swallowed Jonah, I believe it means that Jonah was swallowed whole by a gigantic fish. When it says that Jesus broke a few loaves of bread and fish and fed five thousand people, I believe it happened just that way.

When the Bible says that the walls of Jericho fell or that the Red Sea opened so the Israelites could go through to the other side, I believe that the waters parted and stayed that way long enough for a million or more men, women, and children plus their livestock and possessions to cross.

Substance, not symbolism.

I was told once by a lady of that church that if you were in a movie house when Jesus came back, He wouldn't have time to come and get you.

In my understanding, it all happens in the twinkling of an eye. If you are a believer, I don't think the walls of a movie house can hold you.

It was all so legalistic and rigid, and it seemed to me that I heard so much about the wrath of God and so little about the love of God. It appeared that God was constantly on the lookout for the slightest infraction, and it was a roller-coaster ride of doubt and confusion and a guilty conscience. It all just seemed so impossible that I finally just walked away.

I never stopped believing. I just realized that I couldn't live a totally sinless life, especially according to the legalistic minutia that deemed so many mundane, basically harmless human actions as sins.

I sometimes think that so many churches and well-meaning pastors take for granted that people know the basics of salvation when they walk through the door. They forget that there are those who don't understand why Jesus' sacrificial death brings eternal life to all who repent, believe, and accept.

When people are threatened with hell every Sunday and have drawn the conclusion that the only way they can avoid it is to live a perfect life, they many times become disillusioned and bitter. Then, realizing the futility of such an undertaking, they start imagining God as a vengeful patriarchal-type deity who is just waiting for one little transgression to revoke your salvation.

Actually, the Bible tells us that God is love. He demonstrated His great love by sending His only begotten Son to die the most painful and humiliating death imaginable so that we might obtain life everlasting.

Now, what does that all mean?

I decided years ago to read the Bible and draw, as best I could, my own conclusions. I needed to try to work out my own salvation, as I believe every person has to do.

As the old song says,

You've got to walk that lonesome valley
You've got to go there by yourself
Ain't nobody here gonna go there for you
You've got to walk it by yourself[1]

Why did God do it that way? He is all powerful and could have forced everybody to abide by His will.

While there are many ways to the mountaintop, why do I have to go through Jesus to get there?

I answer these questions based on my own understanding, by my own convictions and beliefs. I have never had any formal theological training and do not, by any means, consider myself an expert.

I do not ascribe to, nor necessarily disagree with, the doctrine of any organized Christian denomination. I have drawn my conclusions according to my own interpretation of the Holy Bible and the interpretations of biblical scholars and teachers whose opinions I agree with.

And from my point of view, here's what it all means.

When God sent His Son to earth, He instituted a new covenant to replace the old covenant, the terms of which had been given to Abraham, Isaac, and Jacob, the forefathers of the Jewish race. Then there were the commandments and laws that were given to Moses during the Israelites' forty-year sojourn in the desert.

The Bible says that without the shedding of blood, there is no remission of sin. The old covenant required animal sacrifice. Animal blood had to be shed to cover the sins of the people.

Why did God do it that way? I honestly don't know. But since His wisdom is so much greater than ours, we should just accept that He knew what He was doing.

Animal sacrifice was not as cut and dry as it sounds. You couldn't just go out into the pasture and cut out some old dry cow that had stopped having calves and take it to the priest to be sacrificed.

It had to come from the very best you had. Your prize stock. An animal without a blemish. I have likened it to giving up one of my best herd bulls or one of my best-blooded heifers. God demanded the best of the flocks and herds for blood sacrifices. It was giving up something that was of real value to you.

And God gave laws and instructions on how to live, dietary guidelines, and outlines for worship. There was the setting aside of Sabbaths and holy days and seasons that were to be observed in specific ways. There was eye-for-eye, tooth-for-tooth justice and laws about how it was to be meted out and the proper time and method to offer the sacrifices.

This was the way to atonement for thousands of years. But humans, being what they are, started trying to exploit the system by ignoring the spirit it represented. They started trying to read between the lines and came to the conclusion that it was permissible to do anything that was not specifically forbidden in the law.

In Jesus' time the religious leaders of the day, known as the Pharisees, followed the law to the letter, even down to tithing the herbs in their gardens. But since the law didn't say you shouldn't force widows and orphans off their land, they did that and other evil things without pity or remorse.

The old covenant law was interpreted in a way God never intended it to be, by legalistic people who ignored the spirit of repentance and fairness. They ignored one of the two most important of the Ten Commandments— to love your neighbor as yourself.

The Pharisees were self-righteous, pompous, and convinced that their interpretation of the Scriptures was the only one that should be accepted. They were so pompous that they didn't recognize the coming of the Jewish Messiah, an event that had been predicted by their own prophets thousands of years ago.

When the Sanhedrin, the Jewish religious ruling body, was debating about whether Jesus was really the Messiah, one of the leaders made a statement declaring that no prophet comes out of Galilee (John 7:52). For it was prophesied that the Messiah would come from the region of King David, which is exactly where Jesus was born: in the city of David, Bethlehem.

But as far as the Pharisees were concerned, He was from Nazareth of Galilee. If they had bothered to ask Him where He was born, they would have found out the truth. In their haste and greed to keep their elite place in the Jewish hierarchy and in their fervor to rid the earth of this young man who healed the sick and raised the dead and threatened their exalted place as arbiters and judges of all religious dogma and theological interpretation, they insisted on nothing less than His crucifixion.

Jesus had given the Pharisees a hard time. He called them whitewashed tombs full of dead men's bones and said that men walked by them never knowing the corruption they were passing.

He called them a brood of vipers and children of the Devil.

They were self-righteous, supercilious hypocrites who presented an outer facade of pious righteousness, calling attention to their acts of charity and presenting themselves as paragons of virtue, tithing "mint and cumin." Under the patina of holiness, they were rotten to the core. They kept the commandments and traditions to the letter but took advantage of weaker people. They justified themselves by there not being a specific law forbidding their evil deeds in the Scriptures.

They kept the letter but not the spirit of the law.

Jesus said that He did not come to do away with the law but to bring it to fruition. He said He came to bring a new covenant, a righteousness not of outward displays of piety but of conscience and heart. His salvation is received not by eating certain foods, observing certain holidays, or sacrificing animals for the forgiveness of sins but by living a life governed by conscience and the inbred common sense of right and wrong our Creator made us with.

Jesus said we must be born again. We must become a new creature with an acute sense of right and wrong and a desire to accomplish the true purposes of God, not because of a set of rules but because we knew in our hearts that it was the way of salvation.

A righteousness based not on laws and traditions but on faith in Jesus. We must believe that He is the Son of God, that He is the only way to the Father, that He rose from the dead and ascended to heaven, and that one day He will return to claim His rightful place as King of kings and Lord of lords.

But since the scripture stated that all have sinned and fallen short of the glory of God and that without the shedding of blood there could be no remission of sin, one more blood sacrifice had to be exacted. It was the last sacrifice that would ever need to be made.

Jesus was conceived not by man but by the Holy Spirit. He was the only human to live His life without blemish or transgression, breaking the cycle of the sin man had been born into since Adam yielded to Satan's temptation in the garden of Eden.

God used the blood of the sinless Son of the living God to break the power of Satan and rip open the curtain of the Holy of Holies, the section of the temple where only designated priests could enter. That made it possible for ordinary men to come into the very presence of almighty God to present their praise and petitions in Jesus' name.

Jesus was crucified, but He rose from the dead and walked among His disciples, breaking the chain of death and in full view of many. He ascended into the sky to sit at the right hand of the Father, interceding for those who love Him and try to live according to His teachings.

The blood Jesus shed on the cross covers the sins of those who are willing to accept His promise of eternal life.

Accepting the salvation of Jesus Christ does not mean a trouble-free life. It doesn't mean that we'll never commit another sin. But what it does mean is that when we sin, and we will, we can ask for forgiveness. If we're sincere and repentant, our sin is covered by the blood Jesus shed on the cross and will be forgiven. The Bible says that if we repent and confess our sins, God is faithful to forgive.

To receive forgiveness, we must also forgive those who have sinned against us, up to and including grievous wrongs anyone has done us. We don't have to approve or agree with what they've done, but we do, in our hearts, have to forgive them to receive God's forgiveness.

When Jesus was hanging on the cross, nailed to it hand and foot in indescribable agony, He asked His Father to forgive the very people who had put Him there because they didn't know what they were doing.

And right there is our example for forgiving. If Jesus in the midst of all His suffering could ask forgiveness for His tormentors, we can certainly forgive those we feel have slighted us.

So, how do we go about this process? How do we receive this eternal blessing of life through Jesus Christ?

In my own personal opinion, one of the hardest things to grasp about the salvation of Jesus Christ is the simplicity. There's nothing you can do to earn it, deserve it, or obtain it. You don't have to be in a certain place. You don't have to be with a certain person or perform some ritual or physical act.

The Bible says that "If you declare with your mouth, 'Jesus is Lord,' and believe in your heart that God raised him from the dead, you will be saved" (Romans 10:9).

First of all you have to believe that Jesus is the Son of almighty God. The God that loves you so much He was willing to send His Son to this earth to suffer the most painful and humiliating death a human has ever suffered so that you can live in unspeakable splendor and peace for all eternity.

You have to repent, which simply means turn away from, change directions.

And it's a "come as you are" proposition. You can't wait to clean your life up by yourself before you present yourself to God because you'll never get it done. It's impossible.

You come with all your wrinkles and warts showing, all your bad habits, all your faults and flaws and prejudices, and with your heart on your sleeve. You must come contrite and broken and truly meaning in your heart, mind, and spirit that you realize that it's going to take something much bigger than yourself to ever give you the peace of mind you seek.

And in this humble, broken, and willing state of mind, confessing that you're a sinner who needs a savior, you ask Jesus to forgive you and take over and help you to make the changes that you need to make in your life.

There is a standard prayer; it's called the sinner's prayer. But I believe that if you cover all the bases and are honestly sincere from your heart, you can do it in your own words, your own vocabulary.

Believing in our hearts, we make our profession of faith. Then Jesus said, "Take up your cross and follow Me."

We follow Jesus, trying to be representatives of His love, trying to emulate His compassion, His forgiveness, and to walk in His way. When we sin, and we will, we acknowledge it, confess it, accept God's forgiveness, put our feet right back on the path and move on, following His teaching and our conscience.

God knew what was going to happen to His Son. He knew that even after giving mankind the most priceless gift possible, the world would turn into an unbelieving and unrepentant cesspool that flaunts its iniquities and ridicules the name of its one way to escape hell.

For there is no other way.

All mankind will spend eternity in one of two places: heaven or hell. One of indescribable joy or one of indescribable pain and horror, and God left the decision up to every individual.

Jesus said He is the way, the truth, and the life. No man comes to the Father except through Him. He did not say a way, a truth, or a life. He said the way, the truth, and the life.

Lots of people will tell you that there are many ways to the mountaintop. But only God is on the mountaintop. His Word says there's only one way up—the Lord Jesus Christ.

One of my greatest joys is that I have seen several of the people in our organization become believers, make their profession of faith in Jesus, and change their lives.

We had lived in the Nashville area for more than thirty years and had gone to a lot of churches. They were good churches with good pastors who preached the gospel and wonderful people making up the congregations. But we had never found a church that we really felt at home in. In other words, we never felt like a part of the church family.

Very possibly the reason for this was that my work schedule meant we couldn't attend on a regular basis. Our attendance was intermittent at best, and we may have gone weeks in between services.

On Easter 2003 I received a request from a church in Murfreesboro, Tennessee, called World Outreach, to do a couple of songs at their annual Easter service. They held it at Murphy Center on the campus of Middle Tennessee State University, the same venue where we did Volunteer Jam 2.

It was a tradition for World Outreach Church to hold its Easter service in the big arena every year to increase the seating capacity in hopes of attracting the unchurched and unsaved who are more apt to attend a church service on Easter.

The praise and worship team and the musicians that make up the band that plays behind them are top notch. The musical worship segment of any service is special and moving. On Easter they bring in extra musicians, turn out the full choir, and perform special songs and arrangements to honor the resurrection of our Lord and Savior Jesus Christ.

In addition, the church brings in a special musical guest, usually a Nashville-based recording artist. This particular year they invited me.

I accepted their invitation. I went and did a couple of gospel songs and stayed for the rest of the service.

Pastor Alan Jackson preached an inspired sermon. The music was great and the people were so friendly that Hazel and me decided to attend a regular Sunday service at World Outreach when we got the chance. After attending a couple of services, it was apparent that we had found the church home we had looked for so long.

Pastor Jackson has a way of preaching that makes it seem that he is preaching to himself at the same time he preaches to the congregation. By admitting his own faults and shortcomings instead of condemning everyone else's, it is an uplifting message about the love of God and the salvation of Jesus Christ.

World Outreach is nondenominational and not bound by the doctrine nor traditions of any organized denomination. With two goals, to reach the lost and pastor the found, they are a Bible-believing, Communion-taking, water-baptizing, and evangelical congregation of hard-working Tennessee people who desire to share the love of the Lord.

We met good Christian folks who were happy to take us into their church family. We've been going to World Outreach ever since and, much to my blessing, I am asked to participate in the praise and worship service from time to time.

CHAPTER 41

Many, Many Years Ago God Came to Abraham, He Said I've Chosen You to Carry Out My Plan

Our church is a rock-solid supporter of the state of Israel and its right to exist, defend itself, and be a sovereign nation that stands in the middle of the total chaos and hostility that surrounds it.

Pastor Jackson's mother and father, George and Betty, live a part of every year in Jerusalem. They have Christian books translated into Hebrew so they can be read by the Jewish people. The church sponsors several trips a year, taking large and small groups who want to experience the Holy Land.

We had always wanted to go to Israel and in 2008, accompanied by our son, Charlie, Dean Tubb, and our grandson, Evan, we signed on for one of the trips.

I had heard it said that going to Israel will change your life. As one who has made the trip three times and intends to go back again, I will attest to the fact.

To see where the Old Testament and the New Testament blend six thousand years of history together in the space of a few square miles.

Where the tenents of the old covenant of animal sacrifice were given to the Israelites.

Where the long-awaited Messiah Jesus Christ was born, crucified, and resurrected, instituting the new covenant.

Where the magnificent temple of Solomon stood.

Where the empty garden tomb is carved out of a hillside of stone a short distance from Golgotha, the place of the skull, where the Bible says Jesus was crucified.

The Wailing Wall. The Garden of Gethsemane. Mount Carmel, where Elijah called down fire from heaven to consume the sacrifice. The caves of Qumran, where the Dead Sea Scrolls were discovered. Engedi, where David hid from King Saul.

The mountain fortress of Masada, where more than nine hundred Israelites died at their own hand rather than yield to the Roman army.

The Sea of Galilee, where Jesus walked on the water.

The gigantic killing plain below Megiddo, where the final war, commonly called the battle of Armageddon, will be waged.

No place on earth more poignantly documents man's inhumanity to man than Yad Vashem. It is the Jewish Holocaust museum, where the murder of six million Jews at the hands of Hitler's Nazis is commemorated in stark and graphic fashion. There are heartbreaking pictures and even boxcars that were used to transport Europe's Jews to their final destination at Buchenwald, Auschwitz, or whatever death camp the Nazi monsters designated.

The slogan at Yad Vashem, and for the whole nation of Israel, is "Never Again." They mean it. No amount of political pressure will ever again remove them from their Holy Land.

When you hear about forcing the Jews to go back to the 1967 borders, the gravity of the situation could not possibly dawn on you unless you have been there and seen the borders being referred to. They would include a goodly portion of the old city of Jerusalem, where there are many important Jewish and Christian holy sites. Plus, it would dissect extremely valuable newly developed commercial property.

They didn't suffer through so many wars and conflicts and live every day of their lives in the shadow of Islamic terror to give back ground with so much Jewish blood on it.

Never again.

Every Jewish teenager, boy or girl, when reaching the age of eighteen serves at least two years in the Israeli military. Even when they're off duty, they take their guns with them wherever they go. They are ready to fight for the homeland at the drop of a hat, whenever and wherever it happens.

One of our trips was during the Feast of Tabernacles. I was asked to play a song with the band they had assembled for an event sponsored by the International Christian Embassy Jerusalem, a week-long event held every year at this time.

I rehearsed "I'll Fly Away" with the band in the afternoon and told them that right before we did it that evening, I would be doing a short piece with the fiddle. That night, right after being introduced, I stepped to the front of the stage and did a solo fiddle version of "Ha Tikva," the Israel national anthem.

It was quite a surprise to the crowd for a hillbilly fiddle player from Tennessee to play their national anthem. It made me glad I had taken the time to learn it.

I have developed a deep and abiding love for the Jewish people and the land of Israel.

My whole family has been baptized in the Jordan River, had Communion at the garden tomb and the Mount of Beatitudes, and walked on the Via Dolorosa where Christ carried His cross to Calvary.

Israel is a mixture of the ancient and the ultramodern, with state-of-the-art shopping malls next to the wall of the Old City of Jerusalem, modern hotels on the shores of the Dead Sea, and superhighways winding through desolate areas where Bedouins still wander the wastelands mounted on camels and living in tents.

The Bible speaks of a day when "The desert and the parched land will be glad; the wilderness will rejoice and blossom" (Isaiah 35:1). That succinctly describes modern-day Israel. Due to wastewater recycled in Tel Aviv and pumped out to the dry areas, the arid lands of the Negev indeed do bloom and blossom. Rank desert becomes productive due to Israeli ingenuity and innovation.

It's a wondrous land, ever fascinating. It is so full of history, with millennia of suffering, victories, and defeats. Home of God's greatest miracles, it is the place where the last few pages of human history will be written and carried out and where Jesus' foot will first touch the ground at His second coming.

I used to wonder why the Jews were called God's chosen people. Now I know. The Bible says that salvation comes to the world through the Jews. The roots of the entire Judeo-Christian faith originated in the land of Israel.

God chose the Jews to bring His salvation to mankind.

The Bible tells us to pray for the peace of Jerusalem.

I do it.

CHAPTER 42

FALLING DOWN AND GETTING
UP AND DIGGING OUT

I n the mid-1980s the music business was changing again.

Our once-dependable album-oriented radio format had achieved a lot of success. The advent of FM receivers in cars and portable radios had vaulted the better-sounding, formerly-shunned FM radio stations to the forefront of broadcasting. This attracted the attention of major companies and mass programmers who snapped them up, fired personnel, and changed formats, which seriously shortened playlists.

Stations that once played everything from James Taylor to Weather Report had their parameters shriveled and their record libraries gutted. The jocks and programmers fortunate enough to survive the takeovers found themselves under the thumb of a tight-fisted consultant in some distant city; someone else controlled their playlists and discouraged the individuality that had once been the keynote of the freewheeling album-oriented stations.

Things had also changed at our record company. MCA had offered Ron Alexenburg a deal any sane person could not refuse. He was given his own label, offices in New York, and the freedom to sign and hire anybody he wanted to. Plus, he was guaranteed an amount of money that would go a long way toward securing his family's future.

Don Dempsey took Ron's place at the helm, and we had success under his watch. But when Don retired, things started falling apart for us at Epic Records in New York.

This was also in the midst of the independent promotion fiasco. A handful of independent promotion men had gained so much power at most of the meaningful radio stations that a company could not get a record played on those stations without going through them.

The ante for this dirty little game started at around thirty thousand dollars and went up from there, which meant that if you wanted to get a record played on the most powerful radio stations, you had to pony up the asking price.

It was never conclusively proven that cash changed hands between the indies and the radio programmers, but there were major-league rumors. There are a lot of guys out there who have to live with the burden of being part of an evil partnership that wreaked havoc on record companies and artists alike.

The record companies could not afford to pay the ransom money to the independents and continue to pay their own promotion staffs. A lot of good people lost their jobs. These were guys who had been with their record companies for years; capable, dedicated employees who fell victim to this disgraceful arrangement.

We were no longer a priority. CDB had lost our main source of airplay, as we didn't fit the mold now imposed on programming and stations. Where we had been a mainstay, now they were forbidden to play our music by the bean counters and number crunchers.

And due to major personnel changes in the upper echelon, we had lost our juice at Epic Records in New York.

This basically meant that the only source of meaningful airplay was country radio, and it seemed that the sensible thing to do would be to move our account to the Epic branch in Nashville.

It was not as if we didn't have credentials in the country format. "The Devil Went Down to Georgia" had made number one. "Boogie Woogie Fiddle Country Blues" made top ten, and several of our other songs, going all the way back to "Uneasy Rider," had done well on the country charts.

Thankfully, the independent promotion scam had not reached country radio, and I had a couple of old friends on the promotion staff. Jack Lameier and Rich Schwann, who I had worked with in Los Angeles and St. Louis, had been transferred to Nashville, which meant a lot because we'd be working with a whole new roster of promotion people around the country.

Another serious situation was unfolding around this time.

When I had signed a management agreement with Joe Sullivan back in 1973, Joe was a successful concert promoter. Sound 70 Productions promoted practically all the meaningful concerts in the Middle Tennessee area and had a constant cash flow.

In addition, we had started Hatband Music, a publishing company to handle my catalog and any other writers we happened to pick up along the way, since our Epic deal contained a small production budget for any artist we wanted to record, Sir Charles Productions.

It seemed like a good idea at the time to form a partnership between Joe and me involving both of us in all of the companies. Money was flowing in from Sound 70 and Hatband Music, and CDB's tour dates were hugely successful. So Joe and I decided to basically split most of the companies down the middle and each become co-owners in them all.

Things went well for a while. Then Sound 70, the concert division, started to slide as other promoters started bringing shows into the area. The saturated market became soft and unpredictable, with a lot of the real money-making shows being promoted by bigger promoters who had more juice with the booking agencies. That left Sound 70 with the smaller, less profitable acts.

Sound 70 turned from a cash cow to a cash pig, gobbling up money with every losing venture it attempted. In a short while, all of the companies I owned half of, which had seemed to have such a promising future, had become a drain and a financial burden. The only entity that was bringing in money was the band.

CDB was becoming the only revenue producer we had left. We were constantly accepting any kind of booking that came along just to stay afloat, and because of our ready availability, the price we could charge for concerts went steadily down. We had a conglomerate of companies and a plethora of employees who worked in our lavish corporate headquarters on the fifth floor of a Nashville office building with its own drive-up private parking lot. With less money coming in, we went a little further in the hole every day.

There were people working at the office who I didn't even know what their jobs were, more than many companies twice our size employed. The payroll was a back breaker, not to mention the exorbitant rent we paid on the suite of offices.

Well, the one thing we had was good credit, and we kept borrowing to sustain the status quo. We let a few employees go, moved into a smaller suite of offices, and cut a few corners. But still the bills piled up, and the bottom line was that every month that went by would see us further in debt.

It was depressing. The band was working all the time, playing every smoky, smelly joint that offered us a payday. Still, because of our excessive availability, our per-show price was dropping, and we were losing ground every month.

We finally had to face the truth. We were slowly drowning in debt and sinking so deep that the time would soon come when we would not be able to swim back to the surface.

When our debts were tallied up, we found we owed about two million dollars.

It was time for a day of reckoning, a time to face the reality that things could not go on this way. As a team, Joe Sullivan and I had gone about as far as we could go. It was time to part ways.

We had a meeting between Joe, me, and our lawyer. The upshot was that all of the companies would be dissolved with the exception of CDB, which would revert to me. Hatband Music would be sold to pay some of our debts.

I would assume all of the debt, the whole two million dollars. I didn't have to, but I wanted out. I wanted to make a fresh start in a hurry, so I agreed.

The mountain of debt I had signed my name to was a tangled web of intercompany borrowing and a spider web of bookkeeping nightmares. I knew it would take a heavy-duty accounting outfit to figure it out.

We hired Kraft Brothers Accounting from Nashville, and Lee Kraft and company set about the tedious task of untying this fiscal Gordian knot that was so tightly wound around my neck.

We owed everybody from bus repair shops to American Express, from thirty-dollar union dues bills to hundreds of thousands of dollars at banks.

David Corlew had started out as a roadie with the CDB in 1973. He had guts, savvy, and a hard-earned knowledge of how the music business worked. He was a quick study and a tough, tenacious bargainer. He was just what I needed to manage the next stage of the kind of career I had plans to pursue.

J. B. Copeland traveled with me as road accountant. He was honest, meticulous, capable, and loyal. He had experience and a history with the band, and he was the perfect one to devise a method and a means to eliminate this monstrosity of debt.

Paula Szeigis worked for Sound 70, but when the split came she wanted to go with me. I was extremely pleased and fortunate that she did. She is one of the most talented and well-liked publicists in the business. People love to work with her.

In the days to come, Paula would become our full-time, in-house publicist. But in the meantime she would be our girl Friday, handling whatever task came up that needed doing.

And that was the staff. David Corlew was manager. J. B. Copeland was office manager and head of all finances. Paula Szeigis was handling publicity and whatever else came down the pike.

We set up two desks and a telephone line in my pool house, and the CDB was back in business.

But there was only one piece missing. Bebe Evans had gotten so frustrated and disillusioned with the working conditions at the old office that she had quit and gone to work for BMI.

She had told me when she left that if we ever decided to split, she would like to come back. And a couple of weeks after the pool house/office was set up, David said, "Let's go get our girl back."

I set up a meeting with Bebe at the Opryland Hotel and talked it over. It was a short conversation. Though I couldn't match the salary BMI was paying her, Bebe was anxious to get back in the game, and she has been running our touring department ever since.

Nobody brings more energy to a project than Bebe Evans. She is competent and efficient and covers every detail of whatever she's working on.

We needed more office space. The double-wide mobile home at the entrance to Twin Pines was empty. We picked up and moved, tripling our office space and giving everybody a little elbow room.

Now we were complete, ready to go out and conquer the world. Although we knew we had a formidable task in front of us, we knew, with the help of almighty God, that we were up to it.

CHAPTER 43

Homesick Heroes

Larry Hamby was head of A&R for Epic Records in Nashville and played a big part in helping me feel my way around. Although I had lived in the Nashville area for more than twenty years, our recording account had always been either in Los Angeles or New York and I wasn't familiar with the infrastructure in Music City.

The faces had changed since the days when I was a part of the Nashville scene. New producers, new studios, and a whole new slate of executives were at the record labels.

I had material for an album, and Larry set up appointments with some of the top producers in town. They were all successful and capable, but I'm attracted to energy, and the most energetic of all the producers I talked to was a guy named James Stroud.

James really wanted the project, and that went a long way with me. Plus he was a musician and knew what it was like to work with a band.

I settled on James Stroud to produce CDB's next album. We booked a studio and started the final phase of rehearsals in preparation for cutting our first record for Epic Nashville.

In 1985 we had a change in the band when Freddie Edwards decided to move back to California to be near his only child, Justin.

We had dropped the two-drummer mode when Jim Marshall left the band. We hired a snappy young player from Niagara Falls named Jack Gavin to take Freddy's place.

We were rehearsed, refreshed, and pumped up to begin this new project. It would be titled *Homesick Heroes* and, thanks to a single called

"Boogie Woogie Fiddle Country Blues," become our first successful album for the Epic Nashville folks.

Things were looking up. We had established ourselves as a viable artist on the Epic Nashville roster and raised our profile at country radio.

But the debt we were under and the steps we would have to take to eliminate it were much more complicated and would take a lot more effort and sensible actions.

Thanks to a long-standing relationship with two bankers, Phil Smartt and Billie Sue Agee, we were able to consolidate our bank debt and make one payment a month.

I called the people we owed and assured them that I was not going anywhere and that every cent we owed them would be paid. Not a single one of them said they were worried about not getting paid. I was determined that, with God's help, we would, as my friend Larry the Cable Guy says, "get 'er done."

The next thing we decided was that the band would not play any more dates for the ridiculously low price we had been working for. We set the bar higher and informed our booking agency that we were not available for bargain-basement prices any more.

Then we went to work.

J. B. Copeland is a big fan of Dave Ramsey, the radio financial guru who has helped get so many people out of debt. Dave believes in taking the smallest debt you owe and putting all the extra money you can come up with toward the balance until you retire it. Then repeat the process with the next smallest bill.

And that's what J. B. did from the day he took over the financial reins until we burned the paid-off bank notes in my front yard at the annual Christmas party.

Thank you, Lord!

Tommy Crain came to me one afternoon in 1989 and said, "Charlie, I just want to go home."

Tommy had given me fourteen years of musical excellence and been prominent in developing our sound and style.

He loved the band. But when a musician becomes burned out on the road, there is nothing for it except to leave it.

With some trepidation, I set about looking for a replacement. Our drummer, Jack Gavin, suggested that I listen to a young man he knew named Bruce Brown. I auditioned several guitar players at the time I auditioned Bruce. But I knew after I heard him play that he was the one, the one who could come into the band and fill a very large pair of shoes.

CDB has to have versatile musicians. We play so many different styles of music, which can stretch from bluegrass to jazz in the course of a few minutes, and Bruce Brown had all the moves and fit right in.

The year 1989 was rolling along. It was time for another album, and as so often happens, you'll set off in one direction, change horses in the middle of the stream, and the whole thing turns into something better than you had envisioned it.

CHAPTER 44

NEXT OF KIN AND SIMPLE MEN

I had been asked to write a couple of songs for a Patrick Swayze movie called *Next of Kin*, a story about a mountain boy who joined a big-city police force and what happened when his mountain kin came into the city to settle a score.

I wrote two songs. One was a slow, high mountain fiddle tune called "My Sweet Baby's Gone," and the other was an attempt at the title song, "Next of Kin."

They accepted the fiddle tune but turned down "Next of Kin." In doing so, they did me a huge favor that would propel our next album to gold status.

We went back into the studio with James Stroud and went to work. Working with James was always a fun experience. He had a great sense of humor and was good-natured about the practical jokes we were always playing on him.

With the help of The Oak Ridge Boys, we did a remake of the Jimmy Dean classic "Big Bad John." I went to the studio one morning before James arrived and dubbed in a vocal replacing the lyrics. It was a version called "Big Fat James," which included a verse that went like this:

> *He didn't say much. He was short and rude.*
> *And everybody knew you had to hide your food.*
> *From Big James*
> *Big Fat James.*

When James came in, we played it for him and he almost had a laughing fit. He loved it and played it for just about anybody who would listen.

We made some great music together, and some of my fondest memories in the recording studio include my friend James Stroud.

The song the movie had turned down became the title song for the album. I just changed the title from "Next of Kin" to "Simple Man," changed a few lyrics, and recorded it. When it was released it started climbing the charts, but not without the usual gaggle of critics who always come forth when you mention anything that they don't consider politically correct. "Take them rascals out in the swamp, put 'em on their knees and tie 'em to a stump and let the rattlers and the bugs and the alligators do the rest" sure didn't qualify.

Some radio stations wouldn't play "Simple Man" and called me all kinds of names, which didn't bother me at all because that was exactly how I felt. I was sick and tired of seeing someone who had stood over a defenseless person and pumped a couple of rounds into his head be pitied because he had been raised in a bad environment.

How about the person he shot? I was a lot more concerned with seeing him get justice. Besides, the CDB fans knew exactly what I was talking about and agreed with me.

I had a line for the naysayers that I'm sure really scalded them even more. "When the wind and the rain have washed the last vestiges of your name off your tombstone, somebody, somewhere will still be doing a CDB song."

Regardless of the backlash at some radio stations, "Simple Man" got a lot of airplay and pushed the album to sales of more than five hundred thousand copies.

I had always dabbled in writing. But I'd never gotten serious about it until several years before, when Ron Huntsman had said kind of offhandedly one day, "You write story songs. Why don't you write stories?"

Well, the more I thought about it, the more I liked it. I went into a motel room one day, sat down, and wrote a story about our "Uneasy Rider" song. That seemed to open the spout, and I went on to write a few more short stories following the story line of one of our songs. Then I started branching out, writing fictional short stories about characters and situations I dreamed up. Most were humorous and some had a small degree of autobiographical content.

I loved writing and lived the stories as I made them up. It was great being able to take the plot anywhere I wanted to, with just as much outlandishness as I wanted. I even wrote one story about Santa Claus being real. And one about a super talkative redneck fisherman who out-fished the local hotshot and his fancy boat and tackle while sitting on the bank with a cane pole and crickets.

When I had written fifteen pieces, it was decided to present it to a publisher. Peachtree Publishers in Atlanta released a book of short stories called *The Devil Went Down to Georgia and Other Stories* by Charlie Daniels.

And just like that the weak-eyed fiddle player, who had barely gotten through high school, was a published author. Go figure.

I have always been up for trying new things and discovering talent I didn't know I had. I would never have played fiddle if I hadn't been adventurous about accepting new challenges and breaking new ground

When The Nashville Network came on the air in 1983, it was an exciting time for Music City. For the very first time, country music would have its very own network. It would be programmed by Nashville people with local personalities and originate in Nashville.

For the first time TNN would be blasting out country-related programming twenty-four hours a day across the nation and eventually in other parts of the world. The possibilities were enormous, and the efforts to fill the airwaves around the clock began in earnest.

There would be trial and error, as some of the early programming was pretty shaky. But what turned out to be the flagship program was a prime-time variety show hosted by long-time local broadcast personality Ralph Emery called *Nashville Now*.

Nashville Now had a great house band made up of some of Nashville's excellent studio pickers. The guests ranged from Randy Travis to Henny Youngman, from the newest country music sensation to the long-time established stars from the *Grand Ole Opry*.

My first real experience of hosting a television show was when I was asked to host *Nashville Now* occasionally when Ralph Emery took a night off.

I found it was something I could handle—introducing the guests and interviewing them and reading commercials off the teleprompter, which could be challenging, but I grew to enjoy my time before the cameras.

There was a show on TNN called *Talent Roundup* that had been hosted by several different music industry personalities over the years. In 1994 Allen Reid, the producer, was looking for a new host and approached me about taking the spot.

The time was no problem schedule-wise. The show would tape on weekdays, with three shows per day for four days and the last one in the series on a day by itself. In total it was five days per season, so I decided to give it a shot.

It was called *Charlie Daniels Talent Round Up* and worked this way.

After going through a series of auditions, the singers, duos, and bands who won got to come to Nashville for a shot at being judged by professionals and heard by industry people who could further their career.

So with a co-hostess, a lovely lady named Lisa Foster, *Charlie Daniels Talent Round Up* was launched and ran for three consecutive seasons on The Nashville Network.

It was an enjoyable and educational experience. It broadened my horizons and bolstered my confidence, and I discovered another talent I had never explored.

We worked with James Stroud on our *Homesick Heroes* and *Simple Man* albums. It was some of the most fun I'd ever had in the studio.

Both albums were successful. I credit James with having a lot to do with it by bringing in a talented engineer named Lynn Peterzell, creating a fun atmosphere in the studio, providing his musical suggestions, and doing the outstanding postproduction work he's so good at.

But the next album we did, *Renegade*, didn't do as well. It seemed like the enthusiasm at our record label was starting to sag a little. We had had a great run at Epic. We'd been very successful and sold a lot of records, but the prospect of overstaying our welcome seemed to be at hand.

I've had several occasions over the years when a business relationship just seems to run out of steam. I have found it best to cut bait and move on. So, after fourteen years with Epic Records, we decided to change labels.

Jimmy Bowen was a renegade, insofar as mainstream Nashville was concerned. He did things in an unorthodox fashion and didn't particularly care what anybody thought about it.

He came to Nashville from a varied background. He had been a recording artist in his early years and had worked his way into the corporate end of the record business. He became an extremely successful producer working with the likes of Frank Sinatra, Dean Martin, and Sammy Davis Jr.

He came to Nashville to run Warner Brothers. Then he went to MCA, where he had worked with Hank Williams Jr., Reba McEntire, and George Strait. But he had recently taken over Capitol Records, where he lit a fire under the label about a young guy they had signed from Oklahoma by the name of Garth Brooks.

I liked his style. You couldn't argue with his track record, and he wanted to sign CDB. So, after a lot of thought, we left Epic records and signed with Capitol. Actually, it was the Liberty label, the imprint Jimmy Bowen started there.

The first album we did was titled *America, I Believe in You*. Jimmy Bowen produced it, and the title song was a single. We had full advantage of the Nashville Capitol office, releasing a video and working well with the promotion department run by Bill Catino.

There was another advantage to signing with Capitol that we weren't even aware of.

I had always wanted to do a gospel album, but major labels like Epic didn't have a gospel department, so we hadn't been able to.

CHAPTER 45

THE DOOR

Promoting and marketing gospel music is a much different undertaking than the methods used for mainstream music. It is a different genre of radio and TV entities, different print media, and different retail outlets. You are basically dealing with a different set of values and principles in content and relationships.

So the major labels left the Christian music to small independent labels, who had developed the experience and expertise to get the job done.

One of the most successful of the Christian labels was a Nashville-based company named Sparrow, which was owned by EMI, the same corporate conglomerate that owned our new label. When we signed with Liberty, the folks at Sparrow asked if we'd be interested in doing a Christian album to be released on their label.

Billy Ray Hearn had started Sparrow and worked hard and taken a lot of chances to make the company one of the top gospel labels in the business. Billy Ray was one of the good guys and respected industry-wide. Along with his son Bill, he had built a company that reflected his character.

Of course, it was a long-awaited desire of my heart. We accepted, and I went into a period of intense writing. I don't ever remember working harder on any project I had undertaken.

I had waited a long time for this opportunity and was determined that it would be special. So I wrote, polished lyrics, and worked out rhyming schemes and arrangements until I had an album's worth of music I would be pleased to call our first Christian project.

Now I needed a producer who had experience in gospel music. It had to be someone who had not only the musical savvy and technical know-how but also someone who understood the parameters on that side of the business.

Peter York and some of the executives from Sparrow came out to our studio to listen to the music we were going to record for the album. They brought along a guy from their A&R department named Ron Griffin.

After spending a few minutes in conversation with him and getting a cursory knowledge of his experience and background, I thought, *This is the guy I'd like to produce our first Christian project.*

He had been around the gospel end of the business for a number of years in different capacities, and he liked our material. I got the impression that the deskbound job he was involved in didn't hold the same fascination for him as being a part of the creative process.

He had a full-time job at Sparrow Records, and it would require taking time away to be involved in the long hours that went into the CDB recording process. But I told him I'd like for him to work with us on the project.

Long story shortened, Ron worked it out with Sparrow and immediately got involved in the preproduction process. He was going over material with me, engaging an engineer, and renting some much-needed outboard recording gear, as our studio was pretty primitive at the time.

We began work on our very first Christian album, and when I say "work," I mean just that.

Ron was a perfectionist and paid attention to every note of music we recorded as we cut the tracks. One off-time drumbeat, one slightly bent bass note, or anything that didn't fit perfectly was identified and replaced.

When we started overdubbing guitars and keyboards, we took hours with each instrument, coming up with licks and sounds, rejecting them, looking for the pitch-perfect and intricate cluster of notes that would enhance what the rhythm section had done.

The vocals and background vocals were the most tedious and exacting I had ever done. But I knew the result was well worth the effort when I heard the finished mixes of the album we would call *The Door.*

We had a couple of number ones on the country gospel charts and won our first Dove Award that year.

I literally had people ask me, "What are your fans going to think about you doing gospel music?"

It was a sort of silly question since we'd been doing gospel music as part of our live show for years, and our fans loved *The Door*.

We were getting ready to do another album for Capitol-Liberty when Jimmy Bowen got sick, sick enough that he had to leave his post as label head. His position was taken over by Scott Hendricks, and I knew our days at Capitol were numbered.

Scott had had success as a record producer, having hits with major artists like Faith Hill and Deana Carter, but he was from another time and another musical world. He neither knew, nor I think cared, about an aging Southern band that paid scant attention to the musical styles and fads that came and went so quickly in the contemporary country-music business.

We were an anomaly, a self-contained band who wrote our own music and did our own arrangements. We were a hard-rocking jam band that didn't fit into any cookie cutter anybody left at Capitol Records could come up with.

One thing led to another, and the pressure mounted for me to make a record with a successful Nashville producer and Nashville session players. What it basically came to was to do it their way or hit the road.

Don't get me wrong. I had the greatest respect for Nashville producers, and as far as I was concerned, the Nashville session players are the best in the world. But there's a sameness about records made that way. They just don't have that unique individuality of music made by a band of guys who make their living playing to people instead of microphones. There's not that spontaneous, spur-of-the-moment, "Hey, listen to this" excitement of a player who comes up with a hot lick that can turn the whole arrangement around.

But, for better or worse, I yielded to the pressure and agreed to their terms. I was paying off a two-million-dollar debt and needed all the help I could get from having a song on the radio.

The one bright spot for me, and the only person at the label who seemed to really care, was a talented and personable young lady in the A&R department named Renee Bell. She seemed sympathetic to my situation and tried to soften the landing by helping me through the confusing situation.

She spent time with me talking about songs and writers and helped me with the process of picking the right producer. I'll never forget what her attention and kindness meant to me.

We talked to several producers, and I settled on Barry Beckett, who cut his teeth in Muscle Shoals, playing keyboard on some of the most classic R&B records ever made.

My friend Herky Williams suggested some writers he felt I'd be comfortable with. I worked with several top writers like Chuck Jones and Craig Wiseman and had an album's worth of top-notch material. Barry Beckett had hired the best pickers in town, and we went to work on an album we would call *Same Ol' Me*.

The album sounded great. It sounded Nashville. It sounded current, but it didn't sound like the CDB. I vowed to myself that come what may, I'd never again go into a studio under duress by a record company and be forced to do a project without my band around me.

End of story.

CHAPTER 46

SAYING GOODBYE TO MOMMA

After my dad passed away in 1973, my mother sold her house on Wrightsville Avenue in Wilmington and bought a small place next to her parents in Brunswick County, near the town of Leland.

She retired from her job, and after both of my grandparents passed away in 1989, she moved to Tennessee to a small place on Twin Pines. Being close to Hazel, Little Charlie, and me, making new friends and a new life, she was the happiest I had seen her in years.

She would occasionally go on the road with us. She got to go to a lot of places she'd never been, lived a full and eventful life, and enjoyed every minute of it.

Her place was at the entrance leading up to our house, and the driveway went right past her door. So anybody coming up to our house had to pass her place.

There are two gates at Twin Pines. One is at the entrance, which is open in the day and closed at night. An inner gate is across the drive to our house, and that stays closed all the time.

One day some guy drove into the driveway to the inner gate that was closed, and he walked up to my mother's house and knocked on the door.

When she went to the door, the guy said, "I need to see Charlie. I'm his brother."

Whereupon my mother said, "Well, I'm his mother, and I don't remember him having a brother."

Poor guy!

In 1992 we found out that my mother had pancreatic cancer and knew it would be just a matter of time. I remember the night I dealt with the fact that my mother was going to die. I was on the road by myself in the bedroom of the bus when I admitted to myself that we had done all we could do. Medical science had run out of options, and it was in the hands of God.

I remember falling to my knees and crying bitter tears, accepting and reasoning with it, and finding a measure of peace.

The last few years of my mother's life had been a constant joy, being close to her family, going places, and doing things she had never experienced before.

Roger Campbell had a mobile home next door to her at that time, and they became big buddies. He was always checking on her and spending time with her. She loved Roger, and she loved all my employees and was at her best at a CDB show.

As the end drew closer, we got a hospital bed and somebody to stay with her twenty-four hours a day. Eventually, we brought in hospice.

I wanted to be with her when the end came and almost made it. I sat with her until late at night, and after I kept nodding out in my chair, I went up to the house to sleep a few hours.

I had barely got to bed and drifted off when the lady who was staying with her called and told me she had just passed. Hazel and I went back down to her place, where I closed her eyes and kissed her on the cheek.

No other experience in life compares to losing a parent, and I had lost both of mine. One was suddenly, and one was after a protracted illness. I don't know which hurts the worst.

We laid my mother to rest on a beautiful sunny day in our family burial plot in Mount Juliet.

Ron Griffin, our gospel record producer who was soon to become an ordained minister, officiated, and my employees, the guys my mother had loved, were pallbearers.

I, at least, had the comfort of knowing that my mother's last years were some of the happiest of her life.

Life is so precious, so fleeting. It seems that when we lose someone close to us, there are always regrets about how we would do things differently if we had it to do over again. We would have spent more time with them or been more attentive.

We should learn lessons at times like these. Although we can't do anything about the past, we can certainly affect the present and remember to make time for those who are dear to us while we still have the chance.

CHAPTER 47

CHANGES GOING AND COMING

In 1994, in a somewhat freak accident, Bruce Brown broke his collarbone and was going to be out of work for several weeks. I needed a guitar player immediately.

I had known Chris Wormer in his capacity as a publishing company employee and knew he was rumored as being a great guitar player. He certainly was and is. When I approached him about coming with the band, he was all for it and never missed a lick filling in for Bruce.

When Bruce's collarbone healed and he came back to work, I decided to keep Chris too. I had toyed with the idea of adding another guitar player, which would increase the versatility of the band and take some of the pressure off of me when I was playing rhythm while I sang.

And besides, it would add another whole twist to the band. We had three guitar players who all played differently and looked at the music from their own unique perspective, putting a little different spin on a tune.

Chris and Bruce worked together like a well-oiled clock, playing their own tasty little guitar parts that put a lot of extra spice into a song.

In 1999 Jack Gavin left to go with another band. I began to audition drummers, but about the third one I auditioned closed the door. He was flashy. He was powerful. He played a dynamite solo and kept the beat like a metronome.

His name was Pat McDonald. He was ready for the CDB, and the CDB was ready for him. Pat was to be our drummer for seventeen years.

In early 2016 Pat came to me and told me he felt that he had to leave the band. He had gone through a divorce, and his ex-wife had moved to Florida, taking their young daughter with her. Although Pat spent as much time as he could with her, it was not nearly as much as she needed. He felt, for the good of his only child, that he needed to be there for her.

I agreed with him. Family has always come first in this outfit. We began auditioning drummers and settled on a locked-in, hard-driving drummer from Soddy Daisy, Tennessee, named Ron Gannaway. Ron is talented and learns quickly. So after a couple of rehearsals, it was business as usual.

In the forty-four-year history of The Charlie Daniels Band, I have had only a handful of musicians. I tell them before I hire them that I'm not looking for a player to come and stay six months. If they don't intend to stay for a while, they'd best just pass on by. I've had very few who have not stayed for a significant number of years.

However, for a variety of reasons, musicians come and go occasionally. Although CDB has an extremely small turnover, it's inevitable to lose a player once in a while.

In 2000 Chris Wormer had some serious personal problems he had to deal with and was going to have to leave the band. After trying out a few players to take his place, I settled on a sharp, personable young picker who was working the club scene around Nashville. His name was Mark Matejka, but he went by the nickname of Sparky. He fit into the CDB like the proverbial hand in glove.

We had it set. The day Chris would be leaving was the day Sparky would be starting. Then Bruce Brown got some devastating news.

He was diagnosed with cancer, and the treatment would require surgery and chemotherapy. Of course, everybody's main concern was to see our friend cured. I told Bruce to go and do whatever he needed to do. When he was well, his job would be waiting for him.

I asked Chris Wormer if there was any way he could stick around for a couple of months until Bruce could complete his treatments and return to the band.

Chris is a great kid with a good heart. He actually put his life on hold to help me out. Even after a couple of months turned into nine months, he never complained and gave it his all onstage every night.

Only after Bruce had completed his treatment, been declared cancer free, and was able to come back to work did Chris leave to take care of his own problems. A personal favor I'll never forget.

But that's not the end of the story.

In 2005, in his off time, Sparky Matejka had been doing some studio work with a band called Hot Apple Pie. They had submitted a demo to a record label and were offered a deal.

The upshot was that Sparky wanted to give it a try with Hot Apple Pie. They had a record being released, and he felt they had a good chance of going somewhere and wanted to leave the CDB. But he wanted to do it the right way, staying around until I could adequately replace him.

I, of course, gave my blessing. Sparky worked out suitable notice and left the band.

Unfortunately, the Hot Apple Pie shot didn't work out, but something really good did work out for my friend Sparky. A few years later, he was hired by Lynyrd Skynyrd.

I love it when good things happen to good people.

Although I have a policy about hiring the same person twice, the situation with Chris Wormer was different. He had left the band not because he had wanted to but because he had to. He had some serious personal problems he needed to work out, which he had done.

Chris was living in Los Angeles and had gotten into writing music for video games and TV shows. When I called him and told him I needed a guitar player, he never hesitated. Arrangements were made, and Chris joined us for a performance at the opening of the Super Bowl 2006. He has been here ever since.

At one time in our band, half of the players were cancer survivors. Bruce Brown in 1999. Then, in 2007, Pat McDonald had a second bout with cancer. He had been diagnosed and treated successfully when he had been fifteen years old. I had been treated successfully for prostate cancer in 2001.

CHAPTER 48

I Ain't Nothing but a Simple Man, They Call Me a Redneck, I Reckon that I Am

I had been asked for years to do the commencement speech at graduation at the University of North Carolina at Wilmington in my hometown.

I was apprehensive to say the least. I had never done any public speaking, but I had never written a book or hosted a TV show either until I just decided one day to do it. So when we received another request to do the spring commencement address for the class of 1996 and since it fit into our tour routing, I decided to give it a shot.

Well, as soon as the news was released, a few of the college students expressed disdain that the powers that be would select somebody who had never been to college and was known more for redneck songs than for the more genteel pursuits of academia. Soon the criticism showed up in the college newspaper and local media.

The pushback came mainly from two seniors named Moore and Leonard. They seemed to think it would be a disgrace to be addressed by someone they considered several cuts below the intelligence level required to speak before such an august body of young men and women who were preparing to go out and make their way in the world.

What they didn't realize is that it was my world they were getting ready to go out into. I had been making my way in it since before they were born and had some things to say about life after cutting the apron strings that could prove just as beneficial as anything they had gotten out of their books.

The chancellor, Dr. Leutze, who had invited me in the first place, called the office and asked Bebe if I would cancel in the face of the controversy.

Bebe replied, "You don't know Charlie. He'll be there."

I figured I should respond to the uproar and did so in the form of a poem I wrote that was published in the college newspaper *The Seahawk*.

ODE TO MOORE AND LEONARD
(NOT TO BE CONFUSED WITH ARCHIE AND SUGAR RAY)

Mr. Moore and Mr. Leonard, the elitist status quo
Feverishly put pen to paper to let all the people know
A non-scholar at commencement?
    Ridiculous, absurd, forsooth
That a redneck fiddle player, gray of beard and long of tooth
Would think he could say something which could benefit this class
Drawing only on experience from his multi-colored past
He'll mount the stage in full regalia when
    we've walked that hallowed aisle
He'll bore us with his drivel, murdered English, verbiage vile
From whence came this wayward misfit
    how dare the powers that be
Give us such an unsung, unsophisticated hick as he
Bring us poets and politicians, novelists, on these we dote
Not some realistic villain who could come and rock our boat
He may actually think differently from us and this we fear
He may tell us of a world we never learned about in here
So remove this sordid shadow falling dark across our land
And let us pea-brained intellectuals stick our heads back in the sand
And if you're wondering my fine young snobs
How I took your bold comments
I'd say your ignorance is outweighed
Only by your arrogance
If I may borrow from the Bard who so
    succinctly states my thoughts
Your words are full of sound and fury signifying naught

And so my fledgling bigots if you're wont to spurn my speech
You can stay away and kisseth all the hind parts I can't reach
I'll See You In May
YeeHaw!!!

On the morning of May 11, 1996, I walked into Trask Coliseum on the campus of UNCW with my speech in hand amid rumors that half the class would walk out as soon as I set foot onstage.

But what nobody but me knew was that the controversy and criticism had spurred me into writing a much better speech than I would have ever written had it not happened.

I wrote and edited and practiced until I had something that I was happy with.

Not only did it tacitly state my point of view on the criticism, but the crux of the speech was about the real world I had lived in for sixty years. The same world they were getting ready to enter, the attitude it took to be a winner, and examples of people who had overcome great obstacles to achieve their place in that world.

It had a modicum of humor and a whole lot of down-to-earth common sense.

We walked down the aisle, the first time I'd worn a cap and gown since graduating high school in 1955. The place was packed. The obligatory preambles taken care of, Dr. Leutze introduced the Wilmingtonian who would be giving the commencement speech to the class of 1996.

I was ready. I had rehearsed every nuance, every rise and softening of the voice. I was ready to tackle my first public speaking engagement.

I stepped to the mic, did the proper thank yous, and launched into my speech. Not only did half of the class not walk out, nobody walked out. I got two standing ovations and an honorary doctorate degree.

I found I thoroughly enjoyed public speaking and would engage in it periodically from that point on. You just can't let somebody else's doubt and criticism affect your deep-seated confidence in yourself. I knew down deep that I could pull this off, and the dissension had served not as a deterrent but as a motivator.

If you want to count, stand up and be counted.

CHAPTER 49

There's a New Train Coming, Get On Board or Just Keep Walking

The record business had changed exponentially by the turn of the century. The compact disc had, for all practical purposes, replaced the big vinyl 33⅓ albums. The music men who once ran the labels had been replaced by lawyers.

The Ron Alexenburgs, Jerry Wexlers, Jimmy Bowens, and label heads who knew the music, loved the music, lived and breathed the music had been replaced by lawyers. Many didn't know a good record from a pot lid. Bean counters and deal makers only had concern for the bottom line.

Not always the most practical of people, in my opinion. It was this mentality that would lead to the biggest goof up in the modern record business.

Record companies have always been behind the curve as far as technology is concerned. It has cost the industry through the years. But it was nothing like the incident that took place in 2000 when twenty-one-year-old Sean Parker and nineteen-year-old Shawn Fanning got together and created an Internet site with a capacity to download unlimited pieces of music free of charge.

They called it Napster, and shortly after launching they had tens of millions of users.

It should not have taken an Albert Einstein to realize that this genie was out of the bottle and there was no way of ever putting it back in. As illegal, dishonest, and thieving as it was, it was obviously the wave of the future. It needed to be harnessed and brought into line before it reached the point of completely obliterating the record industry.

Somebody should have gone to these kids, subpoena in hand, and said, "Do you want to spend the next five years of your lives in court and very possibly go to jail? Or do you want to take this ten million dollars, have all be forgiven, and come and create this thing in a legal way so the artists, songwriters, and record companies can get their rightful due?"

But instead, the record companies did what lawyers always do. They chose to litigate, spending untold dollars of stockholder money and making enemies of every kid under the age of eighteen in the country.

Of course, the record companies did get into downloading. They had no choice. But I personally believe the process could have been less painful, much speedier, and more efficient had a little more thought and common sense been applied to the situation.

Meanwhile, back in the real world.

For the first time in more than twenty years, I was without a recording contract. We were no longer an act that a major label would want to sign. We did not even remotely resemble what was happening on radio, which was increasingly being dominated by younger acts.

George Strait, Garth Brooks, Alan Jackson, and a few others stood tall in the onslaught of image-driven, youth-oriented radio, but for the most part the old guard was disappearing from the airwaves, with the exception of classic country and special nostalgic moments.

The country music industry had tried for decades to attract the younger demographic, to little avail. Now they had found the right button to push, and they weren't about to let it go. Who could blame them? The new country music pushed the format to much higher ratings, and the new artists were packing stadiums and big venues.

We were a band without a radio format but not without a following. As always, our concerts were our bread and butter. We continued crisscrossing the country, playing our music and entertaining hundreds of thousands of concertgoers each year.

I decided that as far as my recording career was concerned, from then on I would record whatever struck my fancy, without being concerned about it having to fit mainstream radio formats, whatever genre, whatever style.

As do most Southern boys, I always loved the blues. So, my first foray into my newfound musical freedom was a blues project I called *Blues Hat*, which did pretty well for an independently produced, independently distributed album.

My manager came up with the idea of our own independent label. We had a recording studio that I had seriously upgraded and was capable of handling any kind of project we wanted to attempt. We had a distribution network. We could hire independent promotion people if we felt the need. Most importantly, we could record anything we danged well pleased, with no interference from outside interests.

So, why not?

Enter Blue Hat Records.

We've done numerous projects under the auspices of Blue Hat Records, including gospel albums, Christmas albums, bluegrass albums, acoustic, electric, movie tunes, and songs for the Nashville Predators hockey team, the Tennessee Titans football team, and the National Finals Rodeo.

Several years ago, David Corlew gave me a plaque commemorating the sale of half a million albums, not a record but a pretty good beginning.

I will never run out of new projects. I've got them backed up in my mind, and when I feel one is complete enough, we just get the band together, call our engineer, and proceed to make some new music.

I did a duet album called *Deuces* with artists ranging from Dolly Parton to Travis Tritt.

I had long wanted to pay tribute to Bob Dylan. Not just because he has had an impact on my career but out of respect and admiration for his talent and refusal to be anybody but himself. He followed his musical star in whatever direction it led, bucking trend and fad and paying scant attention to what the rest of the industry was doing.

Always a leader. Never a follower. He was an innovator who shunned Tin Pan Alley and single-handedly changed the face of popular music. By inspiring all serious artists who came after him, he introduced a freedom of lyric and unconventional approach to chord structure and meter and a "damn the torpedoes, full speed ahead" approach in the recording studio.

I wanted to do Dylan's music but take a far different approach than had ever been attempted before. In other words, I wanted to take his songs and treat them just like we would any other piece of new music we recorded, forgetting his or anybody else's arrangements, tempos, or performances, and to make it a CDB-sounding album of Bob Dylan compositions.

We took the songs one by one and stuck with the ones we could do in a unique way. When we came across one we felt we couldn't do that to, we simply put it aside and moved on to another song. When you're dealing with the Dylan catalog, you never run out of material.

We stayed with acoustical instruments and created the first all-acoustic album we had ever done, giving it a different feel from the hard-driving electric recordings we usually did.

The result was an album we called *Off the Grid—Doing It Dylan*. I must say that I was very pleased with what we had done. We had accomplished what we had started out to do, playing Bob Dylan's music in the CDB style.

We also released a vinyl $33^{1/3}$ version of *Off the Grid*, the first one we'd released in twenty-five years.

As I approach my golden years, I find that the creative juices still flow bountifully. I've got enough album concepts and ideas to take me years down the road, and as long as God gives me the strength, I'll be writing and recording new music.

CHAPTER 50

The Cowards Came by Morning and Attacked Without a Warning, Leaving Flames and Death and Chaos in Our Streets

I was at the Tennessee driver's license bureau renewing a permit when Charlie Jr. called and told me that a plane had flown into the World Trade Center.

Thinking that it was a catastrophic commercial airline accident, I went on about my business until the second plane hit. It became immediately apparent that America was under attack. As the Pentagon was hit and the plane went down in Pennsylvania, we all wondered how far it would go.

How many more planes had been commandeered by terrorists?

Were ground attacks coming?

Did we have sleeper cells among us who were going to come out and start shooting?

As the day wore on, the government swung into action by grounding air traffic, scrambling fighter planes, moving the president to safety, and enforcing the prescribed protocol.

America wanted answers as to what was happening to us.

The news channels had plenty of pictures but were short on explanation. I remember it as being the strangest day of my life.

Then, as the information trickled in about who the hijackers were, that they were all Muslim, the name Osama bin Laden began to surface. It was a name that most of us were only familiar with because of an interview he had done on *60 Minutes* in 1997 when he had talked about shedding the blood of infidels.

In fact, bin Laden had been shedding the blood of infidels long before 9/11. He was responsible for the destruction of US Embassies in Tanzania and Kenya, and had covertly been on the United States's radar for a long time.

Our clandestine services knew that he was dangerous and capable, but nobody ever dreamed that he had the ability to sponsor a successful attack on the American homeland.

The attack was on a Tuesday, and we had concerts scheduled for the weekend.

As we drove across America, all along the route the marquees outside fast-food restaurants and small businesses had phrases like "God bless America" and "Pray for America." Cars were flying American flags on radio antennas, and Old Glory was even fluttering off the backs of eighteen wheelers.

Everybody wanted a flag to proclaim their patriotism, but there were none available. Everybody was sold out.

At least one newspaper printed a whole-page-sized flag so people could at least have one made out of paper.

I wrote and recorded a song called "This Ain't No Rag, It's a Flag," which the politically correct bunch immediately started slamming because the lyrics went, "This ain't no rag. It's a flag, and we don't wear it on our heads," claiming that I was insulting all Muslims.

I didn't care because I knew exactly who I was talking about. Muslim or not, if you didn't have anything to do with those planes crashing into the World Trade Center and the Pentagon, it wasn't about you. Period.

But of course, the usual gaggle of critics refused to see it that way.

CMT, Country Music Television, headquartered in Nashville, planned a show featuring country music artists that would honor the victims of 9/11. We were asked to be a part of it. I thought that "This Ain't No Rag, It's a Flag" would be the perfect song to do. It touted American patriotism and spoke of avenging the lives lost to terrorism.

When CMT heard the song, they said that there was no way they'd have such a song on their telecast. They were afraid of offending people.

Well, what about the families of the almost three thousand people who were murdered on 9/11?

Were they not already offended? What about the millions of Americans who were aching for retaliation?

What about the thousands who had already died at the hands of radical Islamic terrorists before 9/11 even happened?

These were the people I was concerned about. So I told them that if I couldn't do the song I wanted to, I wouldn't do the show.

The upshot was that a lot of people did get offended, but it was not Muslims. It was irate Americans taking exception to CMT's politically correct attitude and letting them know about it.

Whatever bin Laden intended to do to America, it resulted in bringing a nation together and infuriating it to the point of wanting and demanding revenge.

There was an interfaith religious service held at St. Patrick's Cathedral in New York featuring Christian, Muslim, and Sikh clerics, and President George W. Bush kept proclaiming, "Islam is a peaceful religion."

I could never figure out why President Bush did that, knowing that almost three thousand Americans had died at the hands of this "peaceful religion," unless he was saying it for the protection of the Muslims living in America, trying to lessen the revengeful emotions Americans were feeling toward the whole Muslim world right then.

It would be many years before Osama bin Laden would face American justice at the end of a Navy SEAL's gun, but I wonder if his last thoughts were that there was no place on earth where he could hide from the wrath 9/11 had brought down on his head.

America has been at war with Islamic terror for a couple of decades now. It appears that it's a multigenerational fight that will require more drastic action than any of the Western nations are willing to take.

President Bush deployed troops to Afghanistan to defeat the Taliban and hunt down bin Laden. Then intelligence came to light that Saddam Hussein was acquiring nuclear weapons, and troops were deployed there. And just like that, the United States was engaged in a war on two fronts with people and ideologies we knew very little about.

It was a world where the enemy and the friendlies looked exactly alike.

Any young man approaching you could have a suicide vest strapped to his chest. Homemade explosive devices were laid in highways and innocuous places to be detonated at an opportune time.

Mothers were willing to let their sons enroll in suicide squads for the supposedly greater glory of Islam and the seventy-two virgins that bloodthirsty clerics promised those who were willing to sacrifice their lives for the cause.

Not since World War II have US troops fought under rules of engagement that gave them any chance of a clear-cut win. Afghanistan and Iraq were no exception.

I have often wondered why we would even bother to send US troops into war and saddle them with so many restrictions and rules that they fear retribution from our own side almost as much as from the enemy.

Split-second decisions are required in combat situations, and collateral damage is inevitable. When an unavoidable incident happens, by the time it's cycled through the media, innocent soldiers, who were only doing their jobs, are made to appear like bloodthirsty predators and have to fear doing time in Leavenworth.

These wars would be very different from any the United States had ever fought. With the IEDs, the suicide bombers, and no uniforms or flags, there was no way to designate the enemy from civilians, and the enemy had total disregard for their own people, using them for human shields.

September 11 would change the very way of life in the United States in a lot of ways, as we are reminded every time we board an airplane, enter a major building, or even attend a sporting event.

The very freedoms Americans hold so dear make us vulnerable. The freedom of movement and speech and our liberal and lax immigration enforcement policies allow foreigners to overstay their visas and even disappear into society. Our porous southern border, where untold thousands pour across, undocumented, unvetted, and unaccountable: double the danger.

Because of the reluctance of our government to pursue potential terrorists into the mosques and Muslim neighborhoods, they become invisible among the population.

The choosing of political correctness above common sense, the fear of offending taking precedence over national interests, and the release of the world's most dangerous terrorists from Guantanamo Bay to return to the battlefield all put this nation in jeopardy.

Although I have my own deep personal convictions, I am not here to argue the validity of Saddam Hussein having a nuclear device or the right or wrong of the war in Iraq. But a conviction that I will emphatically state and stand by is that the United States should never go to war without having a clear description of the mission and a declared definition of what victory is.

We should vigorously pursue those goals. We should avoid but accept whatever collateral damage and whatever media heat and scathing international criticism we are subjected to.

In my opinion, if we're not going to try to win, we shouldn't go in the first place.

In the case of Iraq, we sacrificed so much blood and treasure securing the biggest part of the country. Under the guise of some political triviality, we turned around and gave it all back, this time to a worse enemy than we were fighting to begin with.

Against the advice of our leading military advisors, we pulled our troops out of Iraq. It created a vacuum that was quickly filled by ISIS, the cruelest monsters since Genghis Khan. They beheaded Christians, threw homosexuals off the roofs of tall buildings, and locked people in steel cages and set them on fire or drowned them.

They have zero tolerance for any religious beliefs but their own. They believe that if they can bring the world to global chaos, it will bring about the arrival of the Mahdi or the Islamic messiah, who will turn earth into a Muslim planet and kill all of those who refuse to convert. They even claim that Jesus Christ will return to earth and tell everybody He was wrong the first time that He came and that Islam is the only true faith.

Unfortunately, there is a general belief among a preponderance of people that the god of Islam and the God of Judaism and Christianity are one and the same. Nothing could be further from the truth.

If that were the case, the Creator of the universe would constantly be contradicting Himself legitimizing the destruction of Jews, the race He called His chosen people.

The Holy Bible of the Judeo-Christian world and the Koran of the Muslims can't possibly refer to the same god.

The conflict between the different factions of Islam has gone on for more than a millennium and shows no signs of letting up. The mainstream Muslims say that the terrorism is caused by a rogue faction that has hijacked Islam and is misinterpreting the teachings of Mohammed. There is so much inner conflict within the faith itself. Sunnis, Shiites, and Alawites are all Muslims, but all have somewhat different concepts and beliefs.

We are involved in a conflict with a people we don't understand, people who for thousands of years lived without a central government. There was an unaffiliated collection of war lords and tribal leaders who formed and disbanded alliances when expedient, claiming no allegiance to any central ruling authority.

Dar al-Islam, literally the Islam world, always has been and probably always will be an enigma to the Western mind. It's extremely difficult to imagine that part of the world being at peace, with or without our involvement.

CHAPTER 51

A Friend Who Affected My Life

Being a huge fan of Louis L'Amour back in 1976, I had named our *High Lonesome* album after one of his books and did a dedication to him in the liner notes.

When Mr. L'Amour found out about the dedication, he got in touch with me and invited me to have lunch with him when I was in Los Angeles. The next time we played there, we made arrangements to meet him at the Polo Lounge at the Beverly Hills Hotel.

David was also a huge fan, and I asked him to go with me. We were a little nervous, to say the least. Now, you have to remember that Louis L'Amour is the bestselling Western writer in the world and the Beverly Hills Hotel is probably the most prestigious address in Hollywood, frequented by movie stars and heavyweight industry people, and it is not the regular stomping ground for a couple of Tennessee country boys decked out in full Western regalia.

We were asked by the gentleman at the Polo Lounge to remove our hats and were led to Mr. L'Amour's table, where we were immediately put at ease. Soon we were talking like old friends and developed a friendship that lasted until Louis's death in 1988.

I treasure the hours I spent with him over the years. He was one of the most knowledgeable and well-rounded people I've ever been around, with expertise in a variety of subjects. But his knowledge of the Old West was unequaled. He knew the facts on every gunfighter, every frontier sheriff, every cattle baron, and every range war. These were not the movie versions but the genuine facts that sometimes made villains out of some of our long-held heroes, or vice versa.

Hazel and I were honored beyond words when Louis dedicated his *Jubal Sackett* book to us. Louis L'Amour made a firm impression on my life. Hazel and I still maintain our friendship with his wife, Kathy, and his children, Beau and Angelique. Thanks to Kathy's efforts and the love Western fans have for Louis, his books are still very much in demand.

Due to our friendship, our family was introduced to the beautiful Four Corners area of Colorado. Louis and Kathy owned a ranch in the area. When they invited us out one summer, we fell in love with the place.

The Rocky Mountains are just breathtaking in that part of the world. The people are friendly, and Durango is the most quality small town I've ever been to, with great restaurants and all-season outdoor activities.

While we were there in 1979, we went to look at some land for sale in the La Plata Canyon. We ended up buying a three-acre lot, which just sat until 1994, when we decided to build a small house on it.

Really, the "we" is a little misleading. It was actually Hazel who undertook the project while I was working. She went out to Colorado, got a builder, designed the house, and furnished it before I ever set foot in it.

When we went out on vacation right after Christmas that year, it was the first time I'd seen anything but a picture of the place. I absolutely loved it.

It's eight thousand seven hundred feet in elevation. The lack of oxygen takes a little getting used to every year when we first get there. We get snow by the foot and spot elk across the canyon. Sometimes eagles perch in the trees close to the back patio.

It's the ideal place for me to unwind after a long touring year, and I never get tired of watching the snow storms work their way down the canyon.

It seems everybody in Colorado is born knowing how to ski. Charlie Jr. took a couple of lessons and loves it when he comes out. I've never even been able to stand up on a pair of roller skates and am not about to try to fly down a mountainside on a couple of barrel staves.

Hazel and I bought some cross-country skis and snowshoes and enjoyed it somewhat, but they're both an awful lot of work so they basically just hang in the garage.

One day we decided to try snowmobiling. We rented some sleds and found out it is a lot of fun and something we would want to do on a regular basis. Renting snowmobiles, especially as often as we wanted to, is very expensive. So we figured we'd just buy a couple and a trailer to haul them around on.

I'll never forget our first attempt at snowmobiling on our own. We hooked up the trailer and drove up to the snow. Knowing absolutely nothing about unloading, I climbed up on the trailer and when I looked down, I may as well have been on top of the house. The thought of driving a snowmobile down a ramp onto the ground, and then having to drive it back up again was not a comforting thought.

Good sense won out. We decided that before we tried to unload snowmobiles, we at least needed to watch somebody else do it.

We called the dealer we had bought our rig from and asked him if he knew anybody we could pay to help us out. We needed someone to go along and teach us about loading and unloading and the basics of snowmobiling in the Rockies.

I soon got a call from a gentleman by the name of Cy Scarborough, who said he'd be willing to take a couple of novice flatlanders into the mountains and help them out with their snowmobiles.

When I offered to pay him, he refused to take a cent. But he offered to meet us on a day in the near future and begin our snowmobile education.

Well, as it turned out, Cy was a musician, too, and had operated the Bar D Chuck Wagon for forty years. The Bar D is a Four Corners institution operating seven nights a week from Memorial Day through Labor Day. They serve dinner and feature the Bar D Wranglers, one of the finest and most-entertaining Western bands in the country.

It turns out Cy plays guitar and does comedy in the show. He works hard for around 120 days in a row. When winter rolls around and they shut the Chuck Wagon down, he's ready to "go play in the snow," as he puts it. He and his wife Jeannie do a lot of snowmobiling, and both of them are excellent riders.

Well, as soon as we had spent a couple of hours together, we knew it was the beginning of a friendship. We probably spend more time with Cy and Jeannie every year in Colorado than anybody else we know there.

Cy was very patient as he showed me how to bring a snowmobile down the ramp and off the trailer. Then he taught me how to reload by goosing the sled up the loading ramp with just the right amount of throttle at just the right time and always having your hand on the brake because you're going to have to stop quickly.

He showed me how to make sure there is plenty of oil and antifreeze in the machine, to always make sure you have an extra belt, and just about everything I know about the operation and care of a snowmobile.

There's nothing like packing a lunch and heading for the mountains with Cy and Jeannie. They know the trails at every location around the area, which ones are too difficult for Hazel and me to handle, and which ones have been recently groomed. We spend a lot of days whizzing around the Rockies together.

CHAPTER 52

CLOSE CALL IN THE ROCKIES

J anuary 15, 2010, was a bright, chilly day in the Rockies. Cy and Jeannie,
Hazel and me, and some other folks were riding in good powder in one
of the most beautiful spots in the Rocky Mountains when something scary
happened.

I think I tell it best in one of my soapbox articles I wrote shortly after
the incident when my memory was fresh and vivid.

I call it "Different Strokes."

* * *

The day was magnificent. The snow was smooth and deep, and the trail
had just been groomed. We were skimming across the snow at a good clip,
doing one of my favorite things in the whole world: snowmobiling in the
beautiful Rocky Mountain backcountry with our snowmobile buddies, Cy
and Jeannie Scarborough and some other friends, hitting the high spots
and just having a wonderful time.

I noticed that my left hand was getting numb and thought that it was
because I had been hanging on to the handle bars of my sled for so long
that it had gone to sleep. Then I felt the left side of my mouth start to grow
numb, and my left foot started getting hard to control. I knew something
was happening to me. I knew I'd better get back down the mountain and
get some help.

I told Cy how I was feeling, and we immediately headed to the trail-
head for the longest fifteen-mile snowmobile ride I ever hope to take.

When we got to where we were parked, Jeannie gave me three baby aspirins and we got in Cy's vehicle and tore out for Mercy Regional Medical Center about thirty miles away in Durango.

I had so little coordination on my left side that I needed a wheelchair to make it to the emergency room, where the staff hurriedly started diagnostic procedures.

A few minutes later, the doctor on duty told me what I was pretty sure of already. I was having a stroke in the right part of my brain, the part that controls the left side of your body, probably caused by a blood clot in the brain.

They gave me a shot of a drug called tPA (tissue plasminogen activator), which breaks up blood clots. In a few minutes I was loaded aboard an ambulance plane and hurried off to Swedish Medical Center in Denver, Colorado. I was hurriedly taken into the emergency room and examined by a very capable staff of doctors, including a neurologist. I was put in the critical care ward, where I was hooked up to a battery of diagnostic machines and IVs and began the many tests I would be given over the next two days.

The early consensus of the doctors was that I had indeed had a stroke in the right part of my brain, as a CAT scan was later to confirm.

The only effect that it seemed to have left behind was a numbness in my left hand and a stiffness in my left arm.

They released me on Sunday morning and I went back to Durango, where I am writing this column.

I begin physical therapy today to relieve the stiffness and numbness in my left hand and arm.

That's kind of it in a nutshell. I'm doing fine, but there are a few details I'd like to share with you.

First of all, if you begin to feel a stiffness in your limbs or face, or if one or more of your limbs start to become difficult to control, immediately chew up a couple of aspirin and head for the nearest hospital or clinic.

Don't procrastinate or try to tell yourself it's going to go away. You only have three hours from the time you feel a stroke coming on to get a shot of tPA into your system to break up the blood clots that are causing the stoke. So don't play with your life—get help.

The other thing I want to share with you is how the fingerprints of God were all over my experience.

First of all, we were snowmobiling on the side of Durango where Mercy Regional Medical Center—the only hospital in Durango—is located. We could easily have been on the opposite side of town and much farther away.

Cy and Jeannie Scarborough—who always haul their own snowmobiles—had decided to ride my two extra sleds that day, which meant that we had a vehicle with no snowmobile trailer to unhook and could hurry to the hospital without delay.

Our other friends, Tom and Anita, loaded our snowmobiles and drove our vehicle down off the mountain.

By the time I got to the hospital and the doctors got me diagnosed, since the drug is time sensitive, I only had fifteen or twenty minutes left to take the shot of tPA to break up the blood clot in my brain.

Swedish Medical Center—the hospital they took me to in Denver—has one of the top neurological units in the country.

Of course, Hazel immediately got on the phone and started calling our pastor and our Christian friends. The prayers were making their way to heaven even as I was making my way to Denver.

I have seen the hand of God extended over me in the past when I was in a dangerous situation, and I knew He was near.

There were so many things that made me know that God was ordering our steps.

We could have easily been snowmobiling a lot farther away from the hospital.

The fact that Cy's vehicle had no snowmobile trailer to remove saved us precious minutes.

Everything worked like clockwork; there was a plane available to take me immediately to Denver.

And here's the mind-boggling part. Mercy Regional Medical Center in Durango had only been stocking tPA in their pharmacy for about three months. If they hadn't had it, there would have been no way for me to get the shot in time to prevent the stroke from doing major damage.

As I said, nothing less than the hand of God.

One other note. My wife Hazel is a very emotional person and will shed tears at the drop of a hat. On the way to the hospital I heard her tell Jeannie, "I've got to be strong for him."

And she was; she has been a rock.

On the way to the hospital, I called my son, Charlie, and after telling him what had happened, I simply said, "Your mom needs you."

He and my manager and friend David Corlew were on the next plane heading our way and met us in Denver.

Thank God for family and friends.

Well, that's about it. I'm doing fine, and I want to thank all of you who got the news and prayed for me.

Looking forward to another great touring year.

See ya on the road.

* * *

We cut our vacation short to get back to Nashville, where I immediately started seeing doctors and a physical therapist to help rehab my left hand and arm.

Although there was no paralysis, the stroke had affected the dexterity and range of motion in my hand, and I needed to do designed exercises to loosen up and strengthen my fingers. My neurologist said that playing my instruments was actually the best therapy I could do.

It was good getting back to work. Our vacation time is from a few days after Christmas until the first part of March, when the year's touring begins.

We set aside a few days of preparation to rehearse a new show, adding new music or maybe going back and adding an old song or two.

When we put a new show together, it's never a problem what to play but what not to play. When you've been around as long as we have and are blessed to have as many familiar songs as we do, when you put a show together, there comes a time when you have to make choices as to what to leave out of the set to stay within the time constraints.

We usually do about a ninety-minute set, which means we play about sixteen songs. We put the skeleton of the set together with our most popular tunes. We always do "The Devil Went Down to Georgia," "Long Haired

Country Boy," "The Legend of Wooley Swamp," and others. When you add a couple of new songs, it takes up most of the hour and a half we play.

Then you've got a couple of slots left to fill in. Do you do "Trudy" or "Stroker Ace" or "Boogie Woogie Fiddle Country Blues," or maybe a blues jam or "Simple Man"?

I may change the order of songs two or three times during the first few shows until we reach a point where the set flows like a river.

The road crew makes sure that all the equipment is in good condition. If we have repairs to make to any of our instruments or amplifiers, we try to have them done during our off time. They change strings, pack the road cases, and get ready to roll.

During our off time, we send both buses to the shop to have them gone over from stem to stern so they can be depended on to roll another hundred thousand miles or so.

When I hear musicians complaining about what a drag it is being on the road, I think to myself, *If you don't consider traveling around the world playing music to be a blessing, why don't you just go home?*

I love going on the road. I love getting up in the morning, going to the front of the bus, and pulling the curtain back to see what motel parking lot we're in. I love looking at the world through a bus window. I love miles and miles of open highway and seeing Lakeshore Drive all lit up when we pass through Chicago late at night. I love to see a full moon hanging over the highway or rolling past a big Kansas wheat field.

I love the fact that I get to walk on stage in front of a crowd of people every night and play music I've created with a bunch of guys I love and admire.

I am blessed and thankful to God for granting me the desires of my heart and to the millions of people who have attended the shows and bought the records, allowing me to live the dream.

CHAPTER 53

Ain't It Good to Be Alive
and Be in Tennessee

I t was a Sunday morning in early May 2010. We were just back home
from a road trip and had gotten off the bus and gone into the house
when the bottom fell out. It sounded like a heavy midsummer shower on
our tin roof. But this was no summer thunderstorm. This was an all-day
rain, straight down for hours and hours.

It had also rained all day Saturday. Thurman, the ranch manager, had
to move some cattle out of some low-lying fields after the fences washed
over, and he helped rescue a lady who had driven into deep water on the
road in front of the ranch.

By the time we got home Sunday morning, the rain had stopped. The
only visible signs of the high water were the washed-over fences and the
standing water in the fields.

But it was to be a brief respite, as the heavy rain began again Sunday
midmorning and continued all day and into the night.

Our house is on a hill and our barn is pretty well elevated, so we were
safe from the creeks and streams that were rising all around us. As the
day wore on and television news began reporting from around the area, it
became apparent that this would be one for the books.

Areas were cut off and isolated. Whole neighborhoods became islands
with people stranded and unable to get out of them, with no end in sight.

The Cumberland River was out of its banks and headed toward the
Opry complex. The shopping mall, the Opryland Hotel, and the Opry
House, the home of the *Grand Ole Opry*, were overrun with the flood

water. There was more than five feet in the Opry House, rising above stage level and flooding out the complete electronic center located in the basement of the Opryland Hotel.

Downtown, an entertainment service complex called Sound Stage, where sound and light companies stored their equipment when they were off the road and country music stars like Brad Paisley, Vince Gill, and Keith Urban stored their extensive collections of guitars, was totally flooded. Nobody was able to rescue anything or even know the extent of the damage until the water went down.

People's homes were destroyed, their livelihoods interrupted, and their lives changed overnight.

I am extremely thankful and proud to live in a place like Middle Tennessee. Nobody waited for any government agency or relief organization to arrive before swinging into action.

Families took perfect strangers into their homes, set up charcoal grills in their front yards, and passed out free burgers and hot dogs to any and all. A location was set up to supply free household items to those who had lost everything. Benefits were planned. Donations were made as the good-neighbor, Southern-hospitality virtue came out all over Middle Tennessee.

Oh, the flood left its marks! The Tuesday night *Opry* had to be held in the sanctuary of a nearby Baptist church a couple of times. The Opryland Hotel and the shopping center were to be out of commission for many months, and private citizens had to wait much too long for insurance claims.

But Nashville cleaned up, rebuilt, retooled, and rolled on, bigger and better.

A little side story. . . .

The Ryman Auditorium had been home to the *Grand Ole Opry* from 1943 until 1974, when it moved into its new home at Opryland. They cut a circle of wood out of the center of the Ryman stage, the place where the legends of country had stood and performed for more than thirty years, and inserted it into the center of the new stage at the new Opry House. It's an honor to stand on the circle of wood where so many country greats have stood.

Well, when the new Opry House got flooded, that circle of wood popped out of the stage and floated away. It was later to be found and reinserted in the middle of the new stage, where it remains today.

I guess it's just supposed to be there.

CHAPTER 54

This Is a Righteous Cause, So Without Doubt or Pause I Will Do What My Country Asks of Me

In 2005 the war in Iraq was in full swing and we had more than a hundred thousand troops in the theatre. They were in a strange and foreign land fighting a kind of war the United States had never been engaged in. They needed some distractions.

Judy Seale, who heads up Stars for Stripes, a service organization dedicated to getting entertainment to our service men and women no matter how desolate the posting, asked CDB to do a tour that would involve stops in Kyrgyzstan, Afghanistan, Kuwait, and Iraq. We eagerly accepted the invitation.

The first leg of the trip was a breeze. We were aboard a state department plane that was laid out like a passenger plane, with wide, comfortable seats and the amenities of a commercial flight. But from there, the travel would become much less luxurious.

We were accompanied by Tennessee Adjutant General Gus Hargett, Colonel Max Haston of the Tennessee National Guard, and Brigadier Russell (Rusty) Frutiger.

I remember there was a light snow falling when we landed in Kyrgyzstan. We went to our quarters and tried to shake off some of the jet lag. Then, rested and fed, we headed out to do our first show, which was a blast for us and the troops.

Next morning, we boarded a C-130 for Bagram Air Base in Afghanistan.

The *C* in the C-130 denotes that it is a cargo plane, configured for large loads of supplies. The passenger contingent is basically incidental, usually some fold-down webbed seats along the sides of the plane.

The C-130 is a four-engine prop plane that is the workhorse of the military. The crews are constantly in the air ferrying cargo and passengers around the battle zone. We were to get quite familiar with them over the course of the next couple of weeks.

On most of our flying trips, I had the honor of flying in the cockpit with the crew. They gave me a headset so I could talk while we were in flight, and I quickly learned the working names the crew used to communicate with one another in flight. "Nav" was "navigator," "load" was "load master," and so on.

They were the greatest bunch of kids. Friendly and courteous, they were always willing to call attention to points of interest along the way or answer my naive questions about flying around a war zone.

As we approached Bagram, it became apparent that we were not going to be able to land. There was a sand storm blowing on the ground that looked like thick, brown turbulent clouds obscuring everything. I'd never seen anything like it.

We had to divert to a base in Uzbekistan called K2. We turned away from Afghanistan air space regretting that there would be no show for the troops in Bagram that night.

We arrived unexpected at K2, and the base commander scrambled to find lodging for us. Although we didn't have all of our equipment, we wanted do a show for the guys.

We had guitars but no keyboard for Taz. All Pat had with him was a pair of drum sticks. Somebody at the base came up with a bass drum pedal. Pat hooked it up to a metal garbage can, and with various objects to beat on, we proceeded to do a show.

The next morning, we boarded another C-130 to go back through Bagram, Afghanistan. We would do another stripped-down show for the troops who could make it to the Pat Tillman Memorial Center in the middle of the day. We continued our flight to Arifjan Air Base in Kuwait City, the jumping off place for everything going into Iraq.

Kuwait was the only place where we stayed off base. We went to a hotel in Kuwait City and spent the night. We were able to look around a little, although we were advised not to wander off more than a few blocks from the hotel.

There was a big mosque down the street. As I walked by it, I pulled out my camera and started taking pictures, when this security guy hustled over and seemed very irate about something.

"You got camera?"

"Well, yes, it's right here."

"No pictures!"

"Okay."

"No pictures!"

"Okay, you can take the stick out of it if you want it. I didn't know you weren't supposed to take pictures."

"No pictures!"

We walked away, no harm done but a little confused.

It turns out that this particular mosque is where the emir, or king, of Kuwait attended. I guess they were uptight about security or maybe just didn't like Americans with cameras. But, whatever, I was glad to resolve the situation without causing an international incident.

The houses up and down that particular street were humongous, as big as small hotels. I found out the reason why.

A Kuwaiti can have as many wives as he wants to marry but has to treat them all the same. If he buys one a diamond necklace, he has to buy them all one. That also applies to living space, which explains the size of their houses. The more wives, the bigger the residence.

It was said that the emir has sixty-four wives. I would think his real-estate bill was atmospheric.

One of the things you notice is that there are big, ugly water tanks on top of these multimillion-dollar houses. The Kuwaitis, at least at that time, didn't have their own adequate water sources and had to have it trucked in from Saudi Arabia.

Most Kuwaitis don't work. It's a small country. There is enough oil money to go around, which allows them to live a life of leisure, like flipping their automobiles and leaving them beside the road.

I don't know where they are going, but they're always going somewhere, zipping up and down the road, flying low, and they are by no means the best drivers on the planet.

There is a big population of expatriates in Kuwait. The laborers work in the oil fields. Domestics do the housework. Even the clerks in the hotels are apt to be from the Philippines and keep things going, while the Kuwaitis are busy doing nothing.

Arifjan Air Base is huge; it's the transportation hub for most of the goods and personnel going into Iraq. We did a show for the troops stationed there one night, and the next morning we boarded another C-130 for the trip to Baghdad International.

I've landed in cow-pasture-type airfields in small planes. I've been tail hooked and catapulted on the deck of an aircraft carrier. But I have never experienced anything like a combat landing and takeoff.

The plane comes in high and begins a downward corkscrew approach, keeping it tight, avoiding the traditional vectors and approaches in an attempt to spend as little time as possible over enemy territory.

We had a female pilot who flew with the Michigan National Guard, and it was apparent that this was not her first rodeo. She was a real professional and performed the sensitive landing perfectly.

When you hit the ground in Baghdad, you don't hang around the airport. I was whisked away in what they called an ice cream truck, and that's what it resembled because of the big armored box on the back.

I was quartered in one of Saddam Hussein's palaces, a huge ornate marble barn of a building with a chandelier that probably cost half the national budget of a small country and tasteless appointments. He may have had money, but he sure could have used another interior designer.

We never went outside the wire and off the base on the ground because of the IEDs planted in the roads. Anytime we left the base, it was always by helicopter or fixed-wing aircraft.

The military complex in Baghdad is huge. Camp Victory, Camp Liberty, and all the smaller support facilities make up a lot of square miles, and there's a lot of fascinating things to see.

We would base in Baghdad and fly to the outlying bases and FOBs (forward operating bases). Our first show in country was at Camp Liberty, and something happened that night that truly touched my heart.

I was backstage before the show in the tent we were using as a dressing room, and a soldier walked in. This guy looked like the epitome of a Rambo-type fighting man—muscles, rugged face, short cropped hair, camos, and long handlebar mustache. He carried himself with the confidence and assurance of a true warrior who could bite a railroad spike in two.

I don't know his purpose for coming into the dressing room, and I'll never know why he did what he did next. But as I walked over to talk to him, he started crying. I can't even remember if we talked. But here was one of the toughest-looking humans I had ever laid eyes on, weeping without any explanation whatsoever.

I don't know if seeing me brought back memories of home or elicited some nostalgic thoughts that were just too much to think about in the middle of this hellhole of a country he was risking his life in. I just don't know, but it touched my heart and reminded me that the strongest men I've ever known have the capacity to shed tears. It's a treasured memory.

One morning we boarded a Blackhawk helicopter and headed out on an all-day trip. We would fly out and do shows at two FOBs (forward operating bases) and end up with a night show at a soccer stadium in Balad.

Flying across the Iraqi countryside in a Blackhawk with a fifty-caliber machine gun mounted in both side doors was quite an experience.

We flew over the city of Baghdad, a crowded beehive of a place that appeared extremely trashy and unkempt from the air. We went out into the countryside, where it was apparent how very poor the people were. They were living in primitive hovels with no infrastructure to speak of and dirt roads and mud fences.

We flew across shepherds tending flocks out in the middle of nowhere, and it was just as if we had gone back to biblical times. It dawns on you just how backward and out of touch these people were. How they were deprived while living in an oil-rich nation ruled by an inhuman dictator who built scores of extravagant, opulent mansions around the country and created game preserves with exotic animals for his private hunts.

Saddam's cruelty knew no bounds. He ruled by fear and intimidation. He took the wealth of Iraq and spent it on military might and an opulent lifestyle for his family and friends while the ordinary people lived in abject poverty and terror. His two sons, Uday and Qusay, were, if possible, crueler than their demented father.

They executed soccer players for not winning. They would send goons to the university in Baghdad to kidnap young girls, virgins, who they would spend the night raping. The next morning they would tease them because they had been defiled, which in the Islamic religion means lifelong disgrace.

There were one-way-in, one-way-out rooms, called rape rooms, where young boys would be taken and left for Saddam's depraved friends to have their way with. It's always stressed that homosexuality is a sin in the Muslim religion. But every week at the military prisons where Iranian prisoners of war were being held, anal repair was one of the regular medical procedures.

While the big bases are isolated enough, the FOBs, small facilities located in strategic areas with a small contingent of troops who carry on reconnaissance missions and work with the locals, are even more isolated.

A lot of the shows that came into the country only hit the high spots at the major bases and never made it out to the FOBs. They were the most appreciative audiences. They were just happy that somebody took the time to come and see them, play a few tunes, sign a few autographs, and let them know how very much they were appreciated and respected by the folks back home.

These guys lived hard. One FOB we played had just recently gotten a mess hall. They had been eating MREs (meals ready to eat) for months.

The temperatures can rise to 128 degrees. When a soldier dons his full battle rattle, a slang name for helmet and Kevlar vest, you can imagine just how miserable it can be.

Many of them carry pictures of their families, and I've seen them reduced to tears when showing a picture of one of their children.

For some odd reason, so many people seem to think that our men and women in the military have an extra gene or emotional governor that shields them from missing their loved ones when they are away for such long periods of time. Nothing could be further from the truth. Men and women in the military love and miss their families just as much and just as desperately as any of us do.

If there's an extra gene involved, it's a patriotic one. It takes a special type of human to give up the prime years of their young lives and volunteer to serve their country in hellholes like Iraq and Afghanistan, facing death and injury every day.

That's why when I hear some self-important, pompous politician blasting our military, my hat starts getting a couple of sizes too small and I want to put my boot to his posterior.

One of the most sickening statements I've ever heard a politician make was when Harry Reid said, "The surge isn't working. The war is lost."

In the first place it was a lie, a blatant, politically motivated lie. I can't imagine what soldiers serving in Iraq must have felt when they heard it. It's hard to imagine how a human could sink so low just to try to accomplish some political goal.

To get back to my story, we played a couple of stripped-down shows at FOBs. Then we headed for the soccer stadium in Balad, where our full complement of gear and sound and light systems were waiting.

When we would finish a show on any military base, we would set up tables in front of the stage and sign autographs, take pictures, and spend a few seconds with everybody who wanted to stand in line.

Sometimes there would be several hundred, but it made no difference. We took care of everybody before we left.

I remember that particular night in Balad. We had a long line, and we signed, hugged, posed, and socialized for quite awhile. It's a satisfying experience to be up close and personal with the boys and girls who sacrifice so much for us, and we relished every minute of it.

We finished up and headed to the airfield for the trip back to Baghdad. Our transportation that night was a Chinook, one of the big double-rotor helicopters. I remember as we got on board, General Hargett commented on the newly installed armor plating on the deck.

The flight to Baghdad was about twenty-five minutes. As we passed over Sadr City, I noticed three lights close together and shining straight up into the air. A few minutes later, I heard a ping under my foot, which I thought was just some piece of equipment on the Chinook. I later realized it was probably a bullet that pierced the skin of the helicopter and was stopped by the armor plating underneath my feet.

Things happened so fast.

On a Chinook there are three gunners, one on each side door and one on the rear door. All of a sudden the pilots jinked the chopper to the left and started firing flares.

It was over in a few seconds. The crew had told us before we left Balad that they would be doing some maneuvers on the way back, and I thought that was what was going on.

I soon found out it was much more than that. We had been attacked by small-arms fire, and at least one RPG (rifle propelled grenade) had come up almost between the rear gunner's legs.

The whole time I thought we were doing maneuvers; we were being attacked, and it didn't bother me at all. Well, you know what they say. Ignorance is bliss.

But I never actually felt in danger in Iraq. I knew it was out there, and there were people who would like nothing better than to kill an American band. But I had so many people praying for me back in Tennessee. Although I suffered some apprehension about it before I got there, it never really bothered me while I was there.

Long ago, I memorized Psalm 91. In times of stress it is a comforting scripture. It starts out, "Whoever dwells in the shelter of the Most High will rest in the shadow of the Almighty." And it goes on about how we are in God's constant care no matter what dangers we face.

We went to Iraq in 2004, 2006, and 2008. All three trips were unique and gratifying, with so many memories.

I could tell you about the night in Al Asad when a sand storm came across the stage like a curtain as we played the first notes of the concert. We had sand in everything.

I could tell you about visiting a small military hospital and seeing an Iraqi family with a young daughter being treated by an army medic. I wondered why none of the media was around to document some real diplomacy.

I see the news reports about ISIS moving into areas I visited where there has been so much American blood spilled, where such hard-fought gains were made. Now it is all under the authority of the most bloodthirsty religious fanatics on the planet. Religious fanatics who we will one day have to destroy, or they will destroy us.

And whether you believe the war in Iraq was justified or not, to see territory that was under US control being turned into part of the caliphate, all because one president refused to leave a small occupying force behind long enough for the Iraqi people to become strong enough to protect their country, is maddening.

I will always treasure the time I've spent entertaining our troops and will always honor the service of the men and women who protect our freedom in the far-flung, desolate spots of the world.

While I was in Iraq, I noticed that although quite a few of the troops played guitar and other instruments, in many cases they had no instruments to play and no way to replace broken or worn-out strings.

So when we got home, I started something called Operation Heart Strings to supply musical instruments, strings, CDs, computers, and other items that would help the guys and girls pass the lonely hours while they were deployed.

The Tennessee National Guard told us that if we could get them together, they would fly them over to Iraq and see that they got into the hands of the troops.

My first call was to Henry Juszkiewicz at Gibson Guitar, who went above and beyond by donating one hundred guitars and grosses of strings. With Gibson's generous donation, we were set and went on to Bridgestone, who gave us computers. Record companies donated CDs; other companies gave us keyboards and bass guitars.

All in all, there were three cargo pallets of equipment. The national guard was as good as their word and flew the load to Iraq to provide some much-needed distractions for the men and women serving their country so far away from home.

Almost everybody has a heart for the troops.

CHAPTER 55

A Heart's Desire Answered on the Stage of the Ryman Auditorium

In November 2007, we were doing a show called Christmas for Kids at the Ryman Auditorium. It's a show to benefit underprivileged children at Christmastime, started by the drivers who drive the touring buses used by the Nashville artists.

On a designated day and place, the tour buses meet and pick up groups of kids. They take them to a big retail outlet, where they are all given a certain amount of money and told they can buy whatever they want.

I'm told that many of them, instead of buying presents for themselves, spend the money on their siblings at home. It's a most worthy event and another example of the big-hearted music community in Nashville. It was for several years promoted by our friend Jimmy Jay and featured several acts and was able to raise quite a bit of money for the cause.

On this particular night we had just finished our first two songs of the set and were about to launch into our third when a commotion started stage left and a lady came walking out onstage.

Well, nobody interrupts our show after it's started. I couldn't figure out what was happening, and then I noticed that the lady making all the noise was Martina McBride. She was walking out onstage with an envelope in her hand.

I'll interrupt a show for Martina McBride any time. Thinking she was bringing some kind of citation or letter of thanks for us hosting the Christmas for Kids show, I turned the center stage microphone over to her.

It was to be another one of those moments when just a few words will change your whole life.

She said, "You have been invited to join the Grand Ole Opry!"

Did I hear her right? Did she really say what I thought she said? At the age of seventy-one, was I really going to realize one of my longest-held and fondest dreams?

Well, Martina was holding an envelope with the official invitation in it. So it had to be so.

I was speechless. I've seen the tape that was shot that evening. I stood there shell-shocked, and it was to be several minutes before we would resume and finish our set.

And it all happened on the stage of the Ryman Auditorium, the mother church of country music. This stage had felt the footsteps of Hank Williams, Roy Acuff, Ernest Tubb, Minnie Pearl, Bill Monroe, Eddie Arnold, and almost every country music star who had ever lived.

The show my whole family and I listened to as long ago as I could remember—I was really being invited to be a member of that very same show, and I would be broadcast over those very same airwaves. Maybe I would be an inspiration to some kid listening in some small town with the same dreams, hopes, and ambitions I had.

We had played the Opry almost at will for the last several years, and they called on us to do it regularly. But I was not an official member, which meant that no matter how many times we played it, my name would never be enshrined along with so many of my heroes whenever the history of the Opry was written. To me, that meant a lot.

I went home a very happy cowboy that night, knowing that one of the biggest dreams I ever dreamed was coming true.

On January 21, 2008, we went back to the Ryman Auditorium, where Marty Stuart, Connie Smith, and Pete Fisher, the Opry general manager, inducted me into the brotherhood known as the Grand Ole Opry.

Marty presented me with a statuette that symbolizes Opry membership and told me that the Grand Ole Opry was a family that I had just become a member of.

The first thing I told the crowd was, "My Bible says that God will give you the desires of your heart, and you've seen that come true on this stage tonight."

Trace Adkins joined Marty, Connie, and the CDB onstage for a rousing version of "Will the Circle Be Unbroken." And then it was official. Charlie Daniels was the newest member of the longest, continuously running show on radio, the *Grand Ole Opry*.

The *Opry* hosted a party in a big room across the street, where friends and family came by to share in the celebration. It was the last time I saw my cousin Walton alive. He had come all the way from North Carolina to be a part of the evening and passed away not long after. I'm so thankful to God that he got to come and see his cousin's fondest dream come true.

In the spring of that same year, I had the honor of doing the same thing to some friends of mine that Martina McBride did to me. I interrupted Montgomery Gentry's performance to inform them that they had been invited to become members of the Grand Ole Opry.

No matter how much success you've had, no matter how many records and concert tickets you've sold or how many guest appearances you've made, nothing can compare with the fact that you've been asked to breathe the rarified air of being a member of the Grand Ole Opry.

It's a thrill like no other, a dream come true, and an accomplishment that no serious country music career would be complete without.

Troy and Eddie were ecstatic, and I knew the feeling.

CHAPTER 56

Ain't No Fool Like an Old Fool

In my formative years, state-of-the-art communications technology was a dial telephone and a party line that at least one other family shared with you. This meant that you heard not only your phone ring but also the phone of the family, or families, sharing your line. The difference would be the number of rings, two shorts or one long, and so on, designating which line was being called.

Of course, it was not unknown for some of the nosier ladies to put their hands over the mouth pieces and listen in. In fact, it was practically a neighborhood hobby.

Technology and I make strange bedfellows. I could never even fully understand the workings of the internal combustion engine and have no idea how radio and TV operate. I certainly don't have the analytical type of mind that understands computers.

In fact, the first computers I remember hearing about back in the early fifties were reputed to be about the size of the average living room. Even understanding what the practical use of such a monstrosity would be went way over my head.

So I decided I'd just ignore the whole thing. When the exponential explosion of digital technology started years ago and the desktop and later the laptop versions of computers started showing up, I still retained my reticence.

But regardless of my greenhorn attitude toward computers and all things technical, our office headed in that direction full tilt. Even our road accounting turned into a weekly computerized sheet called the "road report."

When a young computer-savvy guy named Chris Wyatt came to work for us in 2000, he was instrumental in bringing our whole operation into the computer era. He instigated and helped design our very first website and suggested that, since I am an opinionated person, I should do an occasional column we would call the "Soapbox."

The column soon became a weekly feature, with me printing the content out in block letters and passing it on to one of the girls in the office to type and submit to the webmaster.

Early on it became very evident that I should try to acquire at least a cursory knowledge of computers and the capabilities of cyber technologies. So, with the help of my son, Charlie, who had been dabbling in computers since he'd been around twelve years old, I purchased a laptop and began trying to learn how to put it to practical use.

I had two years of typing in high school, so I was not a complete stranger to the keyboard, but the operation of the more sophisticated bells and whistles was a mystery to me.

I was mainly interested in word processing and storage of my song lyrics and writings I wanted to preserve. In baby steps, I learned about how to create and file away the things I wrote. I had a habit of putting lyrics I was working on and other ideas I wanted to keep in notebooks and forgetting where I put them, only to run across them months or years later. Having a central place for storing them saved a lot of time and effort.

Then came e-mail. It quickly turned into a vital element of communication, as I could e-mail my thoughts and ideas to whomever I wanted to share them with while the thought was fresh on my mind.

It was to be several years before I was ready to tackle Twitter, but when I finally got around to it, it became a part of my daily life. I do regular daily features every morning: a Bible verse, a prayer, and something I call "Let's all make the day count," positive thoughts dealing with everyday life. And I sign off every night with, "Guess I'll hang it up for tonight. Goodnight planet earth. God bless."

I'm fascinated by the instant global communication. With the touch of a key, I can talk to people all over the world, share ideas, and receive feedback, all in the space of a few seconds.

I now carry an iPad around with me. Besides the communications features and centralizing my song lyrics and other ideas, being able to store the books I'm reading on it has become a most useful convenience.

I read the Bible and four other inspirational books every morning. Trying to carry them around, plus the fiction novels I'm always reading, was a little too much for any briefcase I could hand carry on an airplane.

Now I just take along the iPad, and the problem is solved. All of my books are available at the touch of a button.

Even though I have been using cellphones since they were about the size of a brick and have evolved along with the styles and improvements, I am still amazed that I can hold a wireless device in my hand and speak to practically anybody in the world from practically anyplace in the world.

That aspect alone floors me, not to mention the ability to take a picture at an opportune time and immediately send it anywhere or record a snatch of a song I'm working on.

It's amazing how willingly we assimilate the new technologies into our lifestyles and how quickly we become dependent on them. I think of the days when if I had even one telephone interview to do it would prevent me from making any other plans for the day because I had to be in the proximity of a landline. Now that seems like a long time ago.

My introduction to the cyber world has made it possible to write and send in my "Soapbox" columns anytime and from anywhere, which is a huge convenience for me. I sometimes get them finished just a few minutes before I send them in.

My biweekly pieces are available on our website but are also often picked up by other websites or publications. I'm sometimes amazed by the number of people who tell me they read them.

The subjects in my column can range anywhere from my personal opinion on current events to the description of going shopping with my wife, which I rate about two cuts above having a root canal. This is my forum for expressing myself as a private citizen. I don't believe in using my time onstage for anything but entertaining the paying customers. I restrict my personal political convictions to interviews and columns.

The feedback can get heated at times, as I pull no punches concerning my feelings about politicians, fiscal affairs, corruption in high places, bureaucratic red tape, and the irritating habit Congress and the president have of wasting our money.

I approach my writings with what I call "cowboy logic," which is made up of three elements:

2 and 2 is always 4.

Water never runs uphill.

If there is smoke, there's a fire somewhere.

My political philosophy leans to the right most of the time, although I consider myself an independent. I sometimes vote a split ticket in state races, as it is my opinion that an *R* or a *D* besides someone's name does not necessarily demonize them nor is it a valid reason to cast my vote one way or another.

I have very strong feelings about some of today's sacred-cow and third-rail issues. I don't hesitate to speak my mind about them, so I naturally garner my share of criticism from folks who feel strongly inclined in the opposite direction.

For instance, I feel that life begins at conception and that taking that life, except in the case of saving the mother's life, is murder.

The Bible says that God knew us in our mother's womb, knit the pieces together, and scheduled the days of our lives before we were born. And being much more concerned with pleasing God than pleasing people, I stick by my assumption.

I believe that true marriage exists only between a man and a woman.

I have rock-solid convictions about the Second Amendment and fully believe that US citizens have a constitutionally ensured right to keep and bear arms. I do not ascribe to the popularly accepted idea that the Second Amendment is meant to assure sports shooting and personal protection only.

At the time the Second Amendment was written, our nation had just fought a war to escape the tyranny of a foreign government. I believe the framers were including the right to bear arms against oppression, foreign or domestic.

There was a famous statement attributed to a Japanese admiral during World War II. When asked why, since the US Pacific naval fleet in Hawaii had been decimated, the Japanese forces had not tried to invade the West

Coast of the United States, he said something to the effect of, "There'd be a rifle behind every blade of grass."

I hope and pray that the day never comes when hidden cells of terrorists will openly attack on the streets of the United States. But any rational person has to admit that it's a possibility, and a rifle behind every blade of grass would be a good thing.

I believe that an able-bodied man should work for a living, and I have scant sympathies for those who are healthy enough to earn a living and instead find a way to sponge off the taxpayers.

I have no use for a man who brings children into the world and doesn't support them. I believe there should be strong laws that when a mother applies to the state for assistance, she be required to identify the father. It is an easy task with today's technology, and he should be forced to support these children to the age of adulthood or spend the same amount of time in jail.

I totally despise the fact that there seems to be two sets of laws. There is one for the common folks and one for the powerful politicians and high rollers, who seem to get away with whatever they do. How many politicians have you seen commit crimes, and their cronies circle the wagons and let them walk?

I have nothing but disdain for politicians who put personal gain above the good of the country. It's called "public service" for a reason. Too many times elected officials fall into the trap of lobbyists and major donors, developing a quid pro quo situation of give and take, all at the expense of the taxpayer.

These people should be put in jail, but they seldom are.

And, yes, I believe the press is biased and many colleges and universities are more concerned with political indoctrination than they are with preparing young people to be employable and competitive in the real world.

I believe that maintaining not just a strong military but the world's best military is absolutely necessary if we want to leave a safe and prosperous United States to our children and grandchildren. Armed forces with the manpower, the hardware, and the latest technology to defend the United States and US allies and interests.

The United States has not finished a war since World War II. Our enemies know that if they can set the rules of engagement and hold out long enough, the mighty United States will pull out, many times leaving a mess that will eventually have to be cleaned up at a later date.

I believe that Congress should have to live with the same insurance plans that are offered to the public. Our veterans should also be able to be treated by the same doctors and hospitals as the rest of the citizens.

As is usually the case, the government can't operate anything effectively. The current Veterans Administration is a prime example of that incompetence, an organization that can see its way clear to spend a hundred million dollars on art while veterans are dying because they can't schedule an appointment.

And, by the way, the VA is a prime example of the single-payer health plan. Is this the way you treat people who have laid their lives on the line for their country?

I believe there are many things we can do to improve and sustain the environment. Having polluted streams and dirty air is unacceptable and unnecessary. I fully believe that there is technology that can accomplish those goals and that we should be pursuing them.

But I believe that we will be burning fossil fuels for the foreseeable future and all the pie-in-the-sky alternative methods are decades from becoming the answer to our energy needs. In the meantime, we need all of our available energy sources—coal, petroleum, hydro, and nuclear. We should best be about the job of creating ways of using them more cleanly and efficiently.

Insofar as polluting the planet, no matter what the politicians tell you, the Western nations are not the problem, as anybody who has ever been to the Orient, especially China, will tell you. Pollution in China resembles thick, gray ground fog.

If you saw a nighttime picture of North Korea, you would see that 90 percent of the country resembles a black hole. There is no light, and it has essentially been deforested because the people have cut down anything combustible to use for cooking and heat.

The same is true in parts of Africa, where the deforestation is so severe that there is no root system or undergrowth. The topsoil has been blown away by the wind, leaving an unarable desert behind. I believe in protecting the rainforest and in preventing the dumping of hazardous materials and pumping chemical waste and raw sewage into our streams and oceans. We should take steps to preserve the fish populations and protect endangered species of animals.

But I personally do not believe that climate change is the clear and present danger many of our politicians would have us to believe. I believe that the universal thermostat is in the control of the Creator. If the planet is warming, it is His doing, and it is arrogant of humankind to think that we could have an effect on His grand design.

I firmly believe that climate change is about power, pure and simple. It is a way of wresting control out of the hands of citizens and passing it into the hands of what would eventually become a global government. They would leech away personal freedoms, right to bear arms, and right to control what you do with your own property, your children's education, health care, and law enforcement, even down to the plants you can grow in your yard and garden.

The distribution of food and fuel, the dispensing and scheduling of health care, and who lives and who is allowed to die would be controlled by government.

This would be a cold and impersonal confederation, where citizens would be numbers instead of people. Mandatory abortion and euthanasia would be standard procedure. This would be an oppressive regime where everybody would be expected to give up their individuality and bend their collective will to the will of the state.

Sound fantastic?

Take a good look at United Nations Agenda 21.

Told you I was opinionated.

To say that the America I knew when I was young has drastically changed would be a gross understatement. Some changes did great good and some did great harm.

There have been monumental advances in civil rights and the discovery of medicines to cure diseases once thought incurable. Advances in transportation have shrunk the planet. The exponential technological leaps in communications and the Internet have placed the knowledge of centuries at our fingertips, to name a very few.

But where there once existed a pioneer-like spirit of self-reliance and accountability, the acceptance of being liable for one's own well-being, present and future, there is a growing feeling of entitlement. It is a dependence on outside sources to make up any shortfalls in our lives, whether self-inflicted or not.

Too few are willing to accept responsibility for their own future and well-being. They are all too willing to let government take up the slack, which self-serving politicians are happy to do. It creates a cumbersome, inept, inefficient bureaucracy, which trips over its own redundancy and becomes a fiscal black hole that takes 75 percent of receivable revenues just to exist.

Power-hungry politicians are readily willing to exploit society to stay in power. Even if it means pitting races and social strata against each other, they promise more and more and make it easier and easier to receive a government subsidy. In the process, they are creating a segment of society totally dependent on entitlements and ensuring a loyal voting bloc in the process.

They advance the idea that the have-nots have not because the haves have. They are being kept from achieving affluence not by the lack of ambition, drive, work ethic, and good attitude but because the haves are stealing what is rightfully theirs.

An unfair system is holding them down while allowing others to flourish. It's really not their fault, even if they don't make an honest effort to get a good education, even if they go from job to job and do just enough to get by, even if they show disdain and disrespect for other people.

The truth is that opportunities exist for those who are willing to accept the fact that they'll never rise above the fray depending on government subsidies. If you're an unmarried young woman who has had multiple children by different fathers and depend on the stipend the welfare service sends you every month, you have locked yourself into a nightmare. Unless you're an unusually highly motivated person, that's where you're going to spend your life.

If you truly want to make something special out of your life, start with your attitude. If you're going to be bitter, hostile, uncooperative, and disinterested, you can forget it. Nobody wants that kind of employee. As one who has had employees for more than forty years, I know what I'm talking about.

The attitude that is going to get you noticed, valued, and therefore rewarded is to take the job you're doing seriously, no matter what it is, no matter how humble or seemingly unimportant. With the right attitude, you can use it as a launching point, a stepping stone to better things. Here's how:

If you can't get what you want, take what you can get and make what you want out of it.

Why do some things cost more than others?

It's based on their value. Some things are just more valuable than others. It's the same thing with employees. Some are just more valuable than others.

Example A: An employee who has a propensity for running a few minutes late, who does just enough to get by, who stops work at the stroke of quitting time, who complains every time there's a problem, who takes no initiative and is not trustworthy with any kind of responsibility.

Example B: An employee who is the first one to get there and the last one to leave, who has a "let me do it" attitude, who instead of complaining about a problem takes the initiative to try to solve it, who is willing to shoulder responsibility and has the tenacity to stick with a difficult job until it's finished.

Who do you think will get the promotion? The pay raise? Who will move up and continue to be given more and more responsibility and therefore more and more reward? Such people are needed. There's never enough of them.

It all comes down to, if you want to make something out of yourself, make yourself valuable to somebody. Your rewards will be in direct proportion to your value.

Let me give you a practical example.

We have four full-time drivers who drive two buses and a truck.

Now, it's fairly easy to find somebody to just operate the vehicles, to get from point A to point B safely and on time, as long as there's no breakdowns or mechanical problems.

But you can tell the real mettle of a driver by how he reacts when you're sitting beside the road at three o'clock in the morning, broken down, and the next show is still three hundred miles down the highway.

If he calls a wrecker and folds his hands, you've got a dud. If the first thing he does is look to see if he can determine the problem, immediately gets on his cellphone to one of his contacts, describes the symptoms of the breakdown, and finds out the closest shop capable of fixing the problem, you know you've got a winner.

It's the same situation with a road manager.

If a vehicle breaks down in the middle of the night, it is not the fault of the promoter or the folks who bought the tickets. It is his responsibility to get the band and equipment there on time, and it's his responsibility to find a way to make that happen.

If the vehicle can be repaired and rolling in a timely fashion, then all is well and good.

If not, it's the road manager's responsibility to move heaven and earth to make sure the show goes on, on time. It could be getting a replacement bus or truck, renting cars, chartering airplanes, calling limousine services, or whatever.

The show goes on, the band gets paid, and the driver and road manager have proven themselves to be valuable.

If you want to get ahead, make yourself valuable to your employer.

And if you're not rewarded at the place you're employed, there will always be somebody who will recognize your extra effort. There are always companies looking for employees who have a good attitude and are competent enough to take on responsibility.

It's out there for you. You may have to look for it for a while, but it's there for those diligent enough to seek it out and stick it out.

When you develop an attitude of "I'm going to accomplish what I want even if I have to work twice as hard as anybody else," you're going to get there.

CHAPTER 57

And the Lonesome Boy from Dixie Made It Home

On January 11, 2011, Hazel and me were vacationing in Colorado when I got a call that Tommy Crain had suddenly passed away during the night.

It was hard to believe. Tommy was one of the most "alive" people I had ever known. He was always bubbling over with energy and putting a vigor into everything he did, whether he was carrying on a conversation or playing his guitar.

Tommy spent fourteen years in the CDB and had a lasting impression on the style and the sound of the band. His playing onstage had motivated me to reach a little higher than I ever did before. Together we climbed the musical heights night after night, spurring each other on and on until some nights it seemed almost as if our side of the stage would catch on fire.

Tommy had left the band in 1989, but we parted friends and stayed that way, still finding the opportunity to jam together from time to time. I loved Tommy like a brother.

Hazel was suffering with a pain in her back that would soon require surgery and was unable to take a flight back to Nashville for the funeral services. I couldn't leave her alone and had nobody to stay with her, so I was unable to attend.

I called Tommy's wife, Melissa, and his brother Billy. I wanted them to know that although I couldn't be there in person, I wanted to participate in the service in some way.

Billy wanted a prayer to be said. It was arranged; at the beginning of the service, which was a memorial jam, there would be a telephone hookup. The prayer I said would be piped over the sound system so all the people in attendance could hear it.

He was the first CDB musician, past or present, I had ever lost. I felt that my world and music's world had been reduced by a very significant factor.

I don't think the world ever realized the extent of Tommy's talent. He wrote earthy songs in everyday language like "Cumberland Mountain Number Nine" and "Franklin Limestone." I know for a fact that the best of his guitar playing never got recorded. It happened late at night on stages around the world when the rhythm section was honking and Tommy was gritting his teeth and sweating and the notes poured out of his guitar in blazing profusion. If you didn't hear it the first time, it was gone forever because he would never play it exactly the same way a second time.

There were times early on when I wondered if the most important thing I'd done in the music business was to introduce the world to Tommy Crain, to give him a platform whereby the world could hear him.

If I were to pick five guitar players I admire the most in my lifetime, Tommy Crain would be on the list.

Our vacation that year was marred by Hazel's back problem. Although she tried to put a brave face on it, when I saw her hobble downstairs one morning in obvious pain, I said, "I'm taking you home so we can get something done about your back."

We drove back to Tennessee, where the doctors diagnosed a problem that would require surgery, which was done at Vanderbilt Hospital in Nashville. After a few weeks of recuperation, my gal was right back on her feet and ready to attack the touring schedule with me.

CHAPTER 58

THE WAY I SEE IT

Although I love every aspect and facet of my career, the writing, recording, and even doing publicity interviews, the part of the business that keeps me going are the live performances.

I love getting onstage with my band and entertaining a crowd of people.

I have devoted many years of my life to learning how to entertain. I don't mean just standing on a stage playing an instrument and singing. I mean entertaining, exciting people, touching people, making people happy, and always giving them their money's worth plus a little extra.

There is an art to entertaining a crowd. If you've got a bevy of hit songs, you can entertain by simply playing them one after another.

If you're a knockout in size 28 jeans who can take away the breath of the females in the audience by simply walking on the stage, you're entertaining.

But since I have never fallen into either category, I have had to rely on other attributes.

One of the most important things any artist can do is to learn how to pace a set of music.

The way you come on, what you start with, what you end with, and the emotional ups and downs of your set are of paramount importance. The dynamics of a show, the ebb and flow, the streaming of energy from quiet emotion to fever pitch and back again, from start to finish.

No white space or empty spots. Something should be holding the crowd's attention all the time, whether it's dialogue, music, or some unique piece of showmanship. There should be a seamless presentation from the opening song until the last note.

Another highly important thing is dancing with the one who brung you. Play the songs folks are familiar with, the ones they've heard on the radio. No matter how old, no matter how different from what you are currently doing, people come to see you for the music they've heard, not the music they haven't heard.

Doing a medley of your better-known songs and spending the rest of the show trying to sell the crowd your new album is self-indulgent and unfair to the folks who bought the tickets.

Every great entertainer you will ever see knows how to communicate with the crowd.

You don't have to tell jokes or tap dance, but being able to talk to the people and establishing a rapport with them is a very important element of a truly entertaining show.

Sometimes people ask me if I get nervous when I go onstage. Actually, it's one of the few times I feel like I know what I'm doing. I've spent more than sixty years of my life learning what to do onstage, and if I don't know what I'm doing by now, I'll never learn.

Once the show starts, barring a power failure or a meteor shower, it should not be interrupted. Once you lose the momentum, it's extremely hard to get it back.

Plow through. If your favorite guitar is on the blitz, grab another one. If the sound system and monitors suck, make the best of it. It's not the crowd's fault, and they shouldn't even be aware of it if it can be helped.

Did you have an argument with your girlfriend? Did one of your musicians give you notice before you walked onstage? Was the plane late and you didn't get much sleep last night? Did the bus break down on the way to town? Did the record lose its bullet? Did the hotel have bed bugs? Did your dog die?

When you walk onstage, you have to leave it all in the wings. Keep it to yourself. The people paid for a show, and it's your duty to give them the best one you've got, sans frowns and sets cut short because of petulance.

If you claim to be a professional, act like one. Or just stay home and play the local lounges on the weekends and work a daytime job. Because if you ain't got the temperament to do an entertaining show in the face of adversity, you're not going to last very long in the competitive world.

Because if you're not up to it, there are a thousand kids from Des Moines and Fresno and Valdosta and from all across this country just chomping at the bit to knock you off your pedestal and take your place. They're always there, nipping at your heels. If you can't hold your spot, they'll gladly take it.

I know everybody is not as passionate about this business as I am. But whether you are or not, I can tell you this.

If you don't have a fire in your belly and a heart so full of desire that you can't imagine your life without a career in music, don't even put your foot on the path because you're going to get your heart broken.

The music-slash-entertainment business is a slippery, fickle lady that can love you one day and push you off a cliff the next. It's during those times that you've got to cowboy up and look for a new record deal, find another band, sign with another booking agency, and beat down all the doors you have to until you get back on track.

So many young artists get the impression that bigger is always better when it comes to record companies, booking agencies, and managers. This is true only to the degree that they believe in you, only when you have at least one important person that goes to bat for you every day.

One of the problems with any music business entity is that there is always an internal game of musical chairs going on. There is a very good possibility that the person or persons that believe in you will be fired or move on to greener pastures, leaving you to the mercy of those who are not so impressed with you.

I've had that happen to me a couple of times. It can really take the wind out of your sails for a while. But you just have to batten down the hatches and deal with it. More than likely if the new regime doesn't believe in you, it'll be willing to suspend any contracts and let you go anyway. If you're in it for the long run, just pick up the pieces and move along.

So, at least from my perspective of stability and longevity, what you're looking for in representation, labels, agencies, or record producers is people who believe in you, and sometimes the smaller entities are where you'll find them.

Of course, nobody will believe in you if you don't believe in yourself. Now, I'm not talking about arrogance or snobbery. It's just knowing that the foundation you've built under yourself is solid and you have what it takes to take your talent to the world and convince them that you've got something special.

To watch a confident, master entertainer work is a unique experience. Little Jimmy Dickens was a prime example.

I saw him over a span of sixty years. Even in his nineties, he always walked onstage confident, capable, and loving what he was doing. He radiated entertainment with the songs he sang, the jokes he told, but most of all that glowing personality.

One of my heroes.

CHAPTER 59

ANOTHER BLIP ON THE SCREEN

During the summer of 2012, I started noticing that my usual high level of energy was dipping somewhat, and it was resulting in a sort of weakness and affecting my performances onstage.

It got to the point that on the last date on one leg of a tour, I had to sit on a stool to play the set.

I didn't know what it was, but I knew something was wrong. I took a flight back to Nashville and went to the emergency room at Vanderbilt Hospital. Dr. Anderson Spickard met me and kept me overnight for some extensive tests, after which he decided to make some adjustments to the medicine I took to control my blood pressure, which was probably making my heart beat too slow.

These adjustments worked well for a while. But a little later, when the condition resurfaced, I had some more tests, including an EKG. It was discovered that, although my heart muscle was healthy, the timing mechanism was misfiring, resulting in a condition known as atrial fibrillation or A-fib.

This means that your heartbeat is uneven and beats too fast or too slow. In my case it was too slow, and the remedy for this condition is the installation of a pacemaker.

They checked me into Vanderbilt that day. I was put under the care of Dr. Chris Ellis, a brilliant young heart specialist, and we began the process.

First of all, they put you to sleep and shock your heart back into rhythm just to make sure you definitely need the pacemaker. If you do, your heart will go back out of rhythm, which mine did. We started scheduling a pacemaker procedure.

I had my trusty iPad with me, which had our concert itinerary in it. Bebe came by the hospital, and we worked out a schedule that would only mean cancelling or rescheduling a few dates. I told Dr. Ellis we were ready to go.

The procedure itself is simple. You're put to sleep. The device is implanted, and your heart is shocked into its proper rhythm. If your heart starts to drag, the pacemaker goes to work, and it gets back into line.

After a couple of days of tests, I was released from the hospital. With a few adjustments in the device and some changes in medicine, we've been ticking along ever since.

I believe in medicine and have been blessed with great doctors. Vanderbilt University Hospital is one of the finest in the world—state of the art, efficient, and brilliantly staffed and equipped.

Doctors are His tools. They do the treatment, then God takes over and administers the healing.

Over the years I've had cancer, a stroke, and some heart trouble. My heavenly Father has healed me and given me health.

CHAPTER 60

There Are Some Things in This World You Just Can't Explain

In 2011 a gut-wrenching tragedy was to rock my world almost to the tipping point.

On the night of October 12, the Twin Pines Rambler, with Dean Tubb, my driver, and me aboard, pulled out about 9:00 p.m. for Marietta, Georgia. We would be doing a concert the next night, and the Lady LaRue pulled out about midnight with the band and crew aboard.

We had reached our destination and were parked in a motel parking lot when Dean called me on the intercom. He told me that David Corlew was trying to reach me.

I knew it was bad news for David to be calling me at four o'clock in the morning. But the magnitude of what he told me when I called him back had not even crossed my mind.

Taz had left his home in Burns, Tennessee, to meet the band bus to leave for the gig. He was headed in toward Nashville on Interstate 40, lost control of his car, and plowed into a tree. He had been killed instantly.

What David was saying seemed surreal. The words were just floating across the phone, words that just couldn't be true. Taz had been with me for forty years. He had been there from the get-go, through all the ups and downs and sideways we had gone through in the past four decades.

This just couldn't be. But I knew that it could be, and it was true. I had to face the fact that William Joel DiGregorio (Taz), friend, sidekick, somebody who had had my back musically for forty years, who had been there across the mountaintops and through the valleys and rough spots, would never again be sitting at the keyboards, stage right of me, playing the music we had created together.

Jimmy Burton, thinking that since Taz hadn't shown up to catch the bus, he had decided to drive the short distance to Georgia, left without him and was about an hour out.

Dean and I just sat and waited for the band and crew to get in so I could break the news to them.

When they got in, I had Jimmy Burton get everybody on the bus so I could tell them all at one time. When they gathered in the front of the bus, I broke the news, and we headed back to Nashville to bury my friend.

When something like this happens to any of our CDB people, the family can plan on getting all the help they need from our employees, who are extremely capable at sorting out details and making arrangements.

Taz's wife, Danielle, came out to the office and sat with the staff. Bebe got on her computer and helped Danielle with all the arrangements, including a venue for the funeral. They found a beautiful burial plot in a cemetery overlooking a highway, which seemed an appropriate resting place for a traveling musician.

I dread funerals. I guess it's just the nature of finality and closure when you finally have to admit that a person you really loved is gone forever. It's a sobering situation.

Taz's mother, sisters, and children were all there, as were many of his friends and of course the CDB people. The funeral home was packed, with standing room only.

Roger Campbell, David Corlew, and myself were scheduled to say a few words at the service. Since Taz had been in the army, there would be a military graveside ceremony.

After that, a venue had been secured and instruments set up to do a memorial jam with whoever wanted to play. CDB took the stage first, and Taz's son Joel came up and filled in on his dad's organ as we jammed out our goodbye to our friend.

Taz and I had spent more than forty years of our lives together. The send-off we gave him, although we did all we knew how to do to honor him, seemed so insignificant compared to all the experiences we'd shared and all the memories we'd made. Taz's memory will always be alive to us who knew him well, as there's never a shortage of stories and anecdotes that happened along the way.

The old-timers remember a long denim duster and an old cardboard suitcase Taz had on the road in the early days. He carried an iron in those days, and it seemed he could never get the cord to his iron in his suitcase. I can almost see him now, running across the parking lot at some motel in Sioux Falls or some such little town, trying to make it to the bus by leaving time, with that duster tail flying and the ironing cord hanging out of that old cardboard suitcase.

Or the time he broke his arm and, for some reason known only to Taz, painted the cast blue and had to play one handed.

We did a PBS special from Saratoga Performing Arts Center, and some lady watching the telecast called in and wanted to know why we made our keyboard player tie his arm up that way.

I had known Taz for so long that the idea of my world without him in it was a strange and foreign thought. We had experienced so many things, been together in life-threatening situations, and shared some of the most joyous moments of our lives together.

Taz had been working with me when Little Charlie was born. We'd been everywhere from the Arctic Circle to the deserts of the Middle East, climbed a lot of mountains, and walked a lot of dark valleys together. Now, just like that, in the blink of an eye, he was gone forever.

Taz left a lasting impression on our music and the CDB fans. It's surprising how many people have memories of him, some little kindness he showed them, or something he said that stayed with them.

The first few nights the band played after his death, I would catch myself about to turn stage right and half expect to see him sitting behind his organ, his black cowboy hat slouched low over his face.

I wouldn't even face the fact that I was going to have to replace Taz for a while. We just played our shows with the five of us. I knew I was going to hire another keyboard player, but I just wasn't ready.

After about five weeks, we began the process of auditioning a new player. It was a short process because the first guy to audition was Shannon Wickline. He was exactly what I had been looking for, musically and personality-wise. I cancelled auditions and told Shannon he was the new CDB keyboard player.

CHAPTER 61

I'll Always Remember that Song

In the flurry of hit records and superstars and the glitz and glamor of the music business, many times the most essential elements fly below the radar insofar as the public is concerned, the piece of the process without which the whole business would come to a screeching halt and disintegrate.

I'm speaking of course of the men and women who write the words and music, who create the songs and start the ball rolling.

Songwriters are so many times the unsung heroes whose names appear in miniature on record labels. They are rarely known by the public, although they are the sparkplug without which the engine would never even get started.

The act of writing songs is the art of making something out of nothing. It is pulling ideas out of thin air, trial and error, trying to find words that rhyme and still make sense. It is striving to get a whole thought across in a single line of lyric and stuffing a whole storyline into a few verses and a chorus.

Songwriting is a joy like no other when the chords are fitting together and the lyrics are exploding like popcorn, falling into place like the pieces of a puzzle. But if you've got an idea you know is worthy of being a song and you just can't get past the first few lines, it can be some of the hardest mental work you'll ever do.

Everybody has their own method of writing songs. I went through several different phases and methods, and they all worked for me in their time.

Some of the most successful writers in Nashville keep writing appointments with other writers. They go around Music Row with guitar case and notebooks in hand, going from appointment to appointment and turning out hit songs, in what I would suppose would be the Tin Pan Alley of Nashville.

Some prefer to write alone, best handling the creative process without any outside influence.

I have written with cowriters, some very fine ones, and have turned out some good music. I've attempted to work with some I jived with and some I didn't. I have written with my band at a time when I was going through a phase in which I wanted an instant beat, bass part, or keyboard lick, accepting and rejecting ideas as we put the music together line by line.

We would create whole songs, complete with arrangement and solos, without as much as a title. Then I would take the music off by myself and do the lyrics.

That is viewed by most people as a very strange way to write songs, but there was a time when it worked for me. I'm a big believer that if it ain't broke, don't fix it. If it works for you, go for it, proper etiquette and tradition be damned.

I was blessed that I basically served an apprenticeship under Bob Johnston. Our writing sessions were long, laborious, tedious, and exacting. Bob was a demanding taskmaster whose work ethic fell somewhere between Jerry Rice and Simon Legree. The clock didn't exist. It made no difference if it was daylight or dark, morning or night. As long as there was one imperfect chord or one word that didn't rhyme properly, it was back to the drawing board, time after time, until it all came together.

But when you wrote a song with Bob Johnston, when it was finished, it was something you could be proud of.

Bob's intransigent approach to creativity and his never-say-die work ethic left a lasting impression on me. It is one that governs my approach to songwriting to this day.

In my opinion, a good song can't be rushed. You can ruin a perfectly good idea by settling for less than the song deserves simply by giving in to music or lyrics you know aren't your best.

Of course, sometimes after struggling for hours to get it right, it still evades you, and it's best to put it away. You can get back to it when you're fresh and can approach it from a different direction.

But whatever you do, don't ever discard a good idea. If it really is good, you'll find a way to make it work somewhere down the line. I've kept song ideas in my head for years before something finally clicked and I was able to finish it.

In fact, I always have several bits and pieces I'm working on. It may be part of a guitar riff, a few notes of fiddle music, a title idea, or a couple of lines of lyric. I know they are worthy of being part of a song but so far just haven't jelled with any of the ideas I've tried to put with them.

Then, one day an idea hits. You go back and start pulling out those old bits and pieces. One of them starts falling into place, and a song begins to take shape. You know where you're going; you've just got to go through the tedious process of trial and error to get there.

As I've said, most of my songs start with a guitar riff, a set of chords I work out, or a catchy line of lyric. But there are times when lyrics and music are happening at the same time. Other times the lyrics are put on hold until I get the melody worked out.

And when I do finally settle on a melody, I've developed the ability to run a loop of the music through my head at will and fit the lyrical ideas together, even before I go to sleep at night or before I get out of bed in the morning.

Though I enjoy working with other writers, these days I prefer working alone most of the time. It's a lot easier being critical of yourself than it is of another person, and it's no fun when two people have two different ideas about how a song should be written.

The first song I ever wrote was when I was about seventeen; it was called "Does Your Conscience Bother You." It was the most trite, ripped-off, cookie-cutter piece of garbage you've never heard. But you've got to start somewhere. It's all part of the learning process. Crawl, walk, run.

I believe that evolving as a songwriter is much like building up a muscle. The more time you put into it, the stronger it gets. As you develop your discernment by accepting and rejecting lyrics and musical ideas, you get to the point when you know you're finished. You've got your idea across so that other people can understand or at least have an interpretation of it.

I am never without a few unfinished ideas running around in my head. I'll sit and work with a lyric line I'm not happy with, trying different words that rhyme until I'm satisfied. Or I play a lick or a guitar riff over and over until a lyrical idea starts coming to me.

I seem to write well under pressure when there's a deadline to meet. When we were on the major labels and had to deliver a new album every year, I wrote constantly until I had enough songs I felt would make a good album.

In 1983 I got a call from Lou Bantle, the president of US Tobacco, who was involved with Hal Needham in the production of a movie about NASCAR racing. It was titled *Stroker Ace* and starred Burt Reynolds and Lonnie Anderson.

It seemed the movie had been shot and was ready to go into final post-production. All the pieces were intact except one. They had not found a suitable title song and needed one right away.

I got a videotape of the latest cut of the movie in my hands on Thanksgiving Day. After having dinner with my family, I retired to the basement by myself to see what I could do about a title song for *Stroker Ace*.

I sat and watched the movie a couple of times, and a line started surfacing.

Stroker Ace was born to race.

I sat there for a couple of hours, and when I got up, I had the whole song ready to record, which we did a few days later at Woodland Sound in Nashville.

It started off with Tommy Crain and me on twin five-string banjos. It worked on into the story of a country boy who learned to drive fast by hauling moonshine, going onto dirt tracks, and finally onto the big stages in Talladega and Daytona.

We played the song at the premier of *Stroker Ace* in Charlotte, where we met Burt Reynolds and Lonnie Anderson. Jim Neighbors, who played Stroker's sidekick, was one of the nicest guys you'd ever meet.

I've written special songs for the Nashville Predators hockey team, the Tennessee Titans football team, and the National Finals Rodeo. Bits and pieces of "The Devil Went Down to Georgia" have been adapted for TV commercials and even Monday Night Football.

I enjoy having an idea pitched at me and making a song out of it.

I think the most pressure I was ever under as a songwriter was when I wrote the songs for our first gospel album, *The Door.*

It was such a special project to me. I wanted it to be much more than just another gospel album. I wanted the lyrics to have impact and hopefully speak to some of the people who, like me, had such a hard time understanding the gospel message and were falling through the cracks.

I wrote, rewrote, rejected, accepted, started over, changed, and rearranged the songs until I was satisfied with the words and how they fit into the music. It was worth all the effort.

The Door would give us our first Dove Award.

A song that took a kind of roundabout way into existence was "Saddle Tramp." It was originally meant to be an instrumental and was all finished and arranged and ready to take into the studio.

I was in Miami on a promotion trip, riding in a car when the lyrics started coming to me. It was a lonesome story of a horseback drifter, riding here and there, looking for something he'd never find but still riding on in search of it.

We went back into rehearsal and combined the lyrics with the instrumental. "Saddle Tramp" was born; it was the title song for an album that would eventually go gold.

A similar situation occurred with a song called "Carolina (I Remember You)." It's about growing up in my native North Carolina the way I remember it.

The song was recorded and finished, except I had decided to add a string section to the arrangement. As the players were setting up and getting sounds together in the studio, I had an idea.

Years before, I had written a piece of prose that was also about growing up in Carolina. I got to thinking it would be great if the song and prose could somehow be put together into one piece of work.

But one part was sung and the other was spoken. One rhymed and one didn't, and it just wouldn't make sense.

I don't read music and know nothing about writing string scores, but I had a wild idea.

I told Bergen White, the string arranger, "Take the first part of your score and have your players double the value of each note. A quarter note will become a half note, and a half note a whole note, and so on. And let's see what happens."

They tried it. I read my recitation over the music bed it created, and it worked perfectly. We spliced the recitation onto the first part of the song, and it sounded like it had been written that way.

My advice to anyone who finds they have a basic talent for rhyming lines of lyric and putting them to music: no matter how primitive that talent or how trite and terrible your first efforts may be, stick with it. Ride it out and take the time to explore your God-given abilities, to hone and sharpen them and develop your discernment level, always being honest with yourself about what's good and what's not.

You may have the makings of a songwriter, and songs are the fuel that drives this music business. There will never be a time when new songs aren't needed.

CHAPTER 62

We've Traveled Our Highways and Toasted Our Times in Rotgut Whiskey and Fine French Wines, Old Friend We've Been a Mile or Two Together

In August 2015 I received a sad phone call that my dear friend and mentor Bob Johnston had passed away. It came as quite a surprise. I knew he had been having some health issues but had no idea they were that serious.

Bob had been such an influential force in my life. He was the person who had brought me to Nashville and who had taught me the importance of discipline and sweat equity when it came to writing and recording. He had been a part of my life for fifty-six years and had been responsible for so many of the good things that had happened to me. Bob was like my older brother, and I truly loved him.

I told his wife, Joy, and his son Kevin that we would do a memorial event in the near future. The people in the CDB office joined forces with the folks at BMI and organized an event for March 16, 2016, that I feel Bob would have been proud of.

People came in from as far away as California to be a part of it. We paid tribute to a man who had produced Patti Page, Aretha Franklin, Louis Armstrong, Simon and Garfunkel, Marty Robbins, Leonard Cohen, Bob Dylan, and Johnny Cash.

He had written multiple songs for Elvis Presley and had songs recorded by Brenda Lee, Tammy Wynette, Johnny Cash, and many, many more.

With a career that stretched more than sixty years, he was a part of creating some of the most beloved and durable music ever recorded.

Bob had come to Nashville in 1967 to replace Don Law, and Nashville had never seen anything like him.

When Bob had mentioned to the Columbia Records brass that he was thinking about trying to get Bob Dylan to record in Nashville with the local players, the executive he was talking to told Bob that he would fire him if he attempted such a thing.

But in typical Bob Johnston fashion, he defied his boss and proposed it anyway. The results are there for the world to hear. *John Wesley Harding, Blonde on Blonde, Nashville Skyline.*

Fresh off big records by Simon and Garfunkel and Bob Dylan, he hit Music City like a thunderbolt, unmindful and uncaring of how anybody else did it. He was taking sessions into expensive overtime, working through the night into the early morning hours, and expecting everybody else involved to do the same.

It was said that one of the Nashville recording engineers complained to an executive of the company about the hours Bob was working them and some of the unorthodox things he did.

I understand the reply came back something like, "If Bob Johnston tells you he wants a microphone on the ceiling, you need to start looking for a very tall ladder."

The memorial was a celebration of the life of a man who had left wide and indelible footprints across the landscape of American music. He touched the lives of countless people and left the business he loved a better place for having been a part of it for more than a half century.

There were speeches, live performances, and videos of Bob in the studio. It was a truly nice night of remembering my friend.

But something else happened that night that I only wish Bob Johnston could have known about.

CHAPTER 63

ICING ON A VERY SPECIAL CAKE

After the memorial I had to go by the Country Music Association, which was only a couple of blocks away, and take a picture for some publicity thing or another that they had going on.

We said goodbye to all of the people who had gathered to honor Bob and headed over to CMA headquarters, where there was a set and a photographer, and prepared to take the picture they had asked for.

Sarah Trahern, the CMA president, came in the room to say hello, and in an almost offhand way she said, "I know you think you're here to take a picture, but what you're really here for is to be told that you're being inducted into the Country Music Hall of Fame."

At first I was afraid I had misunderstood her. Then it dawned on me that she had really just told me that I was going to be inducted into the Country Music Hall of Fame.

Hazel was standing next to me, and I almost fell into her. Then came the emotion and the tears. As the astounding realization of what had just happened hit me right between the eyes, the whole scene turned almost surreal.

The Country Music Hall of Fame!

That's the one you don't even dare to dream about. It's the one you can't lobby for or compete for, the one you have absolutely no control over, the one with the secret list of voters who are rotated every three years, the one you'd best not even spend too much time thinking about.

God had done it again. He had granted me another deeply held desire of my heart.

Hazel, Little Charlie, Dean, Paula, Bebe, Angela, David, and his wife,

Carolyn, were in the room when Sarah told me. Nobody but David knew it was going to happen, and it was a pretty emotional time for the CDB family.

We were told to keep it a secret until the formal announcement would be made in a couple of weeks, and all three 2016 inductees would be made known at the same time.

I didn't even know who the other two inductees were.

The day of the formal announcement arrived, and we headed for the Hall of Fame to let the world know.

When I got there, I found out that the other two inductees were Fred Foster and Randy Travis.

Fred Foster is a legendary behind-the-scenes figure around Nashville in record production and publishing, founder of Monument Records.

Randy Travis needs no introduction. The singer's down-home, earthy voice personified country music for so many in the 1980s and 1990s.

The weeks between the formal announcement and the induction were busy with interviews, Hall of Fame events leading up to the induction, and, of course, our usual slate of concert dates. But no matter what I was doing, it was always in the back of my mind what was going to happen on October 16, when I would get my first look at the plaque with my likeness that would hang on the walls along with so many of my heroes.

Of course I was elated, excited, anxious, and all the feelings one would be expected to experience in anticipation of such a singular honor. But the two emotions I felt the strongest were gratitude and humility.

I asked my friend and Hall of Fame member Brenda Lee to induct me. On a beautiful October afternoon, we arrived en masse at the Country Music Hall of Fame: family, friends, and employees.

After the walk down the red carpet, media interviews, and receptions, we went into the CMA theater for the ceremony. Here's how I remember it.

* * *

As I write this, it is the morning after the night before. The night before being the night I was inducted into the Country Music Hall of Fame.

The class of 2016 inductees are all from North Carolina. Randy Travis,

Fred Foster, and I are all Tarheels, which as near as I can determine is a first.

Fred and Randy were both in wheelchairs. Fred had had some health issues, and as is well known, Randy suffered a debilitating stroke in 2013. It affected his motor skills and his speech, which he has been working very hard to regain. Just being there spoke of his great inner strength.

The folks at the Hall of Fame did such a great job and made the evening so special, full of memories and surprises, with a slate of performers and presenters that included Garth Brooks, Vince Gill, Dolly Parton, Brandy Clark, Alan Jackson, Brad Paisley, and Kris Kristofferson.

I knew that someone was going to do some of our songs but had no idea who. When Trisha Yearwood walked onstage and just killed "It Hurts Me," I was as surprised as anybody in the building.

Jamey Johnson came out and did one of the best versions of "Long Haired Country Boy" I've ever heard. Then Trace Adkins and violinist Andrea Zonn came on and rocked "The Devil Went Down to Georgia."

Then it was time to walk onstage, let Brenda Lee put the medallion around my neck, and get a look at the plaque that will hang on the wall beside so many of my heroes.

This was my acceptance speech:

The grandiose words it would require to adequately describe the sea of gratitude and the mountain of honor I'm feeling tonight simply do not exist in my vocabulary. I'm not sure if the words to describe the emotions I'm feeling in my heart right now exist at all.

When I look around me at the images of those who I have admired, respected, and emulated, whose very shoulders I stand on, to think that I will be represented in that same manner and on those same walls is a very humbling thought indeed.

A plaque on these walls is not just an award or an accolade. It is a page in a history book, an unending history book, a story that will go on and on as long as talented young men and women with desire in their hearts and fire in their bellies continue to write and perform the songs, travel the miles, and pay the dues.

Many of the faces on these walls laid the foundation and established the infrastructure for those of us who would follow in their footsteps, taking their music down two-lane blacktops into the mountains and swamps to the common folks whose lives their songs reflected.

Through depressions and wars they sung their tunes about lonesome freight train whistles and love gone wrong, played the hoedowns and drinking songs, and helped America remember that no matter how dark the days of war became, there was a star-spangled banner waving somewhere.

The Grand Ole Opry was the force that brought it all together. As the first true stars like Roy Acuff and Ernest Tubb began to emerge, their songs boomed across the Southeast and Midwest on the airwaves of the clear channel voice of 650 WSM. Young men glued themselves to the radio every Saturday night and dared to dream about one day being a part of this wonderful thing that was happening in Nashville, Tennessee.

I know because I was one of them. From the time I learned my first three chords, my life has been devoted to the creation and performing of my music.

It's been a rewarding life, an exciting life, and I would do it all over again in the twinkling of an eye.

For me to acknowledge this most distinguished recognition I must also acknowledge the fact that I would not be standing here were it not for the love and loyalty of my wife and son, the fact that God has granted me yet another desire of my heart, and that I have been surrounded by some of the most incredible people who have stuck it out with me and had my back through some heavy storms.

I've often been asked what is my most cherished accomplishment, and my answer never varies. It's keeping twenty-five people gainfully and steadily employed for more than forty years.

It's been a great ride, gang. We're still in the saddle, and it ain't over by a long shot. Bring it on.

The acknowledgments I make tonight would not be complete without recognizing my dear friend and mentor Bob Johnston, who brought me to Nashville in 1967. Bob passed away a few months ago, but I know if he was here he would take great joy in this event.

So with the greatest respect for the past and the greatest aspirations *for the future, as I humbly accept this indescribable honor desired by so many and attained by so few, I realize just how blessed I am.*

Long live country music.

God bless Music City.

Thank you.

What happened that night is the culmination of sixty years of miles, dreams, grit, and determination, of a few disappointments and a lot of encouragement, of a few giant steps and a million baby steps, of trial and error, of lessons learned the hard way, of anxiety and fulfillment.

But, as satisfying and prestigious as this most-sought-after award may be, the story doesn't end here. It's not a stop sign but a "go" sign, as I will continue my career as long as circumstances allow or until the Lord calls me home.

I still have far horizons that I know are there but haven't laid eyes on yet. A jigsaw of bits and pieces of music and lyrics I have to put together, places I haven't seen, people I haven't met, thrills and excitement I haven't experienced.

My life stretches out before me. I can't see around the curves to tell how far it reaches, but you can bet that however many miles the journey, be it many or few, I will travel it with gratitude and take my music with me. When the time comes, I want to go out with a song in my heart and praises to God on my lips.

All things considered, what more could I possibly ask?

ACKNOWLEDGMENTS

My eternal gratitude to:

Hazel, my wife, and Charlie, my son, without whose love, patience, and encouragement I would have never left the starting blocks.

My manager, David Corlew, who has had my back through the valleys and across the mountaintops.

Bebe Evans for patiently seeing me through multiple incarnations of this book over the past twenty years.

Paula Szeigis for her never-ending sense of optimism.

DeAnna Winn, Angela Wheeler, and J.B. Copeland for filling in the gaps.

My ninth-grade English teacher, Mrs. Ethel Oldham, for helping to develop my lifelong interest in literature.

Our typist, Elaine Roberts, who corrected copious amounts of spelling and made sense of my outlandish vernacular.

I want to thank God for helping me discover a talent I didn't even know I had.